The Lady on the Drawingroom Floor

The Lady on the Drawingroom Floor

with Selected Poetry and Prose by Mary E. Coleridge

Edited by Heather Braun

FAIRLEIGH DICKINSON UNIVERSITY PRESS
Madison • Teaneck

Published by Fairleigh Dickinson University Press
Copublished by The Rowman & Littlefield Publishing Group, Inc.
4501 Forbes Boulevard, Suite 200, Lanham, Maryland 20706
www.rowman.com

Unit A, Whitacre Mews, 26-34 Stannary Street, London SE11 4AB

Introduction and notes copyright © 2018 by Heather Braun

British Library Cataloguing in Publication Information Available

Library of Congress Cataloging-in-Publication Data

ISBN: 978-1-68393-146-1 (cloth) ISBN:
978-1-68393-148-5 (pbk.) ISBN:
978-1-68393-147-8 (electronic)

For my fearless daughter, Madeline,
who inspires me every day to be a better
"Fessor" and a better person

Contents

Acknowledgments   ix

Introduction   1

The Lady on the Drawingroom Floor   25

Selected Poetry by *Anodos*

    A Clever Woman   131

    The Other Side of a Mirror   132

    The Witch   134

    We Never Said Farewell   135

    Doubt   136

    Shadow   137

    The Deserted House   138

    To Memory   139

    Two Songs   140

    Horror   141

    Mortal Combat   142

    Marriage   143

Unwelcome   144

Master and Guest   145

Regina   147

Self-Question   148

True to Myself am I, and False to All   149

Go   150

Gone   151

Lines   152

Grief and Death   153

To One Who Was Nursing a Blind Father   154

To an Old Friend   155

To Time the Comforter   156

Essays and Other Writings

"Words, Words, Words!"   159

Recollections of Mrs. Fanny Kemble   162

The Drawing-Room   168

Gifts   170

The Making of Heroines [From The Reflector, March 1888]   173

Her Grace, the Duchess [From The Theatre, September 1884]   176

Mrs. Gaskell [From the Times Literary Supplement,
    14 September 1906]   192

Queen Elizabeth [A lecture given to some working-girls]   197

The Friendly Foe (story) [From The Cornhill, March 1898]   208

Selected Passages from Letters and Diaries   224

Index   233

About the Editor   237

~

Acknowledgments

I have wished for an updated collection of Mary Coleridge's poetry and prose since I first discovered her as a graduate student at Boston College. I am incredibly grateful to the following institutions and individuals for helping make this wish come true: to Columbia University for giving me a 2014 Library Research Award, which allowed me to begin work on this project in their Rare Books and Manuscripts Room; to the University of Akron for awarding me a 2014 Faculty Summer Research Grant supporting my travel to collections; to James Gifford, Fairleigh Dickinson University Press's new Director, for his role in helping shepherd this book smoothly and efficiently into production; to Jennie Young, for showing me what it means to thrive, especially in the midst of competing pressures and great change; to my husband, Chris Horne, for giving me hours of time and mental space to work and for being my loudest, most relentless cheerleader; to Paul Schlueter, whose expertise with edited collections and whose patience reading multiple drafts gave me the confidence to carry on after each re-reading; and to June Schlueter, whose calm, encouraging voice was always in my head and whose belief in this project was steadfast.

Finally, special thanks to Harry Keyishian, model scholar and human being, and director Emeritus of Fairleigh Dickinson University Press. I am grateful to Harry not only for the faith he had in this project, but also for his many years of devoted service to the Press. With so many others, I also owe him thanks for the indelible courage he displayed years ago in Keyishian vs. Board of Regents, the case that established academic freedom as a "special concern of the first Amendment." I am proud to have this book accepted for publication in 2017, the fortieth anniversary of Harry's directorship of the Press and the fiftieth of his U.S. Supreme Court victory for academia.

Frontispiece from Gathered Leaves (London: Constable and Co., 1911).

~

Introduction
Heather Braun

Poet, novelist, essayist, educator, and critic, Mary Elizabeth Coleridge (1861–1907) accomplished a great deal in her short life.[1] Yet even with her family ties to literary celebrity, she never became one herself. Theresa Whistler opens her 1954 memoir of this "minor" Victorian writer with this declaration: "Not very many people today have heard of Mary Coleridge. However, her poems, when they first appeared, were praised with delight . . . . This is not fame, but it is, in a modest way, to live."[2] Indeed, for more than half a century, Whistler's tribute has remained true. In Mary Coleridge's lifetime, the writer was called "the tail of the S.T.C. comet,"[3] evoking the name and Romantic legacy of her great-great-uncle, Samuel Taylor Coleridge. But Mary Coleridge's style and substance were distinct from those of her celebrity relative. Upon first encountering her work, one is struck by its complexity and timelessness: her characters express conflicting desires for connection and solitude, often in the same moment; they yearn for a deeper understanding of themselves and their own complicated histories. These characters appear at times prophetic, even otherworldly as they disclose their sordid secrets and lingering regrets. Through these voices, Coleridge expresses a persistent warning that our own silence and self-denial will ultimately define us, preventing us from seeing how our past shapes who we are and how we wish to live.

The Lady on the Drawingroom Floor with Selected Poetry and Prose aims primarily to resurrect Coleridge's final published novel, which went through five printings in a year and was praised during her lifetime. Published in

1906, *The Lady on the Drawingroom Floor* explores the constraints of romantic love and femininity (especially for the Victorian single woman) from
the distanced perspective of an unreliable male narrator. The novel offers
a valuable introduction to the recurring themes and questions that have
come to characterize Coleridge's fiction, nonfiction, and poetry, all genres
in which she excelled. The ideas and anxieties that define her signature
novel also find expression in the poems, short stories, essays, and letters in
this collection, which speak directly to the intricacies of the writer's life and
writing. Coleridge imagines characters and landscapes that dispel Victorian
expectations of an "eternal feminine," an impossible ideal that demanded
extreme female passivity, chastity, selflessness, and silence.[4] Collectively,
her poetry and prose challenge expectations surrounding appropriate topics
for women writers, while carving out new spaces for experimentation and
expansion.

This collection of Mary Coleridge's writings celebrates the accomplish-
ments of a lesser-known Victorian woman writer by identifying the preoccu-
pations and mysteries to be uncovered in both her poetry and her prose. Frequently taking the perspective of male or androgynous narrators, Coleridge
vividly describes experiences that were virtually unavailable to women in her
time. Moreover, she imagines the creative possibilities of a genderless identity, possibilities that have yet to be realized fully even more than a century
after her death. This collection also seeks to reveal Coleridge's strengths as a
Victorian writer, uncovering not only her diverse contributions but also her
enduring relevance to questions of gender identity and genre fluidity that
we continue to grapple with today. By highlighting characteristic examples
of Coleridge's poetry, fiction, essays, and letters, this volume provides an ac-
cessible introduction to Coleridge's career for students, scholars, and anyone
interested in nineteenth-century literature and culture.

Biography

Mary Elizabeth Coleridge was born on 23 September 1861 at Hyde Park
Square in London, the eldest daughter of Mary Anne Jameson Coleridge
and Arthur Duke Coleridge. The family later moved to 12 Cromwell Place
in South Kensington, where she lived for the rest of her life. Coleridge was
the great-grandniece of Romantic poet Samuel Taylor Coleridge; her grandfather was the son of S.T.C.'s eldest brother, James; and her great-aunt was
Sara Coleridge, author of the novel *Phantasmion*. Her father was a lawyer
and a well-known singer who sang with Jenny Lind and helped to form the
London Bach Choir. Growing up in a middle-class Christian household,

Coleridge was surrounded from a very young age by intelligent and creative adults. Her well-connected parents frequently entertained artists, musicians, and authors in their home. Among their regular celebrity guests were Alfred, Lord Tennyson, Anthony Trollope, John Ruskin, John Everett Millais, and Robert Browning, whom Coleridge secretly adored. Although she was shy and spent a great deal of time alone, Coleridge, through her writing, was encouraged to connect with creative individuals outside her intimate circle of family and friends.

Coleridge was multilingual and had a great passion for learning languages, including Hebrew, Greek, German, French, and Italian. She also had aspirations to become a painter, but by age thirteen she had begun writing poetry, which soon became a primary pursuit. She was educated largely at home by her tutor, William J. Cory (1823–92), a former Master at Eton. She often spent summers with Cory and his family in Hampstead. Although he had a tremendous influence on her, she privately expressed a sense of relief after Cory's death at being permitted to pursue her own education free from male guidance. As she explained in a letter: "When Mr. Cory died, there came, along with the sense that 'there had passed away a glory from the earth,' another sense that I was free—that I should never fear anyone again in just that way."[5] Later in life, she studied English literature, specifically Elizabethan drama, at King's College.[6] Beginning around 1895, Coleridge tutored privately and began teaching grammar and English literature to students at the Working Women's College in London. Confident that this teaching reflected "her Christian and democratic instincts,"[7] she continued working with these women until her death.

In her lifetime, Coleridge was best known as a novelist and essayist who published under the name M. E. Coleridge. Her first novel, *The Seven Sleepers of Ephesus* (1893), published shortly after her return from traveling in Italy, baffled Victorian readers, though it did get the attention of Robert Louis Stevenson. One critic described *Seven Sleepers* as "a reckless fantasia, the record of seven young men's adventures, . . . too wild an attempt to take with the public, and . . . more or less of a failure."[8] According to Carol Dole, this recklessness was typical of Coleridge, who had a "love for dark, mysterious scenes that fascinate but also bewilder."[9] Despite their murkiness, her novels sold quite well. *The King with Two Faces* (1897), a historical romance about the eighteenth-century court of Gustav III of Sweden, was among her most popular, earning her £900 in royalties and helping to establish her reputation as a novelist. *The King with Two Faces* begins with a scene in which four men wait in a dark house for the man they intend to murder. This novel was followed by three more: another historical romance, *The Fiery Dawn* (1901),

The Shadow on the Wall (1904), and *The Lady on the Drawingroom Floor* (1906). This final completed novel, while well-known and praised at the turn of the twentieth century, has become all but lost: only a handful of first editions can be found today in libraries and rare book stores.[10] *The Lady on the Drawingroom Floor* concerns lost love and romantic longing. Moving back and forth in time, the narrator recounts years earlier, when he fell in love with a woman but never told her; now, what might have happened lingers between the pair yet threatens to be lost forever.

Meanwhile, Coleridge continued to publish essays and reviews for such magazines as *The Cornhill*, Charlotte Yonge's *Monthly Packet*, *Merry England*, *The Monthly Review*, *Times Literary Supplement*, *The Theatre*, and *The Guardian*. In 1899, she published an impressive collection entitled *Non Sequitur*, composed of thirty-two essays as well as stories and reviews. She also loved writing letters and keeping track of her thoughts in her journals. One entry expresses her worry that publishing her poems would insult the legacy of her literary relatives. When she finally agreed to publish them, it was only under the pseudonym *Anodos*, or "pathless wanderer." *Anodos* was the name of the protagonist of George MacDonald's novel *Phantastes: A Faerie Romance for Men and Women* (1858), an aimless wanderer who is haunted by his own shadow until the curse is lifted by the song of a woman from Fairyland. Her first book of forty-eight poems, *Fancy's Following*, was published in 1896 by Charles Henry Daniel at his private press in Oxford in a printing of 125 copies. The following year, *Fancy's Guerdon*, consisting of eleven reprinted poems with seven additional poems, was published in Elkin Mathews's *Shilling Garland* series with the help of Laurence Binyon.[11] A few months after her death, Henry Newbolt published 237 of her poems under her own name.[12] The collection was so popular that it went through four printings in six months. A few decades later, Newbolt's granddaughter, Theresa Whistler, published *The Collected Poems of Mary Coleridge* (1954), which included thirty-one additional poems.[13]

One way Coleridge improved as a writer and gained confidence sharing her work was by fostering close female friendships. She met weekly for intellectual discussions with five female friends who called themselves "The Quintette."[14] The Quintette did not identify clearly with any one definitive group: unlike the Brontës or the Bluestockings, these women resisted taking a stand politically, not seeking to draw unneeded attention to themselves. They were "daughters of well-to-do Victorian gentlemen, they subscribed to the conventions of their upbringing. Their lives were sheltered, though not at all artificial, and none of them had to make their own living."[15] Later, in the 1890s, Coleridge helped to form a reading group called "The Settee," which met for weekly debates and to share their own writing. It was with this group, which later included Henry Newbolt, that Coleridge first ventured to share her poetry. We can now read these poems because her friend Violet Hodgkins, a cousin of Robert Bridges's wife, left the small white notebook of Coleridge's poems where Bridges would be sure to find it. Shortly after, Bridges offered to help Coleridge edit her poems.[16] They met in 1894, and Coleridge described his advice as "the finest lesson I ever had in poetry," though she did not take all of his advice (Whister, 65). Yet their collaboration convinced her to publish two small volumes of poems—*Fancy's Following* (1896) and *Fancy's Guerdon* (1897)—under her pseudonym, *Anodos*.

Although at first glance she may have appeared remarkably private and sheltered, Coleridge lived a full life, unhindered by her choice not to marry or have children. Near the end of her life, Coleridge wrote the preface to *The Last Poems of Richard Watson Dixon* (1905), edited by Robert Bridges. Dixon (1833–1900) was a minor religious poet, and Coleridge was invested in maintaining his reputation after his death, describing him as an acquired taste and his poems worthy of a second consideration.[17] The year of her death, she completed an illustrated biography of Holman Hunt at the personal request of the artist.[18] She had also begun working on a medieval romance set in France called *Becq* (1907), a novel that Whistler called "more gripping than any other she invented."[19]

In the summer of 1907, Coleridge travelled with her family to Harrogate in the north of England for their annual holiday. Coleridge became ill with acute appendicitis. During her illness, she continued reading Shakespeare, informing her family: "Life is worth living, as long as there is *King Lear* to read."[20] Due to complications following an operation to remove her appendix, Coleridge died on 25 August 1907. She was cremated and her ashes buried in Grove Road Cemetery, Harrogate, around the corner from where she died. On her grave appear a large cross, the dates of her life, and the words, "Perfect Love."[21]

Critical Reception

Coleridge once wrote about herself: "I have no fairy god-mother, but lay claim to a fairy great-great-uncle, which is perhaps the reason that I am condemned to wander restlessly around the Gates of Fairyland, although I have never yet passed them."[22] While Elaine Showalter's *A Literature of Their Own* (1977) cued the revival of interest in Coleridge's work, it was Sandra Gilbert and Susan Gubar's 1979 anthology of "feminist poetics," *The Madwoman in the Attic: The Woman Writer and the Nineteenth-Century Literary Imagination*, that proved most influential in reviving interest in her poetry. Gilbert and Gubar emphasize Coleridge's self-proclaimed status as a literary wanderer dispossessed of her heritage. In their feminist reading of "The Other Side of a Mirror," for example, they celebrate Coleridge's "old silent dance of death" as "a dance of triumph, a dance into speech, a dance of authority."[23] While some have read the "hideous wound" of Coleridge's most famous poem as a reference to menstruation, Gilbert and Gubar interpret this as a poem about self-alienation. More specifically, they name "The Other Side of a Mirror" as a poem central to "excavat[ing] the real self buried beneath the 'copy' selves."[24] This description seems surprisingly fitting today, when one's online personas can be duplicated indefinitely. Coleridge's mysterious, often androgynous narrators articulate contemporary concerns about the location of an authentic or "first" self beneath the compelling copies we offer to the world.

Since this brief feminist resurgence, critics have continued to revive Coleridge as a would-be feminist, even though she was far from a vocal advocate of women's rights. Such attention does not adequately account for her marked public ambivalence about gender and women writers. More daring in her writing than in life, Coleridge publicly eschewed claims about her feminist motives. As she wrote to her friend Edith Sichel, "Woman with a big W bores me supremely . . . It is a mere abstraction born of monks and the mists of the North. A woman I know, but what on earth is Woman? She has done her best to spoil history, poetry, novels, and essays, and Sir Thomas Browne and Thoreau are the only things safe from her; that's why I love them."[25] At the same time, she was critical of female contemporaries whom she believed failed to transcend their gender. Indeed, some of the writers Coleridge labeled as too proper or too safe have since been called the leading feminist writers of their time. For example, Coleridge expressed frustration that Mary Shelley and Sara Coleridge must be "so Englishwomanly . . . I dare say I should love Frankenstein. But [imagination] does not play about in their ordinary writings or lend any grace to their lives. It is all cold."[26] Through *Anodos* and in the male or androgynous protagonists that frequent her novels and poems, Coleridge found ways to escape the "Englishwomanly" limitations placed on imagination and the woman writer.

More recently, critics, including Christine Battersby, argue that Gilbert and Gubar's reading may be simplistic since it ignores how the poem may indeed be "*renouncing* sexuality" and destabilizing the position of the woman writer.[27] Similarly, Katherine McGowran discounts earlier readings of Coleridge's feminist resistance and empowerment, focusing instead on her clear "reluctance to assume a gendered identity," a choice that, in turn, granted her a great deal of creative freedom. McGowran's approach most directly confronts and attempts to resolve some of the contradictions between Coleridge's reluctance to claim publicly a clear feminist position and her proclivity for creating empowered, independent characters. Viewed through this lens, McGowran explains, "the business of assuming a pseudonymous identity becomes a positive act, a means of casting off the burden of selfhood in order to enter a new one in writing."[28]

But despite her fleeting moment of fame in the 1980s and a scattering of critical attention in the early 1990s and 2000s, Coleridge has become largely absent from scholarly discussions and literary anthologies that include the contributions of Victorian women writers. A handful of her most famous poems do appear in Victorian literature collections including *The Penguin Book of Victorian Verse* (1999), Blackwell's *Victorian Women Poets: An Anthology* (1995), and *The Victorians: An Anthology of Poetry and Poetics* (2000). Scholarly attention to her prose, however, remains sparse. Despite the strong Gothic features of nearly all her writing (features she shares with her famous relative), there is no mention of Coleridge in Andrew Smith and William Hughes's *The Victorian Gothic: An Edinburgh Companion* or Caroline Franklin and Michael J. Franklin's chapter "Victorian Gothic Poetry: The Corpse's [a] Text." The latter text explores Gothic images of the corpse in poems by Christina Rossetti, Emily Dickinson, and Elizabeth Stuart Phelps, writers whose work is complemented by Coleridge's frequent depiction of liminal or "undead" characters who fail to find a home among the living. Coleridge's writing is forever tinged with images of Gothic longing, death, and despair wholly fabricated from her imagination and virtually absent from her tranquil childhood.[29]

The Lady on the Drawingroom Floor

While some of Coleridge's poems have been analyzed and anthologized since their publication, rarely have they been considered alongside her prose works. Yet reading her poetry and prose together offers new ways of understanding Coleridge's place among the writers of her time. This collection opens with Coleridge's last completed novel, *The Lady on the Drawingroom Floor*, originally published in 1906 in London by Edward Arnold. The *Tribune* called *The Lady on the Drawingroom Floor* "a charming creation,"[30] and a reviewer for the *Manchester Guardian* wrote: "Miss Coleridge has not hitherto written anything so purely charming as *The Lady on the Drawing-room Floor*."[31] A review in *The Athenaeum* stated: "There is such comedy or tragedy or fantasy on every page that the reader feels that to skip even a single sentence is to run the risk of missing something essential to the general effect, and at once

to defraud himself and to do injustice to the writer."[32] *The Spectator* called
the novel one of Coleridge's best, most "charming" works, a novel that deserves to be read as perhaps her most mature and reflective work of fiction.[33]
Despite such praise, however, *The Lady on the Drawingroom Floor* has become
all but lost to readers today.

The Lady on the Drawingroom Floor opens in a London boarding house. Its
narrator is a middle-aged semi-invalid named Oliver, an introvert who refers
to himself passively as "the gentleman downstairs." Oliver is disenchanted,
deeply introspective, and somewhat obsessed with his upstairs neighbor, Lucilla, whom he repeatedly refers to as "the lady on the drawingroom floor."
Lucilla, called Miss Z. by her neighbors, is mysterious, single, and plays the
piano for Oliver at least once a week. Often, she chooses a funeral march,
a genre of which Oliver is particularly fond. Eventually, Miss Z. invites her
neighbor to join her upstairs in her drawing room. As he observes her, Oliver
begins to reflect upon profound and repressed emotions from his distant past.
In particular, he recalls a woman whom he loved many years earlier but to
whom he never revealed his love. He learns later that she wrote to him, but
her letter was lost before he had a chance to read it. The "shocker" at the
end of the novel further highlights the impossibility of escaping one's past or
avoiding future pain by retreating inward and living a life of solitude.

For the first chapters of the novel, Oliver chooses this life, remaining in
his room but listening attentively for Lucilla to move about her apartment.
He observes that she "lived above me, in every sense of the word" (2).[34]
While Lucilla embraces her years of experience, Oliver notes with self-
protective pessimism: "Death sits on the doorstep of any one whom I love"
(2). Despite Oliver's attempts to keep Lucilla at a safe distance, her presence in the house nevertheless has transformative effects on its inhabitants,
perhaps most emphatically on the narrator, who initially interacts with her
the least. Neighbors note how Miss Z. "takes an interest" (11). "She's a lady,
sir, she is!" (11). The narrator is at once envious of Lucilla's attentions to
others and fearful that he will experience these attentions himself. "Nothing remained unchanged except myself. Alarm and jealousy increased. I
entertained a nervous terror of Miss Z." (17). Because of Oliver's conflicting
emotions, the pair does not meet face to face for some time. Instead, they
quarrel about the naming of stray cats in letters sent between their apart-
ments. Oliver's "positive aversion" of Lucilla does not prevent him from
thinking of her almost constantly.

Before they meet, Oliver and Lucilla connect through Lucilla's piano
playing, specifically through their shared love of funeral marches. Lucilla
plays these marches exactly to Oliver's morbid tastes: "a Funeral March

ought to begin like death itself—suddenly, majestically, without preparation. Thus it began when Lucilla played" (19). Oliver becomes obsessed
with the mysterious woman playing piano above him. He begins sending
notes to her, requesting specific marches for her to play. The narrator is
relieved to delay a meeting, content to remain still and listen to the woman
moving and playing above him. He is reluctant to replace his romanticized
image of her with the woman herself: "From that time forward there was a
link, forged by the dead, between us. Fearful of breaking it, of finding out
that words could break a sympathy deeper than words, I had no wish to talk
with her" (26). By focusing on the mournful notes of these dirges, Oliver
delays the moment when his intangible longing for what he has lost in his
past is tempered by the tangible and absolute presence of a woman he can
imagine as he chooses.

Perhaps the most interesting section of this novel is the turn that occurs
in Chapter 13. At the end of Chapter 12, Oliver describes being inexplicably transported to a distant moment in his past. As this flashback begins,
he remains constantly aware of Lucilla's presence in the room: "My past life
seemed to have risen to the same level as the present . . . It was as if I lived
through all that was gone by once more, yet without losing consciousness
of the actual moment, of Lucilla, seated there with her book" (206). In this
moment, Oliver becomes a child again, a child who is fearful of his father
more than his adult self is intimidated by Lucilla: "Wherever my father came,
there also came fear and silence. Wherever he came I shrank away from him"
(210). Oliver's fears of his father help to explain his fears of Lucilla as his
childhood passed much in the way that his adult life is passing: in both cases,
Oliver sees himself as "an exile upon a desert island": "But still I wanted some
one, I always wanted some one. So, like a long, slow dream—not happy, not
unhappy—childhood went by" (212). The only time that Oliver feels free
from his family's abandonment is when he "lived under the piano or between
the legs of the dining-room table" (216) where he could exist without fear of
being observed or critiqued.

Still caught in this reverie, Oliver discloses the single most influential
moment of his life, an event that lasted only a few seconds but nevertheless shaped everything he experienced afterwards. He just turned twenty-
one and has excelled in his studies at University College. Apart from his
friendship with an unnamed student at the university, the narrator has
forsaken all companionship to embrace solitude and the life of the mind.
When he achieves his dream of rising to the top of his class, it does not
bring him the joy he expects. He rushes excitedly home to tell his father
that he has been named first at the College "for an essay on the Jacobites."

But his father responds to him coldly in a sentence that changes Oliver's life: "'That shows it is a waste of time and money to keep you there.' I was taken away from College at the end of the term and set to work as a clerk" (230). Interestingly, Coleridge spent her life pursuing an education and teaching others less fortunate than herself: she thrived among books and the company of her closest friends. At this moment in the novel, however, there is a strong sense that education is predicated upon gender as well as class and is ultimately reserved for those with the means to pursue it fully. From here, the narrative returns to the present. Lucilla asks Oliver about his encounters with a woman whom he has not seen in nineteen years. Oliver recalls an evening when he tried to defend an unnamed drunk woman but fell against a lamppost, breaking his leg. At the time, his only male friend, now dead, nursed him back to health "as tenderly as any woman" (249). This memory causes Oliver to remember another painful, life-changing moment in his past: on the day of his father's suicide, when his crimes of forgery were revealed, Oliver gave away all he had to save his father's reputation.

In this climactic moment of the novel, Lucilla is trying to tell Oliver something by asking him about a woman from his past whom she seems to have known personally. She informs him cryptically: "You have been cruel to her" (250). When Oliver protests that this woman could have written to him, she replies: "I am quite sure she wrote to you" (251) and then "But I *know* she wrote . . . The letter was lost—that's why you never heard" (252). Upon realizing what Lucilla is telling him, Oliver flees to his room, explaining to us, but not to Lucilla: "When first we stir with words dark depths of consciousness that have lain silent for many years, we hardly know what it is that comes to the surface" (253). And yet it isn't until the next day that the letter he seeks falls from the pages of the tenth volume of Boswell's *Life of Johnson*. "The writing bore an odd likeness to her own, I noticed that at once, but the hand was very young and unformed" (264). As Oliver struggles to understand what Lucilla was trying to tell him, Lucilla continues to tell him about the "dead girl" from his past who wrote him this letter: "I think she is still alive, waiting. I think she lives in a little room like mine. I think she keeps a bright fire burning; and she has friends. But she is always waiting" (270).

It isn't until the conclusion of the novel that Lucilla confesses what the reader has long suspected but no character has fully confirmed. Lucilla holds up the old letter sent to Oliver all those years ago and says: "I have written to you before. This is the first letter that I wrote you" (281). But Lucilla's confession does not produce in Oliver an effusion of emotions he cannot contain. The two do not embrace. The novel ends with Lucilla saying she cannot be with him then, that he will now have to wait for her: "'Parting, in middle age, is not the anguish of youthful parting; but the risks increased, the insurance money is higher . . . It may be . . . I shall have started on a longer voyage over that unknown sea whither we are all bound'" (282–83).

Throughout the novel, Coleridge perceives the lives of these two solitary individuals as suspended or even ended at the age of thirty-eight. Their most tangible bond before they part is a young woman named Kitty, who is about nineteen, the same number of years that have elapsed since the nineteen-year-old Lucilla and the twenty-one-year old Oliver last saw each other. The pair take an intense interest in Kitty, seeing in her the vibrancy of their own youth: "She seemed to be my own youth speaking, although, at her age, I could not have spoken. Just in that way I used to feel about the insignificance of death" (158). When Kitty dies suddenly and inexplicably, they stand in shock together: "I looked at the reflection of them in the smooth shining surface of the piano, and thought how it would be with me when that casket of sweet sounds stood locked and silent" (278). The reminder of death is forever present in this novel, as it was for Coleridge throughout her life.

The slow-moving plot of this peculiar novel forces readers to notice the complexity of mood and setting evoked in the deep sense of loss expressed by its two protagonists. The novel's mood is best expressed in the funeral marches Lucilla plays, in Oliver's deep regrets about his past, and in the scenes of silence and solitude. Whistler describes *The Lady on the Drawingroom Floor* aptly when she writes: "It is like a brownish, quietly charming study of an interior with two figures. The story, told with gentle irony through the voice of a middle-aged bachelor, hinges on a romantic loyalty as wildly improbable as anything in [her] other books, but here Mary is careful to relate all minor details to ordinary life, so that one easily accepts it."[35]

What is most enduring at the end of the novel is not the order or plausibility of events but rather the complex desires submerged by this "interior with two figures," an interior that strengthens the sense of loss that Lucilla and Oliver share but cannot articulate. As Oliver observes in the moments after his father ends his scholarly career: "It is the tendency of each one of us to think himself alone and singular in suffering" (232). Hence, in her depictions of solitude, Coleridge excelled. Yet she remained, as Whistler describes her, "always more the spectator in the shadows of the auditorium than the dramatist in control"[36] of the final product.

In her essay "The Drawing-Room," published in *Non Sequitur* (1900), Coleridge writes of the longing to see oneself through another's eyes. One day, the girl who danced around the drawing-room suddenly finds herself a stranger there: "An exile feels as I used to feel when I passed the door.

Within there was quiet, peace, music, and books to read that were never dull" (*Non Sequitur*, 200). It is in the drawing room that Coleridge first experienced literature, specifically romance, and the theatre. Coleridge confesses frequently in her writing that she could not engage with the celebrities she most admired. When she first saw her idol, Robert Browning, standing at her door, she responded: "I should like to think of another child—merrier—not so much afraid of the dark on the stairs outside . . . I should like to think of another girl—as gay, as full of bold ambition and not so shy—acting and dancing where I danced and acted. I hope she will see the greatest man in the world come in, as I saw Robert Browning come in the door one evening, his hat under his arm" (201). It is this "merrier" young girl whom Coleridge wishes could meet Robert Browning without shrinking into shyness. These visions of alternate selves living their lives boldly and visibly saturate Coleridge's writing. She found she could not escape the fact that her contemplative, solitary pursuits led only to more quiet contemplation and solitude.

Selected Poetry and Prose

The second section of this collection combines Coleridge's published and unpublished poems, essays, short stories, diaries, and letters. Of these, Coleridge is best remembered for her poetry. In her 1954 memoir, Whistler describes Coleridge's poems as "fragments of a personal world that was original, solitary, subtle." She understood her poems as "cryptic, unsatisfying, haunting—scattered leaves of poetry rather than its fruit."[37] Many of Coleridge's poems combine ambivalent desire and dread that linger suspended and are rarely satisfied or resolved. In 1882, at the age of eighteen, Coleridge wrote her most famous poem, "The Other Side of a Mirror," which appeared fourteen years later in *Fancy's Following* (10–11). The first-person narrator sits before her mirror and deliberately "conjured up a vision bare" (l. 2): a foreign female who embodies the antithesis of the ideal of the Angel in the House. This creature is "wild / with more than womanly despair" (l. 5–6) and yet is unable to express this despair verbally:

> Her lips were open—not a sound
> Came though the parted lines of red,
> Whate'er it was, the hideous wound
> In silence and secret bled.
> No sigh relieved her speechless woe,
> She had no voice to speak her dread. (ll. 13–18)

This horrified, mute, "mad" woman whose eyes reveal "the dying flame of life's desire" (l. 20) is initially unknown to the speaker, who cannot decipher what she wants to tell her. The climax of the poem occurs when the speaker at last comprehends that this "shade of a shadow in the glass," this "ghost of a distracted hour" (ll. 25, 29), has revealed to the speaker that she is indeed the speaker herself rather than her opposite. Such recognition recalls the uncanny connections of female doubles such as Charlotte Brontë's Jane Eyre and Bertha Rochester or the doublings throughout *Villette* of Lucy Snowe, Ginevra Fanshawe, and the ghostly nun who resides in the attic.

Coleridge was fond of the ambiguous themes of desire, despair, and death and returns to them most emphatically in her poetry. Like her Romantic predecessors, Coleridge was drawn to the flexibility of the ballad form, perhaps for its nostalgic tone, circular structure, and disembodied storytellers. The ballad's repetition and open-endedness seem most fitting for her secret interior landscapes that may appear, at a distance, impervious to social and political constraint. While Coleridge retains the song-like refrain and singular focus of the traditional ballad, she experiments with its ability to perpetuate ambiguity and haunting. "The Witch," in *Fancy's Following* (53–54), for example, consists of three seven-line stanzas that conclude with a ballad refrain and two first-person narrators. The ballad begins with the first narrator describing herself as "a little maiden still," a wanderer in the snow who pleads with the poem's second narrator: "O lift me over the threshold, and let me in at the door!" (l. 7). The title of the poem serves to warn readers and the ballad's second speaker that this supernatural creature disguises her strength by seducing us with female passivity: "my little white feet are sore" (l. 13) contrasts sharply with more ominous declarations such as "the worst of death is past" (l. 11).

Characters who exhibit absolute passivity, selflessness, and silence are rarely found in Coleridge's work, which consistently challenges the Victorian Angel in the House ideal by further blurring boundaries between masculine and feminine. Like her great-great-uncle, Coleridge had a fondness for the ambiguous and Gothic, "the strange and the unearthly."[38] Some critics even interpret "The Witch" as a direct response to S. T. Coleridge's Gothic fragment, "Christabel," in which a vampyric Geraldine disguises herself as a weak maiden in need of Christabel's and Sir Leoline's aid. Once invited inside Sir Leoline's castle, Geraldine quickly gains control over both characters, including their ability to speak and feel. Like Geraldine, Coleridge's "witch" expresses desire to be lifted "over the threshold" and let in "at the door." At the end of the second stanza of "The Witch," the pleading "I" of this ballad switches to an unnamed narrator who declares:

> Her voice was the voice that women have,
> Who plead for their heart's desire.
> She came—she came—and the quivering flame
> Sunk and died in the fire.
> It never was lit again on my hearth
> Since I hurried across the floor,
> To lift her over the threshold, and let her in at the door. (ll. 15–21)

The gender of the second narrator is uncertain, though it is clear that this narrator acts instinctively, almost against his or her will, connecting this witch with women "Who plead for their heart's desire." What remains is the certainty that her presence in this home brings darkness and the death of desire, which dies with the "quivering flame" that "never was lit again."

Coleridge's poetry and prose often feature a reluctance to express desire fully, a suspension of longing in time and space not unlike the "quivering flame" that "sunk and died in the fire" at the close of "The Witch." In her ballad "Master and Guest," also in *Fancy's Following* (22–23), Coleridge once again blurs distinctions between male and female, seductress and victim. Here, she places the opposing emotions of disgust and desire side by side, leaving the contradictions between them unreconciled. The ballad opens with a foreigner arriving at the door of a vulnerable widow, which is quite similar to the plot and power dynamic of "The Witch." Yet in neither poem is the sex of the host stated explicitly. The widow (or possibly, though not likely, widower) in "Master and Guest" is repulsed by the man but unable to refuse him any request: "I asked him in to bed and board. / I never hated any man so" (ll. 5–6). In each short, end-stopped line, the narrator is compelled to comply with the foreigner's wishes, watching in horror as "[h]e ate the offerings of the dead" (l. 12). At bedtime, the widow offers to "light you to your bed" where she is compelled, possibly against her will, to lie beside him in her bed: "I might not turn aside nor stay; / I showed him where we twain did lie" (ll. 15–16). The ballad then jumps abruptly to the following morning, when this mysterious figure informs the widow that she should "mourn" since she has "kissed a citizen of Hell, / And a soul was doomed when you were born" (ll. 17–20). The ballad's final lines leave the reader with even more questions: "The gifts that Love hath given to Love, / Love gives away to Fear" (ll. 23–24). These lines blur the boundaries of attraction and repulsion in ways that anticipate the seductive aristocratic vampires of Bram Stoker's 1897 *Dracula*.

Most of Coleridge's essays, criticism, journal entries, short fiction, and other writings are contained in *Non Sequitur* (1900) and *Gathered Leaves from the Prose of Mary E. Coleridge* (1910). The former includes several essays on literary subjects and travel, while the latter demonstrates her characteristically imaginative, humorous style in essays on various topics—literature, art, and spirituality among them—as well as in a handful of short stories. "The Friendly Foe," for example, in *Gathered Leaves* (79–103), was well-received when it was published in *Cornhill Magazine* in 1898, the first of three stories by Coleridge to appear in this periodical. The short story concerns an upcoming duel between an unnamed male narrator and an unnamed Count. The story also includes a dance with an attractive young woman while the narrator is disguised as a Dominican monk. The Count believes that killing the narrator will free his soul, and he wants the narrator to have the same reassurance. On the night before the duel is to take place, the Count hears the narrator's confession and attempts to absolve him of his sins. As a result of their conversation and the events he witnesses, the narrator's beliefs about his immortality are compromised. One of the most interesting parts of this story occurs in this scene when the narrator notes that the Count speaks to him "as if [he] were a woman" (93). Agreeing with him, the Count and the narrator suggest they reverse these gendered roles and ask to be absolved "as if [he] were a woman" (93). In this final scene, Coleridge once again reveals the arbitrary designations of male and female by having her characters experiment with familiar and superficial markers of sex.

Coleridge experiments with this fluidity of gender in her nonfiction as well. Yet she remains convinced that gender remains an essential part of one's identity. "The Making of Heroines," in *Gathered Leaves* (177–80), appeared in *The Reflector* in March 1888. In this essay, she describes the female sex as more active than passive: "Woman is, as a rule, quicker to take advantage of her life than man; she is less passive. Man at a crisis—unless it be a crisis of war—is a stupid thing. He either makes a fool of himself, or allows the world to make a fool of him, from which fate woman is preserved by her innate self-respect, and by a certain capacity which she possesses for making the most of emotion" (179). Here, Coleridge reaffirms John Keats's famous articulation of longing earlier in the century for "a life of sensations rather than of thoughts!"[39] In her essay "Words, Words, Words!" in *Non Sequitur* (19–24), for example, she distinguishes clearly between the worlds of "intellect" and "feeling," between that "endless spinning and weaving" of waking thought and the "quiet fall of darkness" found both in sleep and sensual images (20).

Coleridge's essays also contain reflections on her female contemporaries that challenge and reaffirm her status as a feminist and a woman writer.

In "Recollections of Mrs. Fanny Kemble," in *Non Sequitur* (183–94), Coleridge recalls an argument she had with Kemble, who was fifty years her senior. Kemble had asked permission to show Coleridge's work to a friend. At one point, Kemble proclaimed: "You deserve to be called *a scribbling woman*. You are that thing men call *a blue*" (186). This reference to the Bluestockings was derogatory at this time, an extreme example of the female intellectualism Coleridge demonstrated though did not proclaim publicly. Finally, in her essay "Mrs. Gaskell," in *Gathered Leaves* (186–93), Coleridge praises *Mary Barton* and compares Elizabeth Gaskell to Leo Tolstoy in "her unending compassion, in her love of the gentleness of the frail and the old, in her clear condemnation of violence as a remedy, her scorn of military prowess" (188). Unlike Charlotte Brontë, who "swept the world away in the storm of her passion," or George Eliot, who conquered it with the power of understanding, Gaskell forced the world "to weep for pity [and] charmed it with the sunny wit of a lady who was never . . . mistaken for a man, even when she signed herself 'Cotton Mather Mills'" (186). Yet despite her efforts to distance herself from her female contemporaries, Coleridge shared a great deal with them. Like many of her fellow women writers, she alternated between emphasizing and downplaying her status as a woman writer in order to excel as a novelist, a critic, an essayist, and a poet.

Conclusion

In many ways, Coleridge's work can be defined by its evanescence: at any moment, her characters seem as though they will evaporate into the deep shadows from whence they came. This quality of disappearing into her poems and novels recalls Keats's "chameleon poet,"[40] a device that further increases our desire to know more about her mysterious speakers and protagonists. Often less concerned with realism and plot construction, Coleridge focuses instead on the elusive qualities of character formation. But despite her fondness for androgynous characters, she often maintains that gender differences were essential to identity. In an 1897 letter to a male correspondent, included in *Gathered Leaves* (233–34), she explains how sex is a crucial component to identity that cannot be eclipsed or separated from one's sense of self: "I cannot think of souls that are not masculine or feminine . . . but just as the negation of sex is inconceivable to me, so is its unification; I cannot think that we shall be men as well as women, and men women as well as men. If we do not retain sex I don't see how we can retain identity. Male and female were created; it is of the very essence of our nature" (233–34).

Interestingly, Coleridge often chose male narrators living in "the age of chivalry," riding off on horses and rarely confined to interior spaces. According to Whistler, "It was not just a love of colour and adventure that appealed to Mary in masculine life, but its freedom from pettiness—and, above all, a man's code of honour."[41] It is in her writing rather than in her life that Coleridge most directly explores the dignity of independent movement and self-possession connected with the world of men.

Because discretion and reserve were so deeply a part of her nature, it is not surprising that Coleridge instructed her family to destroy her private papers after her death. The reflexive, often self-effacing quality of her poems also illustrates Coleridge's awareness of her ties to the Romantic tradition. On the title page of *Fancy's Following*, she refers abstractly to Samuel Taylor Coleridge, "whose name the writer honours too highly to set it here." Her feigned modesty (she could not really have hoped to escape this association with her great-great-uncle) helps her to conjure his ghost directly in ballads that rehabilitate the early meters, medieval imagery, and detached narration of ballad collections such as Thomas Percy's *Reliques* (1765) and Sir Walter Scott's *Minstrelsy of the Scottish Border* (1802–3). Drawing from the anonymity of the ballad form, Coleridge emphasizes themes of secrecy and silence, themes often expressed through the symbol of the mirror, a time-honored image of femininity. In Coleridge's hands, however, the image is often used subversively to reflect not beauty but ugliness, fear, and distress. These disquieting experiences, normally repressed in the "good" Victorian female, are represented as inhabiting another private realm, co-existent with the public realm, but foreign and inaccessible.[42]

A master of poetic versatility and disguise, Coleridge created poetic worlds where gender could be regarded as fluid and subordinate to more compelling questions of poetic anonymity and androgyny. Her connection to the brotherhood of Daniel Press, for instance (like Christina Rossetti's involvement with the Pre-Raphaelite Brotherhood in *The Germ*), helped to make her a prime innovator of "a new prosody, forged in private," "a small elite in small editions."[43] After all, it was male writers who heralded her work during her lifetime and memorialized it immediately after her death. Moreover, Sichel describes her friend's writing as marked by a sense of loss and change and by the "downright cut-and-thrust manliness"[44] Coleridge herself admired in male writers like William Hazlitt. Indeed, Coleridge's writing possesses a forcefulness rarely found in the poetry and fiction of Victorian writers, male or female. Her characters, many androgynous and strangely disembodied, are difficult to describe because they cannot be confined to a particular location or historical moment. Despite their persistence, these voices are neither aggressive nor masculine, defined, according to Walter de la Mare, by what they willfully leave out.[45] Coleridge's writing, Whistler explains, "will only please a quiet reader in a silent place."[46] Hence, it is through the courageous and deliberate act of writing that Mary Coleridge continues to speak today. This collection is a step toward getting her words into the hands of more readers and increasing scholarly attention to her marked influence in her time and in our own.

Notes

1. Portions of this introduction are excerpted from my essay "Mary E. Coleridge, Androgyny, and the Spectral Doppelganger," *Parlour: A Journal of Literary Analysis and Criticism* (Special Edition: "Pushing Back: Feminist Readings as Resistance") 1.2 (2016): 1-7.

2. Theresa Whistler, "Introduction and Editorial Materials," in *The Collected Poems of Mary Coleridge* (London: Rupert Hart-Davis, 1954), 21.

3. Edith Sichel, "Memoir and Editorial Materials," in *Gathered Leaves from the Prose of Mary E. Coleridge*, ed. Edith Sichel (London: Constable, 1910), 11.

4. Sandra Gilbert and Susan Gubar, *The Madwoman in the Attic: The Woman Writer and the Nineteenth-Century Literary Imagination* (New Haven: Yale University Press, 1979), 23.

5. Quoted in Alison Chapman, "Mary Elizabeth Coleridge, Literary Influence and Technologies of the Uncanny," in *Victorian Gothic: Literary and Cultural Manifestations in the Nineteenth Century*, ed. Ruth Robbins and Julian Wolfreys (New York: Palgrave, 2000), 111.

6. Vanessa Furse Jackson, "Breaking the Quiet Surface: The Shorter Poems of Mary Coleridge," *English Literature in Transition* 39.1 (1996): 42.

7. Warren Stevenson, "Mary Coleridge," in *Modern British Essayists, First Series. Dictionary of Literary Biography*, vol. 98, ed. Robert Beum (Detroit: Gale Research, 1990), 75.

8. Sichel, "Memoir and Editorial Materials," 22.

9. Carol Dole, "Mary E. Coleridge," in *Dictionary of Literary Biography*, vol. 19, 78.

10. The original print book is 283 pages and was published in London by Edward Arnold. In 2010 and 2011, Nabu Press published unedited editions of *The King with Two Faces* (1897) and *The Shadow on the Wall* (1904). However, apart from scattered copies of the original 1906 edition and print-on-demand reproductions, no edited or

unedited edition of her last completed and published novel, *The Lady on the Draw-ingroom Floor*, is currently available for purchase.

11. Whistler, "Introduction and Editorial Materials," 67.

12. Mary E. Coleridge, *Poems by Mary E. Coleridge*, ed. Henry Newbolt (1907; London: Elkin Mathews, 1918).

13. Mary E. Coleridge, *The Collected Poems of Mary Coleridge*, ed. Theresa Whis-tler (London: Rupert Hart-Davis, 1954).

14. Dole, "Mary E. Coleridge," 78.

15. Alison Chapman, "Mary Elizabeth Coleridge and the Flight to Lyric," 154.

16. Karen Devlin, "Mary Coleridge (1861–1907): A Brief Biography," The Victo-rian Web, http://www.victorianweb.org/authors/coleridge/bio.html, 1–2.

17. "Lesser Poets of the Middle and Later Nineteenth Century: R. W. Dixon." *Bartleby.com: Great Books Online: The Cambridge History of English and American Literature*, Volume XIII, The Victorian Age, Part One: Chapter VI, 30 August 2004, 1–2. Web.

18. Dole, "Mary E. Coleridge," 79. *Holman Hunt: Illustrated with Eight Reproduc-tions in Colour* (London: T. C. and E. C. Jack, 1908).

19. Whistler, "Introduction and Editorial Materials," 60.

20. Sichel, "Memoir and Editorial Materials," 43.

21. This phrase is corrected from "Pure Love" in Karen Devlin's "Mary Coleridge (1861–1907): A Brief Biography," 2. Correction is based on images from Grove Road Cemetery, like the one here: www.flickr.com/photos/19thcenturystuff/5660928283.

22. Sichel, "Memoir and Editorial Materials," 11.

23. Gilbert and Gubar, *The Madwoman in the Attic*, 44.

24. Gilbert and Gubar, *The Madwoman in the Attic*, 15, 44.

25. Passages from letters and diaries, in *Gathered Leaves*, 234.

26. Passages from letters and diaries, in *Gathered Leaves*, 219.

27. Christine Battersby, "Her Blood and His Mirror: Mary Coleridge, Luce Irigaray, and the Female Self." 254–55.

28. Katherine McGowran, "Re-reading Women's Poetry at the Turn of the Cen-tury," *Victorian Poetry* 41.4 (2003): 585.

29. Alison Chapman observes a similar fascination with Gothic tropes such as distorted identities, specifically those that haunt us from our past. In "Mary Elizabeth Coleridge and the Flight to Lyric." Here she highlights the fact that Coleridge's "re-views, novels, and poetry have not been considered together as part of her aesthetics" and argues that her "fascination with the past" is a feature that connects the genres of her writing (149).

30. Quoted in *The Spectator* 97 (10 November 1906), 751.

31. Quoted in *The Spectator* 97 (1 December 1906), 906.

32. "New Six Shilling Novels." *Mr. Edward Arnold's New Books. The Athenaeum* No. 4123 (3 November 1906): 564.

33. "New 6s. Novels, Second Impression." *Mr. Edward Arnold's New Books. The Spectator* 97 (24 November 1906): 851.

34. Quotations from *The Lady on the Drawingroom Floor* and from other writings by Coleridge will be cited parenthetically.

35. Whistler, "Introduction and Editorial Materials," 59.

36. Whistler, "Introduction and Editorial Materials," 60.

37. Whistler, "Introduction and Editorial Materials," 22.

38. Sichel, "Memoir and Editorial Materials," 11.

39. John Keats, *The Letters of John Keats*, ed. M. B. Forman (Oxford: Oxford University Press, 1935), 68.

40. Keats, *The Letters of John Keats*, 210.

41. Whistler, "Introduction and Editorial Materials," 50.

42. Isobel Armstrong, *Victorian Glassworlds: Glass Culture and the Imagination 1830–1880* (Oxford: Oxford University Press, 2008) examines the transformation of glass from an ancient to a modern material as conceived in the Victorian imagination. Of Coleridge's "The Other Side of a Mirror," she observes that "[t]he language of phantoms haunts Victorian mirror poems. … Which is the 'other side' of the mirror, the reflection of the shadow, the shadow of a reflection" (111). Identifying Tennyson's "The Lady of Shalott" as a precursor to Coleridge's poem, Armstrong explains how the mirror functions as a trap for femininity, a "set" surface in which the "raging, anguished, silent woman" must assume society's artificial ideal as her true identity (113).

43. Colin Franklin, 22.

44. Passages from letters and diaries, in *Gathered Leaves*, 227.

45. Walter de la Mare, "An Appreciation," *The Guardian* 11 September 1907, 2.

46. Whistler, "Introduction and Editorial Materials," 76.

Bibliography

Primary Works

Novels
Coleridge, M. E. *The Seven Sleepers of Ephesus*. London: Chatto & Windus, 1893.
———. *The King with Two Faces*. London and New York: Arnold, 1897.
———. *The Fiery Dawn*. London: Arnold/New York: Longmans, Green, 1901.
———. *The Shadow on the Wall*. London: Arnold, 1904.
———. *The Lady on the Drawingroom Floor*. London: Arnold/New York: Longmans, Green, 1906.

Poetry
Anodos. *Fancy's Following*. Oxford: Daniel Press, 1896/Portland, ME: Mosher, 1900.
———. *Fancy's Guerdon*. London: Elkin Mathews, 1897.

Coleridge, Mary E. *Poems by Mary E. Coleridge*, edited by Henry Newbolt. London: Elkin Mathews, 1918.

——. *Gathered Leaves from the Prose of Mary E. Coleridge*, edited by Edith Sichel. London: Constable, 1910.

——. *The Collected Poems of Mary Coleridge*, edited by Theresa Whistler. London: Rupert Hart-Davis, 1954.

Essays

Coleridge, M. E. *Non Sequitur*. London: J. Nisbet, 1900.

——. *Gathered Leaves from the Prose of Mary E. Coleridge*, edited by Edith Sichel. London: Constable, 1910. 1–44.

Biography

Coleridge, Mary E. *Holman Hunt: Illustrated with Eight Reproductions in Colour*. London: T. C. & E. C. Jack, 1908.

Secondary Criticism

Armstrong, Isobel. *Victorian Glassworlds: Glass Culture and the Imagination 1830–1880*. Oxford: Oxford University Press, 2008.

Baker, Kasey Bass. "'Oh Lift Me Over the Threshold and Let Me In At the Door!': Boundaries and Thresholds in Mary Coleridge's Poetry." *Victorian Poetry* 48.2 (2010): 195–218.

Battersby, Christine. *Gender and Genius: Towards a Feminine Aesthetics*. London: Women's Press, 1989. 148–51.

——. "Her Blood and His Mirror: Mary Coleridge, Luce Irigaray, and the Female Self." In *Beyond Representation: Philosophy and Poetic Imagination*, edited by Richard Eldridge. Cambridge: Cambridge University Press, 1996. 249–72.

Binyon, Laurence. "Mary Coleridge." In *The English Poets*, edited by Thomas Humphry Ward. New York: Macmillan, 1925. 614.

Blain, Virginia, Patricia Clements, and Isobel Grundy, eds. *The Feminist Companion to Literature in English: Women Writers from the Middle Ages to the Present*. New Haven: Yale University Press, 1990.

Braun, Heather. "Mary E. Coleridge, Androgyny, and the Spectral Doppelgänger." *Parlour: A Journal of Literary Analysis and Criticism* (Special Edition: "Pushing Back: Feminist Readings as Resistance") 1.2 (2016): 1–7.

Bridges, Robert. "The Poems of Mary Coleridge." *Cornhill Magazine* (13 November 1907), 594–605, reprinted in *Collected Essays, Papers &c. of Robert Bridges*, vol. 5, edited by Donald Stanford. Oxford: Oxford University Press, 1931. 205–29.

Chapman, Alison. "Mary Elizabeth Coleridge, Literary Influence and Technologies of the Uncanny." In *Victorian Gothic: Literary and Cultural Manifestations in the Nineteenth Century*, edited by Ruth Robbins and Julian Wolfreys. New York: Palgrave, 2000. 109–28.

———. "Mary Elizabeth Coleridge and the Flight to Lyric." *The Yearbook of English Studies, From Decadent to Modernist: And Other Essays* 37.1 (2007): 145–60.

Crump, Rebecca W. *A Critical Study of the Works of Four British Writers: Margaret Louisa Woods, Mary Coleridge, Sir Henry Newbolt, R. C. Trevelyan.* New York: Edwin Mellen Press, 2006.

de la Mare, Walter. "An Appreciation." *The Guardian* 11 September 1907. 1–4.

Devlin, Karen. "Mary Coleridge (1861–1907): A Brief Biography." The Victorian Web. http://www.victorianweb.org/authors/coleridge/bio.html.

Dole, Carol. "Mary E. Coleridge." In *Dictionary of Literary Biography, vol. 19.* Alternate Title: *British Poets, 1880–1914,* edited by Donald E. Stanford. Detroit: Gale Research, 1983. 77–80.

Franklin, Caroline and Michael J. Franklin. "Victorian Gothic Poetry: The Corpse's [a] Text." In *The Victorian Gothic: An Edinburgh Companion,* edited by Andrew Smith and William Hughes. Edinburgh: Edinburgh University Press, 2012. 72–92.

Franklin, Colin. *Poets of the Daniel Press.* Rampant Lion Press, 1988.

Gilbert, Sandra and Susan Gubar. *The Madwoman in the Attic: The Woman Writer and the Nineteenth-Century Literary Imagination.* New Haven: Yale University Press, 1979.

Grimes, Janet G. *Novels in English by Women, 1891–1920.* New York: Garland, 1981.

Jackson, Vanessa Furse. "Breaking the Quiet Surface: The Shorter Poems of Mary Coleridge." *English Literature in Transition* 39.1 (1996): 41–62.

Keats, John. "Letter 31." *The Letters of John Keats.* Ed. M.B. Forman. Oxford: Oxford University Press, 1947.

"Lesser Poets of the Middle and Later Nineteenth Century: R. W. Dixon." *Bartleby. com: Great Books Online: The Cambridge History of English and American Literature, Volume XIII, The Victorian Age, Part One: Chapter VI.* 30 August 2004. 1–2. Web.

McGowran, Katherine. "Re-reading Women's Poetry at the Turn of the Century." *Victorian Poetry* 41.4 (2003): 584–89.

Newbolt, Henry, ed. "Preface." *Poems by Mary E. Coleridge* (1907). London: Elkin Mathews, 1918. v–xii.

"New Six Shilling Novels." Mr. *Edward Arnold's New Books. The Athenaeum* No. 4123 (3 November 1906): 564.

"New 6s. Novels, Second Impression." Mr. *Edward Arnold's New Books. The Spectator* 97 (24 November 1906): 851.

Parascandola, Louis J. "Mary Elizabeth Coleridge." In *An Encyclopedia of British Women Writers,* revised and expanded edition, edited by Paul Schlueter and June Schlueter. New Brunswick: Rutgers University Press, 1998. 162–63.

Pearson, Carol and Katherine Pope. *Who Am I This Time?: Female Portraits in British and American Literature.* New York: McGraw-Hill, 1976.

Showalter, Elaine, *A Literature of Their Own: British Women Novelists from Brontë to Lessing.* Princeton: Princeton University Press, 1977.

Sichel, Edith. "Memoir and Editorial Materials." In *Gathered Leaves from the Prose of Mary E. Coleridge,* edited by Edith Sichel. London: Constable, 1910. 1–44.

Smith, Andrew and William Hughes, eds. *The Victorian Gothic: An Edinburgh Companion*. Edinburgh: Edinburgh University Press, 2014.

Stevenson, Warren. "Mary Coleridge." In *Modern British Essayists, First Series. Dictionary of Literary Biography*, vol. 98, edited by Robert Beum. Detroit: Gale Research, 1990. 73–76.

Welby, T. E. [Stet, of the *Saturday Review*] "Mary Coleridge." In *Back Numbers*. New York: Richard Smith, 1930. 124.

Whistler, Theresa. "Introduction and Editorial Materials." In *The Collected Poems of Mary Coleridge*, edited by Theresa Whistler. London: Rupert Hart-Davis, 1954. 21–81. 954. 21–81.

~

The Lady on the Drawingroom Floor

M. E. Coleridge

London
Edward Arnold
41 & 43, Maddox Street, Bond Street, W.
1907

THE LADY ON THE
DRAWINGROOM FLOOR

BY

M. E. COLERIDGE

AUTHOR OF "THE KING WITH TWO FACES," "THE FIERY DAWN,"
"THE SHADOW ON THE WALL," ETC.

FOURTH IMPRESSION

LONDON
EDWARD ARNOLD
41 & 43, MADDOX STREET, BOND STREET, W.
1907

I

When first I came to know Lucilla, she had lived on this unworthy earth for many years—how many I do not recollect. She told me once, for she was frank about matters regarding which most women are silent, as well as reserved on those which they discuss. I recollect certain words that she used.

"*I welcome the years gladly!*" she said.

They struck me—and I wondered why. Why should she, why should any one else for the matter of that, "welcome the years gladly?" "*Patiently*"— "*submissively*"—"*resignedly*"—these expressions I could have understood. How was it possible that any living thing should welcome "gladly" the harbingers of eyelessness, toothlessness, gout, and sleep?

And then she told me her age; and not caring to think of it, for, to my mind, Death sits always on the doorstep of any one whom I love, I changed the current of our talk. I have no memory for such details. Those who honour me with their friendship do not belong to Time.

She lived above me, in every sense of the word. Light was her object in the geography of life; ease being mine. She wanted to go up as many stairs as possible—I as few. Therefore I lodged on the ground-floor, while she had rooms *au premier*. Her coming into these rooms made such a curious difference that the period before she came is all confusion, like those chaotic periods of History before there were any Kings and Queens.

To the best of my belief, however, I had lived in the house about a hundred years before I grew conscious of her presence. I had looked for a hundred years at the little flat houses in front, each one exactly like the other. I had looked for a hundred years upon the soot-strewn "leads" behind.

After the coming of Lucilla the view changed. Only an effort of memory now recalls to me the fact that once it was dull.

"These houses all alike! Who ever said such a thing? He could have had no eyes in his head," said she.

"Well!" I observed, "you can't see much in the house opposite."

"You can see a story written by Balzac, if you look. That house opposite is *The Old Lady's House*. Nobody lives there except the Old Lady and her dogs and her cook and her maid. It is all in apple-pie order; and she thinks she can never have anybody to stay because there is not room enough and the servants would be overworked. Really, she does not care for other people except in other people's houses."

"But the next house is exactly like it."

"Forgive me—nothing could be more different! The house next door is *The Children's House*. There are six of the children, and only a mother, who's a widow, and one general, to look after them all; but the general does not leave so often as the Old Lady's cook, and they are always having people to stay—sometimes a girl with red hair, sometimes a girl with black, sometimes both girls together. They're not pretty children, but the baby is—well, she is a baby!—and now and then the artist who lives on the other side, and has a knocker made of snakes, will borrow her to paint."

"The next door on the other side of the Old Lady?" I said, with a gasp.

"I have not yet made up my mind as to the next door on the other side of the Old Lady. He must have something to do with a flower shop, I think. There is a palm in the window. I am sure she could not afford to *buy* a palm."

After that I looked out for an Old Lady at one window and a Baby at another, and an Artist at another and a mysterious Florist's wife at another, and life had four new interests. As for the leads, they disappeared. Lucilla covered them up with flower pots and ran a creeper along the wall.

The change without, however, was nothing to the change within.

Yet before she came I had considered myself rather fortunate in my lodgings, as London lodgings go. There was nobody musical in them to begin with. Nobody played scales.

To continue, I was on good terms with the landlord—a small trim, wiry, green-eyed man, wide awake and observant. When not at work he stood with his hands in his pockets, and an oddly wistful air of expecting something that never came. It was, perhaps, his wife, for she would make no response when he summoned her, and he summoned her rather often. He was an ex-butler, and he had a kind of distant regard for a gentleman—even for a gentleman who was not rich.

"He calls me *Sir*—and I like it!" said a young fellow of six, an acquaintance of mine, when I questioned him once as to the character of his butler.

My landlord called me *Sir*; and I liked it.

He finished a bottle of wine sometimes, without asking leave; but at the slightest hint he always made it clear that he would not have done this if he had not thought me a gentleman. I forbore to ask him why stealing from a gentleman was not stealing at all, when stealing from any one else was. He stole nothing besides, and my respect for his character suffered little diminution because his code of justice was not ethically sound. Robin Hood held much as he did. Most likely I stole something from him without knowing it. We are all robbers, if it comes to that, and we live by depriving each other of valuable assets for which money is no compensation. I would not have taken twice the money, to do for him what he did for me, to brush his clothes and clean his boots. Surely he was entitled to an extra glass of wine on occasion.

"Very wrong indeed!" said Lucilla, without paying the slightest heed to my line of argument. "He never touches anything in my cupboard. If you want him to have an extra glass of wine, tell him so!"

I did.

From that day to this he has never touched a drop; which inclines me to think that stolen wine—like stolen waters—must be sweet.

His deference in conversation pleased. It is not granted to every one to talk well about the weather. Shepherds do so, according to a brilliant modern essayist, and sailors likewise. If the essayist had had the privilege of knowing this estimable man, my landlord would have been included. When the weather was very hot, he alluded to the eruption of some distant volcano in a tone implying that, of course, I knew all about it. If there was a hard frost, he mentioned icebergs in the North Sea, and said something respectful about the Glacial Theory as though it were a friend of mine.

The landlady was a much cleverer man than the landlord. Her weekly bills were a marvel of ingenuity. No single item amounted to more than sixpence—in fact it was, as a rule, far below that sum—and yet the total caused dismay. She was tall and rather handsome; hard, black hair; hard, black eyes; the slightly aquiline nose that governs trade. Her husband stood much in awe of her; his instinctive knowledge that I did also, formed another bond between us. Outwardly, she was more honest than he, but she was voluble, and I would rather lose half a bottle of wine any day than the idle froth of fancies that her sharp tongue put to flight. It is open to me to get another bottle of wine, it is not open to me to call back the mood that is gone. The attitude of the landlord always implied that I knew many things which he would give the world to know. The attitude of his wife always implied that I must desire to know many things that she knew, things that I would have given the world not to know. She fulfilled to the letter the terrible description of being a host in herself. Two or three other women might have rushed into the room and made less noise in it than she did. There was no keeping her out. She *would* come in. She *would* tell me why coals had risen and what had gone wrong with the sink. She seemed to think that these mysterious afflictions were in some way due to me—that I was bound in honour to give her an equivalent in solid cash for the annoyance that they caused. Coals and the sink do not interest me. I used to hum the air from "Cox and Box:"

> "Coals haven't got souls
> Any more than they have legs."

I used to wonder why I never could say *Don't come in* when I heard her rat-tat-tat on my door. I could no more say it than Macbeth could say "Amen" to the pious ejaculation of the groom in his sleep. There are things that cannot be said.

Still I preferred even the landlady to the landlady's maidservant. She was always addressed as "Mahry," a cockney equivalent for the French name of *Marie*, which is considered much more elegant than *Mary* plain and simple. Her shoes were down-at-heel: her hair was neither up nor down; her face looked as if she slept in the coalhole. When I asked her to do anything, she said *Yiss*; and when I asked her if she knew anything, she said *Naow!*

Lucilla had not dwelt in the house a week before a subtle transformation took place.

First of all the shoes of Mahry reformed themselves. Instead of flap-flop-ping about the room like a moribund fish, they began to move quietly and steadily. Some one had given her a new pair of shoes, I imagined.

A day or two later, some one appeared to have given her new hair. She arranged it in bright and pretty plaits. She looked like a different being.

Yet later she appeared with a new face and new hands. I did not know her. Not for the world would I have given my landlady a conversational opening; but I expressed surprise and gratification to my landlord.

"Yes sir," he rejoined. "It's Miss Z. She takes a interest in the gurl."

There was an unmistakable air of rejuvenescence about him also. He had a furtive appearance of enjoying occupations that were not in the day's work, nailing up creepers and the like. He never actually whistled, but he looked as if some day he might. He expressed to me, with deference, as if I had provided him with her, his opinion that he had done very well to secure Miss Z. as a lodger.

"She's a lady, sir, she is!"

Was Miss Z. taking an interest in him too?

There was a strange silence on the part of the landlady.

Even the landlady was not the same. She cooked much better than before—or much less badly. I once remarked with hesitation, anxious how-ever, to show that I was not indifferent, how much more enjoyable dinner had become of late. I knew how things ought not to be done; but beyond this I knew nothing. Miss Z. came to the front again at once. Miss Z., the landlady assured me, took a interest in cooking, she knew how things ought to be done, she had suggested certain amendments, certain methods in vogue at all fashionable clubs. The landlord ought to have known about them, but he did not. He never did nothing but read "The Dyly Myle." How was she, the landlady, to know? She was not a idle man, she thanked goodness! But when somebody took a interest in the food that was sent up to them, why you liked to show as you was not a perfect fool! I had taken a deep and mournful interest in the food that was sent up to me before now; but she ignored this.

All these improvements alarmed me not a little. Suppose Miss Z. began to take an interest in the only person now left outside the sphere of her beneficence?

Fear was awake and astir.

Jealousy awoke next.

To the backyard a cat was wont to come, the only thing on four legs that ever had come willingly to me.

Now there are cats and cats. To say "a cat" is as indefinite as if one said "A man."

There is the Gray Cat, the Cat of Egypt, a goddess calm and smooth and careless of mankind, fascinating, as certain women are, from utter indifference. She inherits the stately and gracious manners, the lofty reserve of a long line of ancestors, one of whom, no doubt, gazed with gold eyes upon the Pharaoh of the Exodus. It is a privilege to look after a cat like that.

There is the Persian, redolent of Omar, catching, if ever she caught anything at all, nothing inferior to a bulbul; fed, like the Roman gluttons, upon the tongues of nightingales. "Is she not an angel?" I have heard my cousin cry enthusiastically, as the chosen of her hearth stood up and waved a tail as big as a Turk's head. But my cousin was wrong. The angels have nothing feline about them. "Where there are birds there are angels." That cat is a Sphinx, like her sister of Egypt.

There is the White Cat, dear to fairy tale, amiable, gentle, not so fond of her claws as other cats—a perfect lady.

There is the Black Cat, green-eyed, not a single spot of snow on her breast. Why she, of all cats, should be considered lucky, I have never been able to imagine. She brings with her a Faust-like sense of expeditions on a broomstick, of the revels of witches out for the night on their unsabbatical Sabbath.

The Back Street Cat was none of these. It was an outcast cat, a cat with a past, a cat whose paw was against every other cat. Pity for its forlorn condition one rainy day induced me to set out a saucer of the stuff called "milk" which Mahry brought me with my tea. I never talked *cat* to it. I am not good at languages, though very fond of them. But I named it Katerfelto, and by and by it answered to that name. The landlady kept it only because she kept mice. If it did not get enough mouse to eat, that was not her fault, for there were plenty on the premises: but it looked thin and jagged, and I think she threw boots at it. I cannot say that it became a friend, but it was less of an enemy to me than other cats. We established an armed neutrality—at least I did, for Katerfelto was armed rather than neutral, and showed his claws whenever I showed my hand. He had forgotten how to purr, if ever he knew how, but he swore like a trooper, and I believe he knew that I liked to hear him swear at the landlady. He never swore at me. At night, when he was in good voice, he sat upon the roof and sang. Then, indeed, I have awaked to find myself wishing that Katerfelto were dead.

One day he did not come as usual for milk. I thought perhaps he had gone a-hunting. He did sometimes; but then he always returned an hour or two later. As he never came at all, I questioned the landlord.

"It's Miss Z., sir," said he. "She takes a interest in cats, sir."

He offered to fetch Katerfelto for me, but I declined. I was not going to have the cast-off cats of Miss Z. to tea when she was tired of them. She must be very fond of cats to have grown fond of Katerfelto.

Next day—it was the day we heard of the relief of Kimberley—I was in high spirits, having just telegraphed the news to my cousin, whose boy was in the Relief Force. As I came in at the door, I saw a beautiful cat walking downstairs with great dignity, a "Union Jack" ribbon tied round its neck in a bow. It had been brushed and combed until its tabby fur stood round its head in a ruff. It looked all but a Persian. With difficulty I recognised my old acquaintance.

"Why, Katerfelto!" I said; and Katerfelto rubbed himself against my legs and purred.

"Persica!" cried a voice from above.

Katerfelto jumped upstairs, two steps at a time.

"I beg your pardon," I said primly, addressing space, "but that cat's name is Katerfelto."

"I daresay it *was* Katerfelto," said the voice, "but it's going to be Persica now. Purrsica—*PU* double *R*—I taught her to purr yesterday."

"Allow me to point out," I said, "that this is a Tom-cat."

"That can't be helped," said the same voice. "I've called it Persica."

I never heard mere air, converted into word of mouth, sound so decided. There was the noise of a door shut.

I felt annoyed. I persuaded myself that I was really fond of Katerfelto—that I resented the attitude of the *fâcheuse troisième* who had thrust herself between us. He never came near me after that. He always went up to tea with Miss Z. I believe she gave him cake.

Mahry had become another girl. The landlord had become another man. Katerfelto had become another cat.

The change in my landlady alarmed me more than all the other changes put together. Even the landlady had changed. Nothing remained unchanged except myself.

Alarm and jealousy increased. I entertained a nervous terror of Miss Z.

II

Positive aversion was the next stage. Bump-thump-bump-thump-bump-thump—what was that going upstairs?

"If it were to come down," I said to myself, "it would come down like the Ode of Klopstock that Heine heard, tumbling from the top storey to the bottom. Good gracious! what can it be?"

I rang the bell.

No one came.

I rang again, after a fashion to let people know that an angry man was ringing. My landlord appeared, very much out of breath. "I beg your parden, sir," said he, "I was a-helping of Miss Z.'s pianner into her room."

She had a piano then, and it was her piano that went upstairs like that. "Light as fairy foot can fall"—she had a piano.

She let me know it too. That evening—it was a Thursday—without a single preliminary chord that might have suggested what was coming—she struck up Chopin's Funeral March.

Now, if I have a weakness for anything on this earth, it is for Funeral Marches. The only fault I have to find with them is, that they do not last. No one is ever half long enough being buried to please me; and they do not begin soon enough neither. In my opinion, a Funeral March ought to begin like death itself—suddenly, majestically, without preparation. Thus it began when Lucilla played. She struck into the mighty chords without any preface or prelude.

I sat with bowed head, listening.

We had heard that day of the relief of Ladysmith. I had been living lightly but unsteadily, fluttered by an excitement that was too giddy for joy. After the long interminable months of waiting—after the fury of grief as one attempt failed after the other—my brain reeled, I think, at the tidings of success. I was not the only one.

The huge placards—the shouts—the flags—the chiming bells—the signals, roused a wild passion of vanity that shamed me after an hour or two, as if I had drunk champagne when I ought rather to have fallen upon my knees. It was not that I had forgotten the dead, but I had wilfully turned away from the quiet place of their rest. Now, at the touch of a hand that I had never seen, they came back. At the touch of a hand that I had never seen, my solemn rejoicing in their glory stilled the feverish clatter of triumph, unworthy thinking men, that had possessed me. I looked again at the little figure of Gordon above my mantelpiece. I thought of one lying far off among the sands of Egypt.

The next day I buoyed myself up with the hope that Chopin's Funeral March would begin again in the evening, I heard the dead leaves blowing over him as I sat at work among my musty books and papers—dead leaves too, but of another kind.

There is this about a mechanical occupation, that it sets the mind free to follow her own bent when business hours are over. Often have I envied the artist, the musician, the literary man, whose business is his pleasure. Yet it is not the musician who most enjoys the music. He knows too well—for himself and even for another—the agony of failure. Fingers too cold or too hot—feelings too hot or too cold. You may praise him up to the skies, but he has not earned his own approval. Comfort him if you can! What is the hideous clapping noise of a thousand hands to him who has heard the music of the spheres and rendered it wrongly? If it were not for his bread and butter, poor wretch, he would rather be hissed! The artist, if he sees beauty beyond our ken, frets himself often almost to death because others are blind and do not care to buy that which it is more than meat and drink to him to paint. Even the literary man, to whom his books are daily breakfast, dinner, and supper, does not know the taste of a book as he does who has been kept from it for nine hours out of a sixteen.

As soon as I could get free—and never had the office appeared to demand more attention—I hurried home to be in readiness for the funeral.

Dinner ended, I threw myself into an armchair, put my feet on the fender and prepared to pass into another world.

I looked at the little statue of Gordon, and I waited. Alas! a piano listened for bursts into song no sooner than a watched pot boils! The hour came and went—the piano remained dumb.

The next night came, and the next night. Still the piano kept silence.

Did it never sound except when a siege was raised?

The rest of the week passed, as many weeks of the wonderful thing called *life* do pass, in a blank heedlessness. I have no recollection of it. A strong conviction forced itself upon me, that I should hear that piano again on the day week that followed the relief of Ladysmith. As nine o'clock drew near I could hardly control my eagerness. Lucilla had begun at five minutes to nine a week ago. I sat by my fire under the shadow of Gordon, listening, listening.

Nine o'clock struck.

Still never a note.

Half-past nine.

I could bear it no longer.

I knew now that I could not sleep till I had heard that Funeral March once again. Perhaps Miss Z. was not at home! When this thought flashed across me I grew desperate, and summoned assistance.

"Mahry," I said, "is Miss Z. at home?"

"Yiss, sir," said Mahry. (She now said "sir.")

"Be so kind as to take her up this note, and to wait for the answer."

The note ran thus:

"The gentleman downstairs presents his compliments to the Lady on the Drawingroom floor. He would be greatly obliged if she would favour him with a repetition of Chopin's Funeral March."

The answer descended after an interval that, measured by the clock, appeared short. It was written in pencil, in a clear, bold hand, that asked for plenty of paper. There were no stops of any kind, but the words were spaced so that the meaning was clear.

"The Lady on the Drawingroom floor presents her compliments and she will be happy to play Chopin's Funeral March again if the Gentleman Downstairs will kindly mention the name of the hero in whose honour he would desire it played She cannot play it except in memory."

Here was a crux. I wondered whether the lady had an accurate mind. Her fingers were accurate enough; but her ideas? Was she the kind of person likely to have a Dictionary of Dates at hand? I decided to risk it. There was no time to be lost. I have observed that women, even women who know about history, do not as a rule read the Peninsular War.

"To-day," I wrote (Heaven and the Duke forgive me) "is the anniversary of the death of the Fiery Crawford."

For all I knew, it might just as well have been the anniversary of the death of Robert Bruce, but I dared not risk that, for she might have been better acquainted with Robert Bruce. Apparently she was satisfied, for, in a few minutes, a tremendous chord fell plump upon my ear. It was not Chopin, however. When I came to know that piano better, I learnt that it would never play the same air twice in succession. This was at once heavier and more electric; it suggested to my mind a funeral among the hills and in the mist. I heard the drums all night long.

The Lady on the Drawingroom floor and the gentleman downstairs were now on thinking, rather than on speaking, terms with each other. We did not meet face to face. She had heard my voice—in contradiction. I was aware that she spoke with the refinement of a woman who reads, and with a certain quality of decision which proclaimed at once that she was born to be king. Her fingers were more eloquent than her lips. She told the piano what she thought, and the piano told me. I did not reason it out. I knew she felt as I did about those who have died worthily. From that time forward there was a link, forged by the dead, between us. Fearful of breaking it, of finding out that words could break a sympathy deeper than words, I had no wish to talk with her. It was to me as if she had known him whom of all others I counted dear. I did not care to be told what I knew very well, that she had never even heard his name.

So far as I could make out, few people came to see Lucilla, but those who came stayed a long time. Sometimes I heard a bell ring and the door opened. An hour or more would pass before the door opened again; and no bell rang in the meantime.

I came to know, later on, that Lucilla never mingled nor confused her friends. It takes two to make one; it takes three to make two; in this sense she understood arithmetic. To say the same thing in another way, she had the precious gift of holding each friend in himself to be the only friend she possessed for the time being. Sensitive people are flattered thus—flattered even more successfully than they are flattered by other sweet women whose besetting virtue it is; to try and make every friend of theirs the friend of an earlier friend.

I learnt also that she was not quite such a recluse as I at first imagined. Most likely I did not hear her play on the long dark evenings between Chopin's Funeral March and the Funeral March Among the Mountains, because she was entertaining some one with the sound of his own voice, or because she had gone out to hear some one else talk. This explanation dawned on me at a large, unwieldy dinner-party in my cousin's house, to which I went, because, an invited guest having failed, she came herself and commanded my attendance in terms that did not admit of refusal. I was most unwilling to go. Suppose Lucilla took it into her head to play the Funeral March that evening? But "I want a man!" my cousin said, and bitter experience had taught me that my cousin—unlike her country—never wanted a man but she got one.

The youngest daughter of the house, a tall, pale Maypole of sixteen summers, who had to be encouraged to take her proper part in society, fell to my share. I looked forward with dread to the innumerable little bits of meat and pudding which, by order of her Mamma, we should be compelled to accept or refuse together. I am very much of Hazlitt's mind as regards a young girl. If she giggles, I detest her. If she is not shy, I do not like her. Shyness is the natural condition of a young girl, as it is of a fawn. At the same time I find her shyness dull and infectious. I do not know that any outside person could have made up his mind as to whether Frida was most afraid of me, or I of Frida.

Having discussed soup, fish, and the first *entrée* in almost unbroken silence, Frida, moved, I fear, by the fact that from the end of the table, her mother "gave her a look," made a sudden determined frightened rush.

"Cousin Oliver," she said, "are you a Wagnerian?"

She had heard a lecture by the distinguished musical critic of *The Times*, it appeared, and she thought that the whole duty of a man was to be a Wagnerian.

"I think I must be a Wagnerian," I said. "I heard a Funeral March the other night, and it was not like any other funeral march I ever heard, so I suppose it was Wagner's.

Most certainly I admired it."

"Was it like this?" she asked, and she actually beat the drum on the table-cloth with her little unformed pink fingers.

"Yes," I said encouragingly, "it was just like that."

In my heart I apologised to Lucilla as I spoke.

"Then it was Siegfried's Funeral March," she cried joyfully. "You heard it on the orchestra, of course."

"No—a piano."

"Who was playing?"

"Nobody that you know. A fellow lodger of mine, a Miss Z."

Frida's expression changed in an instant.

"Oh, Miss Z.," she cried, and broke off. It was as if she were lighting candles before a shrine and swinging incense. She asked no more questions. An intimation was conveyed to me, somehow or other, that I had uttered a name that was, in her eyes, too sacred for discussion; but she was attentive and kind throughout the evening only because I lived under one roof with Miss Z.

After dinner the conversation turned again upon music. They never talked of anything else in that house, except dancing.

"Were you at the Pop last Saturday, Mrs. Hopgood?" enquired a fatuous dark young man, rather stout, with too many rings on, and eyes that were like bad rings. "I heard your daughter mention Miss Z. at dinner. I saw her there. Awfully taking woman she is." He broke off as though he could have said much more but that he was too far in Miss Z's. confidence, or she too far in his.

"Charmin'!" echoed a fair young fellow of whose prowess at cricket I had often heard. "Met her at Lady Dartry's the other night."

And he, too, broke off meditatively, as who should say, "I know something about *her!*" or "She knows something of the utmost importance about *me.*"

I have heard my cousin assert, not without gentle malice, that she had begun to make a list of the gentlemen she met, each of whom wished it to be understood that he was the only intimate friend of Miss Z., and that in the course of a month the names ran up to forty. I can believe this, although my cousin's statements are not always made upon oath. Lucilla gave to every one who crossed her threshold a sense of intimacy. She made no acquaintances; either she did not know people at all, or she knew them well. The sense of intimacy, however, had nothing to do with what she said, and I doubt whether the visitors who went away well content knew her so well as they thought they knew her. She seldom either asked or answered questions, disdaining the cheap and obvious methods to which common minds have recourse in the effort to understand. She took the trouble to think over everyone in whom she felt interested, as if he had been a carpet, a wall-paper, or a piece of needle-work—with surprising results.

Women varied more in their opinion of her than men. They were not spellbound like the young girls—like the weak members of the stronger sex; quite the reverse.

"Rather too fond of having her own way, don't you think?" said my cousin.

As Miss Z. lived by herself, I did not see whose way she could have had except her own. True, she might have had the land-lady's way! That she did not adopt, and the landlady had grown censorious in consequence. But the landlady caught a bad cold a few days before this dinner-party. Miss Z. (I heard it from my landlord, who was impressed with the quality of the dish) went down into the kitchen and made arrowroot for her. After that the landlady fell silent. This rather annoyed me at the time; it was unlike the idea that I had formed of Lucilla that she should do anything useful, and there was too distinct a moral about it. I began to see in imagination regiments of *ci-devant* landladies who had "seen better days" marching up to receive flannel petticoats and packets of tea and sugar; and I felt certain that I should have to give notice. I hate the Ministering Angel kind of woman. I like the flower, the star, the fancy.

I was recalled from these meditations by the voice of my cousin as she stirred up the white cat with her foot.

"Is she well off?"

"I do not know. I should not think so, as she lives in Back Street."

"She is very independent," said my cousin, who likes to confer a benefit. "Sir Simon Smear, who is, of course, an R.A., recommended her to me as the best person he knew for copying miniatures. So I asked her to do Aunt Sally—you know, Oliver, Aunt Sally with the red hair, who used to give us rice puddings on Sunday, because it was good for the complexion. She did it well, I daresay, but she took a long time over it, and her charges are enormous; so I gave Uncle John to little Miss Twitter. It may not be quite such a pretty picture, but then Miss Twitter got it done in three days, and she was so pleased to be asked to stay to luncheon. It kills two birds with one stone, you know, because Miss Twitter is very poor. I am surprised to find that Miss Z. has so many acquaintances. I should hardly have thought she was in a condition to dine out."

Secretly I felt glad to learn that Miss Z. was independent. She might condescend to work now and then, because she liked to paint and could paint well; and if she did she would insist on proper remuneration. As I remembered the stately strains that floated down to me from the drawingroom floor, I could not think of her as a poor little harassed, down-trodden drudge like Miss Twitter. I had seen Miss Twitter, and I had seen Miss Twitter's miniatures.

"Her clothes are so peculiar," the critic went on.

"Indeed! Does she sport a turban?"

"Did you never see her?"

"I have not had that pleasure."

"How odd, when you live in the same house! Oh! well, I daresay you would not have noticed anything! Men have no eyes."

This, by the way, is the only remark about men that all the women I know have concurred in making.

"Tell me, my dear cousin, you who have such surpassing eyes, what it is that they see when they see Miss Z.?"

"Oh, I can't answer that kind of question!" said my cousin. "She wears coral—and nobody wears coral nowadays. And a big cameo brooch, a Roman cameo, the size of a frying-pan. And a little close bonnet that fits tight to the head. It's very becoming; I daresay she trimmed it herself."

"She is clever, then?"

"Oh, no, not in the least! She did not even know where Wilton Place was when someone mentioned it the other day."

I pondered over Lucilla's old-fashioned ornaments, over her coral and her cameo brooch, as I walked homewards. Inherited, of course. It seemed to me that she wore these things because she liked them. We have all our weaknesses; I, nameless thing that I was, felt pleased to learn that Lucilla had a grandmother; that grandmother had had a grandmother, probably.

The thought that Lucilla was poor—even the idea that she might be—was repellent. Surely the piano indicated wealth—unless, indeed, she was one of those, like myself, to whom certain luxuries are more necessary than the needful. Yet she could not be rich. No one would have lived in Back Street who was rich enough to live out of it.

Perhaps she was merely playing at poverty. She was, perhaps, a great lady in hiding. It is an odd game to play at, but people do odd things for amusement, as they do odd things for money. So long as she was poor by her own will, it made no matter to me. There is all the difference in the world between chosen poverty and poverty that cannot be helped. When Francis of Assisi took Lady Poverty to wife, he was richer than the head of the Rothschild family; but poverty, when she is not treated as a lady, poverty unsought, unclaimed, struggled against, degrades the poor like some insidious illness of the brain.

I speak of the only class of which I have personal knowledge—of the genteel poor; not of those who are born and die in the slums. When I reflect on the life of these last, I am filled with panic-stricken admiration—I am standing at the bar on the Day of Judgment, without defence. Their very vices put me to shame.

Only drunk? Only dishonest?

The Pharisee who saw a man going by to be hanged, and said to himself, "There, but for the grace of God, goes John Bradford!" had not eyes to see that the man who was going to be hanged was probably the better off of the two. He had no vanity, poor fellow, no ridiculous "appearance" to keep up in the eyes of his brother men!

The ideas of the genteel poor and of the poor who are not genteel are very different.

The genteel poor do everything that they can to conceal their poverty, short of telling a lie *in words*. They will go out to dine to hide the fact that they have no dinner at all.

I have done it myself.

They will spend hours sitting in a cold, stuffy Museum, or tramping the streets, because they would rather people did not know that the coals have all but come to an end, and there is no money to buy more.

I have done it myself.

They shut themselves up in their poverty and make an excuse of it not to help others, when, if they were as rich as Crœsus, they would not help.

I have done it myself.

But they will never tell a lie *in words*.

Now the poor who are not genteel have no regard for truth *in words*. They look upon her as she is *in love*. They will say they are poorer than they are, if they see the slightest advantage in doing so. They have their want-of-all-things in common, they make an excuse of it to help each other everywhere.

I could not nurse a foul, foul-tempered old woman for eight weeks, without ever taking my clothes off, any more than I could tell a lie to earn sixpence; but I am glad, and for the sake of humanity, I am proud to take the part of the hundreds of men and women who can, against myself—to own that this exaggerated love of literal truth is a poor thing as compared with the love of my neighbour. There is much about my neighbour in the Ten Commandments and little about truth, except as it concerns him. All virtue is involuntary. "Here stand I, God help me, I can no otherwise!" It is virtuous to speak the truth—well and good; but between the man who speaks the truth because he cannot help it, and the man who is the slave of others because he cannot help it, there is a great gulf fixed, although both are virtuous. The slave is on a higher level than the other. I cannot choose, the choice was never granted me. I follow the cold and blue star, Truth—not the red star of Love. I cannot follow another man's nor he mine. I can, I must admire the beauty of his following; but he does not enjoy my society, nor I his.

III

One day, when I came home from work, I found a tortoise on the hearth-rug. There it stood with its head straight out, as if it had stood there since the beginning of the world.

Words fail me to describe my embarrassment. In silence, though not in tears, I gazed at it for some time. At last I poked it with my stick.

The tortoise might have been stone-dead for all the notice that it took. Still I made no doubt that it was alive, horridly alive; if I ventured to read a book or write a letter, it would begin to crawl about.

I sat down and watched it; but it did nothing at all. At last the situation became unendurable. I rang the bell.

"Mahry!" I said, "where did that tortoise come from?"

Mahry shrank away towards the door with an expression of agony.

"Don't you ask me for to touch it, sir!" said Mahry in a smothered scream. "I can't abear them reptiles. I'd rather meet a lion any day. I couldn't touch him, no, not with a pair of tongs—no, not if you was to offer me £5, sir!"

She took a corner of her apron, as if prepared for tears, and backed out of the door.

Now Mahry was not in the least likely to meet a lion any day—nor did I wish her to remove the reptile with a pair of tongs—nor could I, in the state of my finances, have offered her £5 for this important service. Whether I should have taken it myself, had any one offered me so much on condition that I removed the tortoise, I do not know. My sentiments—bar the encounter with the lion—were exactly the same as those of Mahry.

Still, helpless as she appeared to be, I felt myself obliged to recall her. I could not be left alone with that beast.

"Mahry," I said, "it is your fault. You must have left the door open when you brought in the tea; otherwise this most untoward event would not have occurred. Whose is the tortoise?"

"Please, sir, it's Miss Z.'s tortoise, sir, which she bought it off of a man in the street this morning, sir."

"Did she indeed? She hardly intended to make a present of it to me, I suppose. Is she at home?"

"Naow, sir."

Mahry was edging towards the door.

It is all very well to have a musician on the drawingroom floor, but I had not the slightest desire to see a menagerie established there.

"If Miss Z. cannot keep the tortoise upstairs," I observed, "I shall give it back to the man in the street."

I wondered, as I spoke, whether it would be possible to find him before Miss Z. came home. There are so many men in the street.

"Yiss, sir," said Mahry, getting still nearer the door.

"Kindly give her this note as soon as she returns," I said, and indited the following: —

"The gentleman downstairs has received a visit from a Tortoise, which belongs, he is told on good authority, to the Lady on the Drawingroom floor. As he is not accustomed to receive Tortoises, he is unacquainted with the etiquette to be observed on such occasions. Would Miss Z. be so kind as to tell him what is the next move? For the Tortoise makes none."

Tea was impossible. I might, at any moment, find the thing on my knee. I took a book, sat down opposite it, and longed for the return of Miss Z. as a sleepless invalid for the approach of morning. I could not read. Once I began; but the tortoise put its head out a little further. I tried to write a letter; but then the tortoise drew its head back.

I began to wonder how old it was.

I remembered, under a glass case at Lambeth, certain remains of a venerable tortoise that had played with Archbishop Laud. This present tortoise now before me might have heard the voice of Strafford at Whitehall. Rupert of the Rhine might have stroked its back; it had, perhaps, accepted a dandelion from the white hand of Henrietta Maria. I did not suppose it had anything to do with the Puritans. Tortoises are, I feel sure, Erastian and cavalier.

In the midst of these reflections I heard a key turn, and the front door opened.

Miss Z. had a latch-key, then, a boon constantly denied to me since I lost the three first and refused to pay a pound for the fourth. There was a momentary pause. Mahry, no doubt, was presenting my note. The next instant Miss Z. might be upon me. I had never thought of that. I was beginning to feel that even the society of the tortoise might be less embarrassing, when I heard her go calmly along the hall and up the stairs.

If I had been alarmed lest she should come, I was now twice as much alarmed lest she should not. I could not spend the evening with that creature. I made up my mind that I should go out to dine.

Suddenly, however, Mahry reappeared, grim, determined, armed with a black tea- tray.

"Well?"

"Miss Z. says I'm to bring the 'orrible reptile upstairs at onest," said Mahry, in a voice which convinced me that she would have laid her now tidy head on the block in a second, if Miss Z. had required it.

She put the tray down on the rug, and proceeded to urge the tortoise on to it by the application of the shovel behind. He stood upon the order of his going, but go he did. I dare be sworn he went upstairs much faster than he came down. Once he had crossed the Rubicon, and was safely landed on the tray, Mahry dropped the shovel as if it had been red-hot, and fled to the Drawingroom floor as though a policeman were at her heels.

A note came to hand five minutes later.

"The Lady on the Drawingroom floor regrets that Barnaby Rudge should have caused the Gentleman Downstairs inconvenience She will know better how to restrain him in future."

She kept her word. Rudge never darkened my doors again.

It was long, however, before I got over a nervous fear that he might.

Some time after, having been without news for a longer period than usual, I inquired what had become of him.

"He has disappeared," said Lucilla. "Tortoises always do. I have had three, and they all disappeared."

This comforted me, and I inquired no further.

It seemed appropriate. Barnaby Rudge could not have taken such a definite step as to die. No; like many a tyrant before him, he "disappeared."

Lucilla showed, on this occasion, all the kindly indifference that has often amazed me in people who devote themselves to pets. They will behave as if the adored object were the only thing in life that deserved their affection; they will sacrifice their own comfort and the comfort of others remorselessly, to attend to its lightest want; but when it "disappears" they accept the fact with a philosophy for which their previous warmth has not prepared one. Their very sympathy with animals gives them, I believe, a touch of the indifference of animals over the inevitable. I do not forget that Sir Walter Scott refused to dine out on the night of his dog's death; and I have myself seen Lucilla unable to speak when—but I anticipate.

IV

For a few days after the Rudge Raid there was peace.

Often of an evening Lucilla talked to the piano, and the piano talked to me. I used to wonder afterwards what it was that she said—I wondered what she looked like as she said it.

If I myself could have remained unseen, I should have wished to see her. She was, I fancied, small, fair, dignified as becomes the little women who rule; alarmingly, yet rather charmingly reserved.

Complexion—ivory, stained with faint rose-leaf. Eyes—blue, Irish gray, something between:—

"Eyes too expressive to be blue,
Too lovely to be gray."

Well-plaited hair, and plenty of it. I have not the indifference professed by Benedick as to the colour of a lady's hair. Black hair is disagreeable to me; there should be nothing black about a lady. If it had pleased Heaven that her hair should be black, I could not but feel disappointed.

I was pondering over her appearance one afternoon when a loud and very hoarse voice, a dreadful travesty of my own, said, close to my ear, "*Mahry, shut the door!*"

There, on the back of my chair, sat a little green parrot, and, without any more ado, he walked on to my shoulder, where he began to sing "Tom Bowling's gone aloft."

"I'll not have you calling me Mahry, nor Tom Bowling neither. You'll go aloft yourself—and very shortly!" I said with decision; and marched upstairs, taking no time to consider.

If I had hesitated one moment, I should have been lost, but the firm grasp of the parrot's claws, rooted in my coat, gave me confidence, and I knocked at the first door on the landing.

"Come in!" said the voice there was no disobeying: and I turned the handle.

That is a strange moment when we see for the first time one at whom we have looked hitherto with the eye of the mind alone. I remained dumb. She was not in the least what I expected.

She was tall—taller than myself. She was pale, not as those are whose roses have faded, but as those who are born under an alien star. She was dark, and her hair—black hair—curved like a shell as it rose on either side above her great calm forehead. She had large dark eyes. Whether they were softer than they were deep—deeper than they were soft, I never knew; they had not the penetrating look that makes one so uncomfortable in the presence of some women. She never seemed to be reading her interlocutor as if, *faute de mieux*, she were reading a book. There was distance in her eyes; they appeared to be resting on things beautiful exceedingly, but far, far away. Whether the image reflected in them were of the past or of the future, who could tell? Of both perhaps; for what was will be.

Thus she stood for an instant, gazing. But when she really saw the sight before her there was a sudden change, the change that comes on water ruffled by the wind. She did not laugh aloud, but she covered her face with her hands, and her stately form shook.

There is nothing (except fear) more infectious than laughter. We laughed in company—we laughed for several minutes before a word was spoken. After that she made a perch of her finger, coaxed the little parrot away, put him back in his cage, and thanked me as well as she could for laughter.

"It is a great mistake to have pets," she said, "especially other people's. You never know what they are after. Still, I think I can promise that they will not annoy you for the next half-hour at any rate; they will be too busy eating and drinking. We are all going to drink tea together. Will you not take a cup with us, to show that you bear no malice?"

Therewith she lifted down from a shelf a pretty, half-transparent cup and saucer.

"I dust them every day," she said apologetically, and we sat down.

Katerfelto was purring over a saucer of milk. Barnaby Rudge was sucking out of another, the parrot waddled down off his perch and began to eat bread and milk from a Japanese bowl. Where a cat, a bird, a tortoise, and a woman, were all comfortable together, why should not a man be happy too?

He was.

A quiet sensation of well-being stole over me, so soon as I felt myself one of their company.

The light, bright, airy room was the perfect expression of the taste of one person, and that person a lady.

Over and over again I have seen a charming room spoilt because too many people have been permitted to adorn it. Unity—purpose—repose—are frittered away by crowds of photographs—the last new baby of the last great friend—the girl the husband's brother is engaged to—Sarah Bernhardt dressed as a man—Dan Leno dressed as a woman—the gloomy brows of Kitchener—

the amiable tightness of "Bobs." Lucilla had no photographs in public. In private she had many, but she kept them in a heart-shaped box, covered with blue linen, and suffered no eyes but her own to rest on them, except by special favour. To my mind, she honoured the originals with more delicacy by this exclusive preference. She would not, could not expose them to the common light of day, nor bare the features that she loved to the chance criticism, the flighty admiration of a casual visitor. She did not even think that she herself was always in a fit mood to behold them. She observed times and seasons.

One photograph, however, she displayed, "The Unknown," Painter Unknown, from the Louvre; and she displayed it in the post of honour, over the fire. There he hung, his eyes full of affection and unrest, his lips disdainful, every inch of his odd face contradicting every other inch of it.

What kind of man was he, I wondered? Why did Lucilla care to have that face—of all the faces in the world—before her?

He was not all of one piece, I think. His virtues would have despaired, had it not been for his vices; and his vices would have had it all their own way, had it not been that, "when he wandered here and there, he then went most aright."

"You know many things," I said once to Lucilla. "But even you do not know whether that fellow is in Heaven or in Hell."

"He is not in Heaven now, but he will be!" she replied with earnestness.

I laughed.

"You speak as if you meant to meet him there."

"I do!" she said, still in the same serious tone.

We held this conversation long after our first interview, at a time when she went often to the National Gallery under my escort.

"I bet you my Tintoretto—if I had it—to your Fra Angelico—if you had it—he is in Hell. The mouth is bad."

"The eyes are good," she said. She was looking at me as she spoke, not at the portrait.

"Character shows most in the mouth. Our other features are kind to us, and keep the secret. But the mouth is the traitor; and the mouth, I repeat, is bad."

"You have no call to abuse it," she rejoined. "It is very like your own."

To which, of course, there was no answer. When I reached the seclusion of my bedroom, I consulted a looking-glass, and found to my disgust that she was right.

No other face, whether of man or woman, adorned her walls.

Nor was there any sketch, picture, or photograph that could, by any possibility, be made to bear the title of *The Old Home*.

On one wall hung a print; a long, long avenue of thin, tall trees, such as are to be seen in the North of France, an avenue that led straight on to the sky. Beside the mantelpiece hung a tiny sketch of a bit of bough, a bird with outstretched wings, and—far below—the sea. Unless she were an angel or a mermaid, it would have been rash to come to any conclusion from these as to the place of Lucilla's origin.

The space at her command was doubled by an oval mirror in a frame of carved woodwork. There was a motto underneath, but I took many months to decipher it in the old, unfamiliar lettering. *Hier c'est demain* it ran. What had that mirror reflected yesterday?

In the centre of the mantelpiece, opposite the round mirror, there stood a bronze statuette of Charles George Gordon, the counterpart of that which I possessed. I recognised it with a feeling of pleasure, but without surprise—as if I had known all along that it must be there.

When I went back to my own apartment, it seemed bare and stupid by comparison, wanting alike in definite meaning and in suggestion of the world without. It was also very dusty. Lucilla's looked as if she dusted it morning and evening. I have no doubt she did. Mahry is not fond of dusting. I myself am not so fond of dusting as Mahry.

V

"You will come to tea with me again, this day week!" Lucilla had said, without a note of interrogation in her voice, when I rose to take leave. I cannot recollect whether I made any answer. That seemed unnecessary. She decided the matter as she decided every affair, great or little, within her ken; and it became a custom that I should drink two cups of tea and eat one piece of bread-and-butter and two of cake on the Drawingroom floor of a Thursday. Habit makes half the pleasure of meeting; and Lucilla knew this. An occasional visit is a duty to be discharged, but one paid regularly becomes agreeable, even if it was mere duty in the first instance; how much more when the first step cost nothing but a laugh?

I began to find the study of my neighbour one of the pleasantest studies imaginable.

For many years I had cared little about society. The memory of the one friend I had never lost, even by death, was company enough for me.

My lameness sets me at a disadvantage among sportsmen and athletes—the dryness and shyness of my manner is, I have often thought, repugnant to scholars and men of taste.

Even if I could move about as others do, I doubt that I should have had the strength of mind to fish or to shoot. I should have been the salmon, plunging and dashing in his efforts to escape; I should have been the fluttering wounded bird, the terrified hare. I have enjoyed a fight now and then. I enjoyed very keenly the fight in which I was lamed for life; but I cannot enjoy a struggle in which I am myself on the weaker side. I have seen, now and then, a human being look out of the eyes of an animal—as I have seen that more dreadful thing, an animal looking out of the eyes of a human creature. It is perhaps because I am weaker in body than a man should be, that anything yet weaker always seems to me like a woman. I have none of the huntsman's instinct concerning Woman neither. I have seen men who regarded her as a superior kind of game; and I have seen her look upon them as huntsmen—whom she could sometimes hunt. It filled me with inexplicable shame. Diana must hunt, I suppose, though I would rather she did not; but all the laws of forestry are against our hunting Diana.

Why I should care to defend Woman in this way, I know not. Strength for strength, some women are stronger than the strongest men. Lucilla was one of these.

At first I only saw her quality in negatives. She was never *in extremis*. She did not say "Good gracious!" when "Dear, dear!" would do just as well. She neither scolded nor complained. She controlled enthusiasm as if it were a spirited horse that must not be allowed to run away with her. She ruled her ardent sympathies in the same way; and thus she kept herself from entangling the threads of the many friendships that she held in her hand.

She did not surprise me much; but she surprised me constantly in little things.

On the second Thursday when she did me the honour to invite me, we sat long over the tea-table in the long, late spring twilight. During the pause that followed on some remark of mine that gave her reason to meditate, I suddenly became aware of a little fat hand resting on the coverlet of the sofa. Something beneath it stirred, it was thrust lower down, there lay revealed a babe of about three years old, so sound asleep that I had not noticed her from the time I came in.

A cat—a tortoise—a parrot—and now a baby: what should I find living in that room next? Whose baby could it be? The creature was pretty enough; but I felt instant disapproval.

Lucilla, who is quick to detect any change in a companion, looked round and smiled.

"It's only little 'Liza!" she said defensively. "I call her Betsinda—Betty for short; and when she is a very good girl, Tricksy Wee. She's the landlady's little niece. I don't encourage her. I am not fond of children. But she has taken a kind of fancy to me. She crept upstairs all by herself, and, of course I could not turn her away. She was sitting by my side on a stool, looking at pictures, for an hour before you came. She is as good as gold, I must say that for her, but she got drowsy, so I just laid her down to sleep her sleep out. Her Aunt will come to fetch her presently, and take her home."

"How very dreadful for her to have an aunt like that!" I observed.

"Not at all!" said Lucilla. "The landlady likes her better than anything else in the world."

For my own part, I felt certain that the tiresome baby would wake up and scream. It did nothing of the kind, however, and in a few minutes I had forgotten its existence. On the whole it caused less interruption than the parrot; and at any rate it did not crawl like the tortoise.

"A wonderfully good child!" I said, as I rose to depart.

"Children are not naughty with me," said Lucilla. "I don't make a fuss with them." And tenderly she laid the little hand, that had grown cold, under the coverlet.

In the solitude of my room downstairs, I wondered why she had no children of her own.

She said she did not like them, it is true, but—though she was a woman of her word—if ever I saw Theory go one way and Practice another, I saw it now. In theory she did not like pets any better than children. She had only taken care of Katerfelto because it was a public disgrace to see such a neglected looking animal about the house. She had only bought the tortoise because the man had too many tortoises on his cart, and there was no room for them to move, and she chanced to have a shilling in her pocket. There was some other explanation—I forget what—of the parrot. He belonged to a friend who did not understand him, I believe. Betty, of course, explained herself. I did not wonder that she came upstairs.

She seemed to have no relations; that was another thing I liked about Lucilla, though I found it hard to understand, because, in the rest of my experience, women of large sympathy have been women with large families. She was never full of satisfaction because dear Tom's wife had got a little boy— never mournful and abstracted because Hetty's fifth daughter looked white and thin, and nobody could make out what was the matter. She pursued the even tenour of her way, quite unaffected by domestic incident of any kind.

Nor did she adopt a whole parish instead of a family, as many single women do. "All the world is my parish!" Wesley said; and I have often thought "My parish is all the world!" must be their motto. She did not take a motherly interest in telegraph boys, in Deep Sea fishermen, in cinder-sifters, in the inhabitants of Sierra Leone. She disclaimed a motherly interest in anybody or anything. Somehow or other, animals and children insisted on making her their mother. She always carefully assured me that it was not her fault.

She had an almost morbid horror of official charity, and I have it on her own authority that she seldom gave more than twopence in church.

"Money is a hard thing," I heard her say once. "It does more harm than good unless you wrap it up in soft words—or a warm jacket—or something to eat and drink. It is only a stone itself—not bread—not anything a man can live on."

Her ideas about time were as unconventional as her ideas about money.

She did more, and she did what she did more thoroughly than anybody, man or woman, whom I have known. Yet she was always at leisure. She seemed to keep a private supply of time on hand. She laughed once about a motto that she had seen over a clockmaker's shop, "Time is Money." The clockmaker did not take the responsibility of it; he put the name of *Campbell* underneath.

"To think that anyone can talk such nonsense!" she said, "let alone the man who wrote 'The Battle of the Baltic.' People who have time never have money. All the rich people hurry and hurry from morning to night. Why, even I might have money if I had no time!"

"Time is thought," I said, "but it cannot be thought and it cannot be money, both at the same moment. And you want time to think, more than you want money."

"Time is tea-time," she rejoined. "I want my tea, and so do you."

For a woman who delighted in thought, she was oddly shy about talking of it.

"I like to talk over the thoughts of other people. I always feel as if I were telling lies about my own," she said.

Dull talk put her out. She did not think it in the least worth while to talk of any thing dull.

"Life is short," she said. "I have no time for kettle-holders."

An instance of a theory long held by me, that proverbs are the invention of Woman, on the spur of moment. They must generalise; to them nothing is unrelated. I wondered that she thought life short. To me it appeared long—not that I wished it shorter.

When she went out, it was not so much her talk that I missed as her music—and above all, her silence. The other women whom I know are ceaselessly occupied. Their heads must be working, or their hands. They must have something to show for the time spent. Lucilla insisted on large clear spaces of doing nothing. She would scarcely answer some remark of mine, but she would sit still, brooding, and at the end of many moments there shone into my mind a light that came from hers. For the most part she compelled me to answer my own questions, though how she did this I hardly know—oftener by a look or a gesture than by any words, I think.

Those great brown eyes of hers—and mine—were made upon a different pattern; and, though we might be sitting side by side, one always saw what the other did not.

"That inner eye,
Which is the bliss of solitude"

was in her so clear and direct that, with her outer eyes, she scarcely saw at all.

"Dante is your favourite poet, is he not?" I enquired one evening.

"How did you know? I never let a day pass without a few lines of The Divine Comedy," she rejoined; not as if she were surprised, but rather glad.

Few things astonished her, yet she was full of wonder and reverent admiration. There were times when I thought some strange experience in early life must have left her cold to all passing events ever after. She kept her marvelling for children—for the old and the poor—for heroic people. At the call of any of these it awoke. I feel sure that in this characteristic lay the secret of her power to confer repose.

"He that wonders shall reign, and he that reigns shall rest."

"You care for Dante," I said, "because everywhere in this world he saw the next. Earth to him, is *not* earth; it is Hell, Purgatory, Heaven."

"I suppose you care more for Shakespeare than for any other poet," she said with a sigh.

"How did *you* know?"

"People always care for one of those two poets more than for the other. We are only grown-up children; one child likes Hans Andersen better than Grimm, and another likes Grimm the best. They are never equally fond of both. You have read Dante through, and I have not done that, but you do not read him every day as I do."

This was true. She still looked mournful.

"Why do not you read Shakespeare every day? Shakespeare understood women."

"He never cared for any woman as Dante cared for Beatrice."

There she was right, perhaps. Yet her opinion was not founded on study. She would take a tragedy or a comedy, and think, in one afternoon, that she had one with it.

In the earlier days of our friendship I used to speculate as to her origin, as to her history. I did not think that she came from the North, nor yet from the East. She had no liking for cold winds and frost; in the warmth of a soft, wet day she would open out like a flower. I could not but believe that she had been born in the West, where women are tall, gracious, brown-eyed, and the many golden sunsets of their childhood give them a serenity that is not lost in after life. She had lived in a spacious home, I thought, among loaded apple-trees, close to the blue sea, where September, lingering, crests the hedges with foam of honeysuckle. I often wondered at the space that she gave to her little room. I believed that it held within its narrow walls much larger, airier rooms; in some strange way she made me feel as if I sat or moved in them when I was with her. Yet there was never any word—nor the slightest allusion.

Was the past then indifferent to her? Had she banished all connected with it? Did she exist, "the day to the day," without a memory? Or was it, like my own, woven and tangled in with the present, so much a part of the tissue of every hour, that it could no more be spoken of than those fleeting, intimate sensations that we cannot make known even to a friend till they are well behind us?

The weeks had two days in them now, Sunday and Thursday. On Sunday Lucilla played—on Thursday I went to tea with Lucilla. She played on other nights; but on Sunday she played for me, and there was often, "by special request," a Funeral March.

Spring became summer, and summer autumn, and autumn winter, and winter spring again; and this not once but twice.

I began to note the seasons more than I had noted them formerly, because I gave my friend Lucilla flowers. To speak by the book I gave her one flower, and one flower only. I never thought anything but a rose was good enough. In the winter, when roses were scarce, I gave her a bunch of them. In the summer, when there were many, I gave her one. She was no more indiscriminate in her love of flowers than in her love of human beings. She did not fill anything that came to hand with masses of this, that, and the other, jumbled up anyhow. She chose a delicate bowl or cup; a small, fanciful vase—she set them in the best light—against the looking-glass—she played with every blossom as a child plays with a toy. I always thought that flowers lived longer in her room than anywhere else. I said so to her once, and she replied in the prosiest way that it was because she took the trouble to cut a little piece of the stem off, to slit it at the bottom, to put a scrap of charcoal into the fresh water that she gave them to drink every morning. I felt sorry that she made the mistake of telling me this. Why should she give me rational explanations of things that seemed to me romantic? Afterwards I let such incidents alone, and enjoyed the sense of mystery.

Many are the subtle differences between men and women. I had always understood this in the grand sense. In fact, until I knew Lucilla, I should as soon have thought of making a friend of a Parsee. Women are Fire-Worshippers. This is the great difference: but now, for the first time, I began to know the difference there may be in little things as well as great.

A woman, for instance, will be friends with you, year in, year out, and never feel the need of defining you by any name at all. With me it is otherwise. A dull crystallization of feeling impels me to name my friend always in absence, occasionally in presence. I cannot get on without a name. I used to wish that I had earned the right to call her as I chose, not as the whole world called her. I cannot help thinking that she divined this—that when she spoke of it, she was uttering my thoughts rather than her own.

"I wish," she said one day, "that we had individual names for each other. We are not the same to every person that we meet. What do you call me when you are by yourself? I am sure you do not call me *Miss Z.*"

"Why should you think that I am so deficient in respect as to call you anything else?"

"You say it awkwardly whenever you have to say it—as if you had forgotten—or were trying to remember. Confess! You call me something else?"

"I call you *Lucilla*," I said, straight out. "I called you *Lucilla* before I ever saw you."

She looked surprised—not disagreeably surprised.

"Why?"

"I can invent a reason if you like," I said.

She laughed.

"If you had given me one, I should not have cared. But will you not call me *Lucilla* always? I have no objection to answer to the name, now that I know it. And frankly, *The Lady on the Drawingroom floor*, every time you write a note is becoming tiresome."

"Must I be always *The gentleman downstairs?*"

"Always!" returned Lucilla, with precision.

VI

"Kitty is coming," Lucilla said one evening.

"Who is Kitty?" I asked, vaguely alarmed. "Is she another cat?"

Lucilla's low, clear laugh murmured round the room.

"No, Kitty is just—Kitty. I will not tell you what she is like. You shall judge for yourself. She will be here the next time that you come."

"Oh, will she?" said I. "Then I intend to make the most of the time without her."

And I talked about something else.

As I was going away, however, my fears returned upon me in full force.

"Only tell me one thing," I said. "Kitty won't be here always—she is not going to live in the house?"

"No," said Lucilla evasively, "not in the house."

She was going to be here always then.

Of course Lucilla had every right to avail herself of the company of Kitty, if the company of Kitty was what she desired. Nevertheless I felt aggrieved.

Kitty is coming! I pondered again over the words, over the tone in which they had been said. There was something like girlish delight, a kind of triumph in them, as if the coming of Kitty were almost too good to be true. From my heart I wished that she were not coming. Girls are pretty things, but they are hopeless for purposes of conversation. They live in the shining of their own eyes, in their singing voices, and in their dancing feet, but they have no experience of life at all. Why cannot people be satisfied? *"Toujours le mieux est l'ennemi du bien."* We were very well as it seemed to me, Lucilla was quite happy. Why should she care about this girl? But she had spoken in such a way that I could not forget it, and all day, every day, whenever I chanced to be alone, I heard the mockery in my ear, *Kitty is coming*.

At last she came; and I drew breath again. There was nothing to be afraid of, Lucilla would not prefer her company to mine.

"Well?" inquired Lucilla, when we had all drunk tea together and Kitty was gone. She went soon after tea, whether by instinct or by arrangement I did not know at the time. I feel sure now that it was by instinct.

"She is plain," I said.

"Is she?"

"She is rather dull."

"*Is* she?" said Lucilla, still more markedly.

"She seems to me to be just like any other girl."

"Oh!" said Lucilla.

The quiet depth of her disagreement annoyed me.

When, however, I saw Kitty again, a week later, I began, to my own surprise, to disagree with myself. At the end of three weeks I felt bound in honesty to let Kitty's protectress know that I had changed my opinion.

"Very uncommon," I remarked, in a tentative manner.

"She is not at all pretty," said Lucilla regretfully, as if she wished to be contradicted, but felt it impossible. "You are right about that. I wish she were more like her mother. And yet"—was it my fancy that Lucilla's voice softened a little? "I was so much pleased to see the likeness to her father—he is the one I know best, you see, that I never noticed it is not pretty until you said so."

"She is very graceful. Her voice is charming. I have never seen any other girl at all like her."

I thought it best to give way all along the line—to attempt no reserves. Lucilla smiled.

"What are you laughing at?"

"Shall I tell you what Kitty said of you, the first time that she saw you?"

"Certainly, if you think it will give me pleasure."

"'Auntie,' she said, 'he has pale eyes like a fish, and I thought he was deaf and dumb.' But last night she informed me that you must have looked like Raphael's Portrait of Himself when you were young, and that you were quite different from any other man she had ever met."

"Miss Kitty and I are going to be excellent friends. I can see that."

"I hope so," said Lucilla demurely.

"We began with being excellent enemies—a very good beginning of friendship between people of different ages," I said. "And now that I have made up my mind about her, be so kind as to tell me who is she."

"Her mother comes from the border country up North, and her father from Orleans. The aunt with whom I used to live down in Cornwall (I never knew my own father and mother) gave him a start in life. He had a turn for mechanics, but no money. Now he owns a mill in Yorkshire and gets on well there. He is an old friend of mine. I promised that I would see something of his child. She likes to play and sing—she has come up to London for a year at the Royal College of Music. The mother is a *malade imaginaire*—a very sweet woman and all that, but rather helpless—not able to go about with Kitty. They thought she would be quite happy, lodging next door to me, and so she is, dear child! I shall get her to play to you."

"How does she play?"

"Not at all in the style of the Funeral March."

"I shall not like it then."

"You ought to beware of rash statements by this time," Lucilla said.

I have often thought a piano one of the strangest things in the world. If it did not stand solid and square in every drawingroom, should we cease to wonder at the magic box that holds within itself so many different voices? When Lucilla's piano spoke for Kitty, I could hardly believe that the actual material, wooden keys, the metal strings were the same. An elf, I think, had got inside and changed it all.

Kitty preferred to play "out of her head," as she called it. Hers was the one gift that Lucilla lacked—invention; it came naturally to her to extemporise rather than to read or to remember. She neither could nor would play anything at any other person's suggestion. She embroidered the air around her with fanciful grotesques of sound that were, now "beautiful exceedingly," now odd to the verge of absurdity. Sometimes this delighted, sometimes it rather distressed Lucilla.

"Her sense of time is not good. And I don't think she practises her scales enough," she observed one day.

I smiled in my turn; for I knew that it was not in Kitty to practise her scales.

There as she sits at the piano—the only place in the world in which she ever, for one minute, could sit still, let me draw her.

I have tried again and again for my own satisfaction, not with any success—never, to speak truth, with the hope of it, but because there are certain tasks that attract by virtue of impossibility.

As there are some women who cannot be painted with colours, there are others who cannot be described in words. Colour and words suggest something too definite, too strong, too much finished. All the while I am writing a critic is contradicting me; and I know (women are women's critics) that she is as right as I am.

But that the music her little slender hands are making sways Kitty gently to and fro like a breeze, the wand-like figure would be almost prim in its unrounded, youthful straightness.

"Too thin!" the critic says.

Her hair is like the back of a thrush in colour, soft it may be, but not shining, nor very abundant, and she brushes it up into bird-like crest.

The forehead?

"Low," the critic says.

Her eyes are grey—and not a pretty grey—too mouse-like, one of them has a speck of brown. I shall leave out her nose and her mouth—the first because I cannot remember it, the last because I remember it too well.

A plague upon this inventory of her features!

When I wished to please Lucilla, I used to say she was a pocket Gainsborough that had not quite succeeded. If that cunning artist had taken it into his head to paint a miniature, he might have given the stiff, maidenly grace, the unconscious candour of some transient attitude that betrayed the elfin spirit. But he must have caught her upon the wing; she could never have sat to him, she could no more sit still than a bird, and when she sang, it was as a bird sings, clearly, sweetly, without a note of passion. I apologise for speaking thus to the nightingale, Romeo of birds, but Kitty had nothing of the nightingale. The lark was her fellow.

From the first she put her foot down on the Funeral Marches.

"No, no, Auntie," she said. "Don't play that, it's too sad. It makes me think of all the dead people. I don't know them. Nobody I loved has died. Nobody shall."

Something in her frightened voice, her frightened eyes, made me turn away.

"Darling," Lucilla said, "that's not the way to think of it. They are not dead really. They are more living than we are."

But Kitty was not to be persuaded. For my part I had more sense than to try and persuade her.

"I want it to be always here, always now," she cried. "Always you. Always father and mother. O Auntie, Auntie, why will you be older than I am?"

"One day you will be just as old yourself, my child."

"Oh dear!" said Kitty. "That makes it better—I never thought of that."

We all three laughed, but Kitty had her way and the Funeral Marches were banished.

"How very old she does think people of our age," Lucilla observed when she was gone.

"She has made me remember my years, and the number of my days what it is," I said. "I shall go down to my own room and meditate. Miranda was only fifteen when Prospero declared that every third thought should be his grave. I have heard a middle-aged man say that was the right proportion, I daresay Prospero was younger than I am."

Lucilla paid not the slightest attention to this neat Shakespearean essay.

"I cannot bear the child to be frightened," she said. "She would not be so much afraid for us if she were not afraid herself. I never had that fear. I do not understand it. She will be less afraid when she knows what it is—when she has lost some one."

"Will she?" I said. "Do you not think it is a matter of temperament?"

"Perhaps."

Lucilla spoke with courtesy rather than with confidence. I think she distrusted the modern word *temperament* very much as she distrusted the words *heredity* and *environment*. They seemed to her faithless.

"I wish," she continued, after a minute's pause, "that some one could teach her how to think more accurately. She lets her feelings run away with her."

Again I smiled. For I knew that there was more power of accurate thinking in Kitty than in Lucilla, and I was not so sure that if she did begin to think, Lucilla would like it. Kitty had the fatal power of seeing things as they are.

In minor matters, however, she was inaccurate enough, and I am sorry to say she had not the slightest regard for accuracy. She had been taught—or she had chosen of her own accord—to call Lucilla, who was no relation in the world to her, "Auntie." She had taken the *Unknown, Painter Unknown*, over the mantelpiece, for Raphael by Himself, and even after she found out her mistake, she persisted in calling me "Mr. Raph," because of the fancied likeness that she detected as quickly as Lucilla. I think names meant much to her, for she named everything that she came across.

Katerfelto accepted her as a matter of course. The parrot liked her better than Lucilla, and would sit on her shoulder and lay his gray bill against her cheek. She taught him to say, "How are you?" and was inordinately vain of the achievement. She lost her heart at once to Tricksy Wee, and to my surprise I found myself building card-houses and blowing soap-bubbles to amuse that young person, who had never seemed to want amusing before. She was also much naughtier; Kitty excited her.

Kitty was, of course, devoted to Lucilla; I never met the girl who was not; and as I had formerly profited by Frida's devotion, so now I profited much more by hers. Her pretty feeling for her guardian extended itself to her guardian's friend; and, with a feeling of pleasant wonder, I began to understand what Lucilla had foreseen, I suppose, from the first—that my friendship with her would grow yet more pleasurable from our common interest in the life so much younger than our own.

We were always holding little committees of two on Kitty, her sayings and her doings. Lucilla would half pretend to find some fault. I would defend the absent, and she was not displeased. After our first conversation about her I never attempted independent criticism, nor—to be quite fair—did it occur to me.

"I think the child ought to see some pictures," Lucilla said one day. "You know all about pictures. I only know the few that I love; but she ought, of course, to be shown the different Schools. Would it be troubling you too much to ask you to take her to the National Gallery?"

I leapt at the offer; not thinking honestly that Kitty would ever care much about pictures, not minding much whether she did or did not.

She was delighted to come. Her merry nature found mirth in every journey to and fro. Lightly she ran up and down the steps of 'bus after 'bus; airily she settled beside Lucilla on the top and looked upon the streets as on a garden, every inch of which had been laid out to charm her.

I could not climb the steps, but in spirit I, too, sat on top. I understood that she could not be caged inside; and I heard what she said, for Lucilla told me.

It pleased her when she heard her brother man address her brother man as "Now then, Four-Wheel Cab!"

It pleased her to see a carriage full of plump, rosy, fair-haired children—to know that one of them would some day be King of England.

"Just like little fat Cupids," said she. "What a lovely place London is! Look at the little darling Cupid on that house! There is another! And there's another!"

I had never seen these Cupids on the houses in Piccadilly before; it amazed me to find how many there were. Sometimes, as I go past them now, I look for them and think of Kitty. They did not interest Lucilla, but she was kind to them for Kitty's sake.

When we reached Trafalgar Square, however, such a diversity of tastes became apparent that I wondered whether we should, on any single Saturday morning, find any single picture at which we could all three gaze with satisfaction. The initial difficulties were tremendous.

To begin with, no one could persuade Kitty to look at things in order. You might as well have hoped to persuade a squirrel. Through an open door she would catch a glimpse of a baby—of the head of a Cherub—of a Lady at a Harpischord—and she was off. Michael Angelo himself could not detain her. It mattered nothing to her who had painted the picture if she did not like it; and very little if she did. She would settle on the picture itself as the squirrel stops and settles on the bough, crack the nut for a minute as if she had nothing else to do, and race away again.

Now Lucilla liked to take one room at a time, and to consult the Handbook. She wanted to be told, not only who every painter was, but whether he had a wife and children, whether he lived in Venice, Florence, or Rome, whether he died a natural death or "disappeared." Two questions were, although she did not ask them in word, for ever present with her as she looked; the first, the eternal child's question, *"Was he good?"* the second, the eternal student's question, *"What did he mean?"* Having determined in her own mind that the early Italians were good (we know so little about them) and that they meant something (which is true occasionally), she went, by preference, to the Early Italians. She would stand for half an hour patiently making out the emblems of every bright particular star in Fra Angelico's Paradise, or in Botticelli's, quoting in a hushed voice remembered lines from Dante.

To her pictures were signs and symbols; if they failed to connect themselves with something invisible, she did not care about them.

To Kitty pictures were memories of something that she had seen for herself, and recognised with joy—suggestions of something it would be good to see some day.

To me pictures were pictures.

Both my companions displayed equal indifference to colour and drawing, and the only point on which they could agree concerned my supposed pedantry in such matters as these.

"That arm is all wrong," I would say to Kitty, before an enchanting Sir Joshua.

"As if it matters about an arm!" she would reply indignantly. "It's just the most darling little child I ever saw."

"That leg is preposterous!" I would say to Lucilla, before a Blake.

"As if it mattered about legs!" *she* would reply indignantly. "He was thinking of souls."

Yet Lucilla, in whom the quality of a teacher ran strong, although she never, to my knowledge, filled any educational post, was teachable, as teachers always are. With infinite pains I taught her to respect Velasquez' "Admiral." I induced her to lay out some of her spare time on "Bacchus and Ariadne."

She thought the Admiral voluptuous and cruel, and to this day I remain uncertain whether she really showed anything more than an amiable desire to meet me half way on that subject; but she did at last become an enthusiastic admirer of Titian—though even then I am afraid she found it easier in that "Bacchus and Ariadne" is an allegory, and Ruskin has an elaborate theory of the significance of it.

Kitty I never tried to teach: she taught me often by wise, instinctive flashes, as a child teaches.

"Let us go down these steps! Kitty ought to see the statue of Gordon," Lucilla said, after our first visit.

So we went down among the lions and the fountains.

If she had not spoken thus, I should have made an excuse and stayed behind, for I could not leave Trafalgar Square without going to stand bareheaded before the greatest Englishman of our time. As we gazed at the statue no one spoke; and even Kitty stood still.

I think Lucilla, who had a purpose in everything she did, may have cherished the hope that the early Italians would open Kitty's eyes to the light invisible. If so, it was not fulfilled. We find what we bring with us, and Kitty being still a child, saw everywhere not Heaven but Fairyland.

It was much the same if we went on Sunday, as we sometimes did, to hear a famous preacher at the Abbey or at St. Paul's.

What pictures failed to accomplish, preachers might suggest perhaps, Lucilla thought. I knew instinctively the trend of her reflections; and I was further complimented by being asked to help in the second experiment. I was not a regular attendant at church myself. The ancient spell under which I had lived in my youth was broken, and I had lost the habit, but I fell into it again gladly now there was some one who wished me to go.

"The child ought to hear the great preachers," Lucilla said. "Would it be troubling you very much to find out who they are? I myself never stay for the sermon, if I can help it. When I was her age though, I felt differently. She ought to have the chance. Perhaps you would be so very kind as to take her some afternoon?"

Lucilla's custom was to go to church early in the morning—I used to watch her leaving the house with her little prayer-book—and sometimes of an evening. She did not like a crowd, she hated emotion and excitement. An empty, quiet, unpopular church was the church of her choice, and wherever she went she made interest with the sexton to get a window open. It rather annoyed her to be considered "orthodox," and she had little sympathy with those whom she called "dogmatic." I vexed her once by the assertion that *orthodox* only meant *straight thinking* and *dogma* an *opinion*. They meant, according to her, something much worse and quite different. Of course, if I did not understand, she said, she could not explain; people who knew Greek never did understand words. I am convinced that in her heart she thought *dogma* had something to with *dogs*, whom she disliked, not personally, but because cats disliked them, and cats were weaker than dogs.

What her heterodoxy consisted in I do not know, unless it lay in the fact that she believed that all men were made to be made good—and therefore happy—in the end. She did not tell me this in so many words; but I gathered it, partly from that unquenchable hopefulness which was, in her, the result not so much of nature as of thought—partly from the extreme indignation with which she visited the landlady when she found that Tricksy Wee had been terrified by descriptions of hell.

"If I could ever believe in it at all, I could believe that it was made for those who frighten little children!" she said, her eyes gleaming so fiercely that I did not know them.

She was tolerant of different opinions in religion, so long as they were not cruel, though very clear as to her own.

Fanaticism alarmed her. I have seen her lips grow white when she encountered a detachment of the Salvation Army.

We were waiting on a doorstep to let them pass. I had turned to her with some commonplace remark, but it froze on my lips. I suppose I asked a question.

"It is," she said, "that if that woman with the timbrel and the beautiful eyes knew the right word, and said it, I should be marching by her side tomorrow."

I could not have believed these expressions if I had not heard them. They seemed to me wild—inconsistent—absurd. Yet, as I pondered over them in solitude, I began to feel that in religion also Lucilla might have to bridle and restrain enthusiasm that would otherwise have run to madness—I came to understand why it was that she disliked excessive ritual, yet could not bear the absence of all ritual; that—dearly as she loved music—she preferred to accomplish the highest act of worship in silence.

There was one title the use of which never failed to provoke her quiet scorn.

"If people say *Our Lord* we all know what they mean," she said. "If they say *Jesus Christ* we know what they mean. But *The Founder of Christianity!* It was left for the pedants of the twentieth century to find out that; they alone know what they mean by it."

Kitty was quite as well pleased to go to church as she had been to visit Trafalgar Square.

She had the sweet, natural devoutness of all good girls, oddly combined with a dash of scepticism, inherited, perhaps, from her French father. She would ask difficult questions now and then as to the meaning of words, and Lucilla, for all her ignorance of Greek, did not know how to answer.

"Auntie," she said one day, "I feel so happy on Sundays, when I've got on my new hat. Do you think it is quite true to say so very often that the burden of my sins is 'intolerable'?"

"I hope that you will never live to think it more true than you do now, my child," Lucilla said. She spoke as if she were pained, as indeed she always was if any remark were made as to the words of the Liturgy. Yet Lucilla had that morning put on her little close-fitting bonnet—the bonnet that became her so well—to go and say that the burden of her sins was "intolerable."

Nor is there any doubt in my mind that she believed it was. Only when we are very young and logical do certain words appear to us to contradict certain facts in this way.

It was a foregone conclusion with me that the child would care most for St. Paul's; but the fact that she did so baffled and disappointed Lucilla, who liked to go there that she might hear any one who happened to be with her say how much more beautiful was the Abbey. To her the shadow, the mystery, the manifold associations of the dim shrine of St. Peter outweighed the beauty of the shafts of light struck through the dome, of the vast concourse of human beings kneeling and standing together as one man.

Wherever she might be, whether in the Abbey or at St. Paul's, Kitty sang and prayed with the best of them; but I observed that she took an unobtrusive little red pocket-book with her, and that she employed the interval of the ser-mon in sketching. She seemed to find the study of minor canons more inter-esting than theology in a less concrete form—or perhaps it was the Cupid over the organ that she drew. While she sketched, Lucilla sat listening for morals and for reasons. If morals were drawn, if reasons were found for her, she re-mained content; she had a fine disdain of mere rhetoric. *Is he good? What does he mean?* Again I recognized in her the everlasting child, the eternal student.

With music it was different. There the artist came in, and she boldly threw significance to the winds. Once or twice, when I ventured out of the condition of blind enjoyment to inquire what this, that, or the other *meant*, she looked at me as if I were making a fool of myself. She asked me once to go, when she and Kitty attended a concert, but I refused. I had heard them talking together. They said things not to be understood by any one except a member of the Royal College of Music. I preferred the concerts given in Back Street, where there were two soloists and an audience of one.

Sometimes they essayed a duet—to their own great satisfaction, but not to mine; for on these occasions the piano spoke with two voices, and I did not know what it said. In fact, they were doing what good manners would have prevented their doing in any other way—they were both talking at once; but they never found it out.

They were not even so good to look at as usual, for while the treble moved to and fro, the bass sat fixed like a rock. Two sisters—twins, if possible—are the only people who ought to play duets on the piano. Difference of tempera-ment is too strongly marked in all others.

Often Lucilla, who loved an opera, would play one through, recalling the story as she went along.

"We ought to take Kitty to see it," she said one evening, when we were all three very happy over "Romeo and Juliet."

"No, no," said Kitty eagerly, glancing up from her seat on the fender-stool. "Don't let us go. It's much more nice as you play it, Auntie. It's much more nice with only you and Mr. Raph here. I've been once, and I don't like it. I don't like the ugly, painted ladies. And I hate to see people making love to each other. I'd like to run away when I see that."

"Kitty ought to go oftener to balls and parties. She ought to have more companions of her own age," Lucilla said thoughtfully when she was gone. "I cannot tell what to do about it. If I invite Frida they are very polite to each other, but one is always glad whenever the other leaves. They both want to talk to me, not to anyone else; and Kitty does not get on with Mrs. Hopgood, and won't accept Frida's invitations. She likes the masters at college well enough, but she does not seem to care for the boys and girls that she meets there; she will not let me ask them to come. I don't want her to lose touch with her own generation. It's not right."

"Were not you rather surprised just now?" I said. "I thought that all young ladies liked operas and plays, and people falling love."

She sighed.

"They are so different nowadays. We were much more sentimental. Kitty often makes me feel ashamed of myself backwards."

"She is wonderfully attractive," I said, with a curious feeling that the room had grown darker the minute she left it.

"Yes," Lucilla said. "We shall not keep her much longer."

The words fell like stones on me.

"Surely," I said, startled, "she is very young—too young to think of anything of that kind. You will not lose her yet."

Lucilla sighed again.

"I do not know. She is nineteen. Older than—some girls."

Lucilla finished that sentence wrongly. *Some girls* was not what she meant to say when she began.

What had she meant to say?

In a moment, without a moment's warning, I had come close to the edge of something that I should have liked to know. But I was stopped upon the edge; I went no further.

VII

My cousin had asked many little services of me, seldom in vain. The time was come when I meant to ask something of my cousin. The conviction that she would be very much astonished, and not altogether gratified, made me laugh in my sleeve. Hitherto, whenever we enjoyed a friendly contest, I had always been defeated, but now I meant to win.

Time, that brings round many greater things, brought round the occasion that I desired. Frida was coming out, and a ball had to be given in Pont Street in honour of the event.

"I'm not going to ask *you!*" said my cousin. "You can't dance."

A fact, undoubtedly. Why should any one dislike to have that taken for granted which is self-evident?

I thought of the power of the human eye.

"No," I said, fixing it upon my cousin with the firmness of a man determined to conquer or to perish. "You are not going to ask me, because I cannot dance, but you *are* going to ask some one instead of me, who can."

"Oh, some man friend of yours? Delighted!"

"No, not a man friend, but a girl."

"A girl!" repeated my cousin, with disapproval as pronounced as if I had said "A porpoise!" "You, of all people! And why, pray, should I ask a girl?"

"Because she will enjoy it more than any one else you could ask."

"It is not at all a question of her enjoying it, said my cousin severely. "It is a question of my finding partners. If I invite her, will you promise to come yourself? You can't dance, of course, but at any rate you can take her in to supper; and you look like a man."

I weighed the matter with a sigh, and said "Yes."

"Where does she live?" asked my practical cousin. "She has a mother, or an aunt, or something, I suppose?"

"Miss Z. is, at the present moment, her mother and her aunt.

"Oh, I see!" said my cousin. "*She* asked you to ask me, of course?"

"On the contrary, she knows nothing whatever about it."

"Oh, well, Frida insisted on her being asked, anyhow—the invitation's written—so it only makes one more. Here's a card. You'd better take it yourself, and then Miss Z. can give it to the girl."

"*Fancy Dress!*" I said in some alarm as I glanced at it. I had wished to please Kitty; yes; but had I wished to please her to the extent of appearing in fancy dress?

"I quite agree with you," said my cousin. "It's an awful nuisance. But somebody has put it into Frida's head that she is like a Botticelli, and she wants to wear a dress that nobody could wear at any ball, except a fancy ball, and a cock's feather sticking straight up in the middle of her hair; so what was I to do? It's all very well for you, you're a man; you can borrow a uniform, or a pink coat. *You* needn't complain."

"I shall bring a bundle of parchments tied up with red tape, and appear as what I am—a solicitor," I observed. "It is rare for any one to appear in his own character; the most fanciful thing he can do, in fact."

After tea that evening, as she sat down to the piano, I asked Kitty if she were fond of dancing. In a minute half the fairies of the "Midsummer Night's Dream" were flitting over the keyboard. Presently she began to speak in a far-away voice, not like her own, playing louder between the words, and lightly when she wanted me to hear.

"*So the Fairy Queen said there should be a dance in the forest. There were no birds, of course, because it was dark. And they did not ask the Nightingale, for if he had come they would have listened instead of dancing.*"

Here the nightingale got into the piano and had it all his own way—but not for long. With Kitty, nothing ever was for long.

"But the bluebells rang, and the daffodils blew their trumpets. The moon was not shining, you know—they had forgotten to ask her—but all the stars were out; so they danced, they danced, and they danced till the jealous angry moon put her yellow face through, and shot an arrow at the Fairy Queen, so that she dropped down dead. Then they were all very sorry, and they had a Fairy Funeral, and this is the Funeral March. Auntie says you like Funeral Marches, Mr. Raph. Do you hear the rose-leaves blowing about over the grave?"

I did indeed. The room was filled with the tramp of tiny feet, and tiny tears were shed, and tiny wings folded. And with some other consciousness I was aware that Lucilla feared lest Kitty were going where she should not, and wished to stop her, and knew not how.

"But the wind drove the clouds across the yellow jealous moon, and drove the rose-leaves off the Fairy Queen, and she woke up again, and they all danced for joy till the Cock cried 'Cockadoodledoo.'"

With which performance of the cock Kitty concluded.

"There, Mr. Raph," she said demurely. "Never ask me again if I am fond of dancing! I should like to dance every night of my life until I dropped."

She rose from the piano, and took her usual seat on the fender-stool, with the sudden gravity of a kitten after it is tired of playing with a ball of worsted.

"Your fairies kept bad time, Kitty, and they danced in the oddest place I ever heard of," said Lucilla. "Daffodils and bluebells and roses, all out together!"

"I can't help it, Auntie. There are no clocks in Fairyland, and everything nice happens there all at once. Do you—I mean, did you—like dancing, Auntie dear?"

"Yes," Lucilla said. "I liked it very much, but not in that way. This was how I liked it. Only *you* must dance now, or I cannot play."

She moved to the piano.

Kitty sprang to her feet, caught up a Japanese fan that was lying on the table, lifted her white cotton skirt daintily with the other hand, and faced her own reflection in the mirror.

"Play, Auntie, play!" she cried impatiently. "Play the lovely old Gluck Minuet that you played the other night! I know some of the steps. Father taught me."

Lucilla sat down, obedient, to do as she was bid. For a second ere she began, she glanced at the child over her shoulder. The evening sun streamed full upon her, lighting up the words on the old mirror opposite, *Hier c'est demain.*

But I have only one pair of eyes; when Lucilla goes to the piano, they belong to her; so I know not what Kitty did. The mirror knew, I suppose, for she danced to her own reflection. As the Minuet ended, she dismissed it, with a low curtsey and a wave of the Japanese fan.

"If you went to a Fancy Dress Ball," I said, "what would you wear?"

"'Little Turk or Japanee,
O, don't you wish that you were me?'

Or would you be a fairy? Or would you be a lady with powdered hair?"

"What a hard question! It would take me at least a week to answer it properly. No, I would be the china shepherdess on Auntie's cupboard, in a white dress, with lilac flowers and a lilac sash and a crook. Auntie should be a great tall beautiful Vandyck, all in black velvet, with a ruff round her neck. As for you, Mr. Raph, you should be that queer man over the mantelpiece of course—in the slouchy hat,—the man I used to think was Raphael. Oh why—why are we not all going to a Fancy Ball together? What fun it would be! I have never gone to a Fancy Ball in my life."

"Well, you are going to one now, my dear!" I said, with an odd sense of self reproach for not having seen to this most important matter before. "So is your Aunt.

So am I. But this will be the first Ball that I have ever attended. Will you take me as a *débutant*? I am going in character, to the tune of a bundle of parchments tied up with red tape."

I felt it necessary to be firm and clear about this, as I drew the card from my pocket.

Kitty snatched it from me, waltzed round the room with it, tossed it to Lucilla, who was still sitting with her hands on the keys, laughing softly.

"Auntie!" she said, "I always knew that Mr. Raph was the kindest person in all the great wide world."

What is there in the midst of our mirth that checks us suddenly, in the sweet gratitude of the young? Is it shame that when so little is needed to make them happy, we have taken so little trouble to give it them? Is it the quick instinct that they will soon need more?

"How very kind of Mrs. Hopgood!" Lucilla said. "Of course I should never have thought of asking her. Frida begged me to go, the other day. She said I told her once that she was like a Botticelli. So she is, dear child—the thin, willowy figure, the pale delicate, sensitive face! She wanted me to see her dancing like Simonetta in Simonetta's dress. I told her that I never went to dances since I had given up the pleasant habit of being young. But, now I should to go; I should like to take Kitty."

"Do you know, Auntie, that this is Mr. Raph's first dance—the first he's ever gone to in his life? We must start very early, so that he may not miss one moment of it. I'm going to give him a flower for his button-hole. What shall it be?"

"A bachelor's button," I said. "Will the Gentle Shepherdess and the Duchess by Vandyck do him the honour of dining with him at his club, before they go?"

"What fun! I did not know you had a club Mr. Raph. When do you go to it?"

"My club is the South Kensington Museum," I said. "I pay sixpence a week whenever I want to belong, and I meet the Gods of Greece there—and all the best company!"

If Kitty was not much like the china shepherdess on the cupboard, or any other shepherdess in or out of Arcadia, she was more like herself than I had seen her yet, on the night of the ball. I cannot in the least describe it. There are these radiant moments for boys and maidens when first the sense of power blossoms out, and on a sudden they become aware of homage in the eyes of those who behold them. Proud and delighted, Lucilla looked at me with triumph as who should say, "There!—But you doubted! *I* knew long ago."

Kitty had sprung on to the sofa. Her little silver shoes sparkled and shone under her white and silver petticoats. She held her silver crook, adorned with shining dewdrops, like a sceptre. A wreath of soft green leaves lay on her hair. Before her stood ranged her humble Court—Lucilla, stately in her sweeping robes of black—the charmed, obsequious landlord—the landlady, fussy and critical, but softened for once to true benevolence—Mahry in the seventh Heaven of frightened admiration—the middle-aged Solicitor, armed with parchments, who bent towards her, lifted her light hand to his lips, and placed in it a branch of lilac. She threw it over her shoulder like a sheaf.

"It's just too beautiful!" she cried. "Oh, Mr. Raph!"

This also was like Kitty. She very rarely said anything so common as "*Thank-you*." She expressed pleasure—which is a prettier thing than gratitude—by a cry, a gesture, a glance.

Thus, with all the good will in the world, amid the nods and becks, and wreathèd smiles of the inhabitants—the Old Lady peered at us under her blind, the children stood staring in a barefaced group on their doorsteps, the Artist happened to be entering his door and paused, knocker in hand, and I caught the Florist's wife peeping behind her palm—we started for the club dinner.

As regarded the club dinner, there had been a slight difficulty a few days earlier.

"I think—if you do not mind," Lucilla observed to me in private, "we will dine at the Museum first, and come home to get ready. Then we shall start fresh. If we were to go in our fine clothes, Kitty would only rumple her gown. She would be far too much excited to eat anything, and she would want to be off every minute. It will be much better to dine in peace and comfort. We shall have a long night before us. I know the child. You are not responsible. You may get home before dawn, but I am sure to see the sunrise. You remember how the Fairy Queen danced till the cock said 'Cockadoodledoo!'"

In secret I was disappointed. I had looked forward to a white vision of the child among the snowy fauns, the still Bacchantes of the Hall of Statues. Yet more I wished to see Lucilla, clothed like the Night, moving amongst them. I assented at once, however. Single people who rule their own lives are glad to be ruled for a minute or two, if they get the chance. But Kitty had been left out of the reckoning, and she disapproved with the utmost vehemence when her chaperone suggested to her that we should come home to dress.

"Auntie!" she said, "I am surprised at you. It was not you and me, it was a Duchess by Vandyck, and a china Shepherdess that Mr. Raph invited to dine with him. I couldn't think of going as my own self. It wouldn't be proper at all. I've not been asked. Nor have you."

So it was a Duchess and a china Shepherdess who sat down with a Solicitor, parchment in hand, to eat beefsteak in the blue-tiled Grill Room, after all.

"What lovely cooks!" Kitty said, with a sigh of content. "I never saw such nice cooks anywhere. They look like statue cooks in their white aprons."

She had regained her spirits after a brief eclipse in the Hall of Statues. In that faint, shadow-veiled light, in that world of frozen dancing girls and maidens gone a-hunting, a momentary silence fell upon her. She seemed to change like a chameleon, to take the same dumb huelessness. Lucilla walked along the solemn avenue as if she had a right to be there, as if she could at any moment, if she would, become a sister statue.

The cooks, turning and basting their beefsteaks at the fire, put fresh life into Kitty on an instant. She laughed and chattered until I felt sorry for a remote young art-student, dining in solitary state at the next table, clearly envious. I knew he would have liked to flirt with her.

Others came in—an odd, shady party, with bad clothes and good faces, and that strange touch of over-coquettishness in the girls, over-familiarity in the men, which marks those whom study in common is lifting, but has not lifted quite high enough. To Kitty they seemed like people in a play. I am afraid she liked them all the more because they threw bits of bread at each other across the dishes. One was quieter, more refined than the rest—a Sir Joshua Reynolds of the future perhaps. He stared very hard at Kitty when he thought no one was looking; and once I caught him sketching her on the table-cloth.

To my amusement it was Lucilla, not Kitty, who betrayed excitement, nervousness, a certain fear of being late, a certain dread of being early—it was Lucilla who pretended to eat, and then asked me the time. Kitty did not hurry herself in the least.

Beefsteak, according to her, had never tasted so delicious; to see it grilled yourself before you ate it gave a kind of personal charm to the most national food in the world.

"Your health, Mr. Raph!" she cried, lifting her glass.

I returned thanks in a speech, to the great amusement of the art-students.

Vain man that I am, I was conscious of the many admiring glances shot in the direction of the Duchess and the china Shepherdess, for all that they sat cruelly muffled up in soft white clouds, as careless of mankind as if they had been true Olympians. I liked to think the students were wondering who the Solicitor was, and what he had to do with them.

Proserpina graced my speech, and Demeter. In the unspoken thoughts of the deep heart, I rather held that Lucilla resembled the Goddess of the Hearth, beautiful Hestia, who stayed at home and kept the fire bright while all the other Goddesses went out. I believe she would sooner have stayed at home that evening.

"Hush! Hush! You will turn the child's head. It must be nearly time for us to go," said Lucilla.

Not much of Kitty's company did she and I enjoy after that; but, for my part, I did not want it.

As my two ladies fluttered and swept into the drawingroom in front of me, I experienced something that I had never felt before, I saw that my cousin was impressed, that Kitty was not what she expected, that other people were impressed likewise.

Frida, the cock's feather in her hair, came up shyly, almost devoutly, to kiss and welcome her friendly Duchess; and they were quickly surrounded.

One fantastic, eager young gentleman after another, soldier, sailor, tinker, tailor, appeared with great alacrity, murmured a word in Frida's ear, made Kitty a bow, seized the minute pencil hanging by a thread of blue to her card, inscribed his name.

"There seems to be no great difficulty about finding partners," I observed.

"I never thought there would be!" said Lucilla, with a smile in which lay something of the satisfaction of prophecy fulfilled.

As the evening wore on I forgot that, for the first few minutes, I had felt like a bat in sunshine. I passed through various stages of fresh experience.

There came first the unusual gratification of delicate, bright lights, of softly shaded roses, of rhythmical music, of flowers and feathers and flashing jewels, of graceful, curving movement. I watched, with sympathy quite new to me, each young figure as it entered—the hope, the wondering, the fear, the welcome, the aversion, the merriment, the dreamy surrender, on every face in turn—their formal stiff approaching of each other, their conventional greetings, the quick understanding or misunderstanding, followed by laughter or by embarrassed silence, the partners firmly held or fearfully, the rushing or gliding or measured steps together, the relief or the reluctance of the bow and the bended head, as the maid returned to the matron, and the young man sought another.

Sometimes I almost felt as if I could have danced myself. I learnt once, at my cousin's instigation, long ago, in the hour of my wealth, when she looked upon me as the eligible partner-for-life of a certain relative of hers. Not all her descriptions of this young lady's charm, however, had persuaded me to cross the threshold of a ballroom in those days. I was far too shy. By what caprice of fancy was it that now I almost felt as if I could have danced myself? The thought brought back to me with a pang the recollection that I was middle-aged and lame, that I was here on sufferance only—the wraith of a man who, for the dancing world, had never lived—not the father, not the uncle even of any boy or girl in the room. That moment I felt alone, and bitterly alone, I wished that I were back in my dingy quarters in Back street. I kept a friend there always. Here he had left me.

"It makes one feel rather like a ghost, does it not?" Lucilla said. And from that moment I was no longer one by myself.

"Were you· really fond of dancing?" I asked.

"Yes—and no. I was very fond of it in my girlish days, when I learnt from an old French dancing master with a fiddle, who used to say, 'Now, my dears, there are rats in that wall, and they will bite you if you lean against it!' He taught us pretty, sliding, curtseying steps and ways—not to look glum, not to frown at each other—not to go squarely through a crowd, but like a smiling human wedge—not to "waddle or toddle or walk in two parishes at once," (that was the way most Englishwomen walked, he said) not to bang doors behind us, always to smile and to look gracious. When I came out into society and found it so different—found that people gave themselves no time to be gracious, and me no time to practise my careful steps—I was disgusted. I always liked the minuet, the long slow polonaise, much better than waltzing. I should have danced in the days of Louis XIV., I think.

"I am very glad you did not."

"I could always keep step with one person—and that was Kitty's father. Because he was French, I suppose."

To have danced with her—to have made her like to dance with him—not to have married her! What manner of man could Kitty's father be? French I supposed! French like the dancing master, to whom, according to her own account, Lucilla owed her graciousness of manner.

"Kitty inherits that. She dances well, does she not? She makes her partners respect her. That thickset Guardsman over there, who tumbled down a few minutes ago, did quite well so long as she had him in hand. Do you see the Nabob standing by the conservatory? He is a famous cricketer. I sometimes think he is inclined to pay attention to Frida."

"He seems to be paying considerable attention to Kitty," I observed. "He never takes his eyes off her."

"Oh, that's only because he doesn't want people to see he is looking at Frida!" Lucilla said with comfortable assurance.

At that moment Kitty was whirled past us, and I marked the curious distinction, the air of dainty fastidiousness, that made her other than the others.

All this time Lucilla had been absorbed in her. She had only one interest in the room, and that was Kitty. Everything else was only Kitty's background. She had spoken of the ghost feeling because she wanted to answer something that I had not said; not because she had any time to feel like a ghost. She had not wandered away to herself, to the rooms where she dwelt alone. It was because I had done this, that all this youth made me feel old, cold, solitary. It was because she had not done this, that she seemed to me younger, farther away from me again.

Rows of what is, I suppose, the usual kind of mother, were seated along the wall. No doubt, because I have not much acquaintance with them, they seemed to me all very much alike, and very much like my cousin.

I wondered how women felt when first they introduced a daughter into society; whether they were most pleased or frightened, as the murmur of admiration went round; whether they were relieved if she danced just as everyone else danced, and that was all; whether they recollected their own girlhood and sighed or smiled.

Lucilla appeared to have gone through most of these phases.

At first, she confessed, she was lost in the study of Kitty's dress.

This amazed me; surely there was no room for uneasiness on that score.

"You are quite wrong," Lucilla answered seriously. "I had forgotten the wall-paper."

"Dear me," I said with a glance at it. "If you had recollected, would you have dressed Kitty in pomegranates?"

"I might, or I might not. Dress is much more a matter of relation than people think. That is the vexatious thing about a dance of this kind, you never can tell what other people are going to wear. I could have dressed Kitty even more becomingly if I had known beforehand who her partners would be. It does not matter later on; but a girl ought not to be too original, she should harmonize with her surroundings. However, one must leave something to chance, and to her own taste.—Charles I.'s costume goes best with her, as to colour, I think?"

Charles I. was the young man with bad agate eyes whom I had met before at my cousin's. I resented his assumption of the character, I could not feel certain that, if he were beheaded, anyone would be able to write of him:—

> "He nothing common did, nor mean,
> Upon that memorable scene."

He seemed to me to be doing common things every minute.

It was altogether disheartening to see how few people understood the parts for which they might, with fitness, have been cast, in other ages, or in the golden East. The Nabob for instance, was a fair-haired, blue-eyed Saxon as any you would wish to see. A good blowsy, frowsy dumpling of a girl, who might have made a passable Audrey, appeared as Joan of Arc, at sight of which profanation it was all I could do not to use bad language. But Charles I. was very foolish indeed. He made despicable jokes about his silly head, and I saw Kitty laughing at them too, which annoyed me.

"I cannot think why he was introduced to Kitty," I said. "I don't like him."

"I do not think there is any harm in him," said Lucilla. "He was not born in the purple, of course. That sort of person always does want to be Charles I. Now Kitty has some right to call herself a china Shepherdess, has she not?—Frida looks very picturesque."

I thought myself that Frida looked very odd; but I contented myself with remarking that she showed great devotion to Botticelli. *Picturesque* is a favourite word of Lucilla's when she wishes, but does not venture to say that a girl of whom she is fond "looks pretty." I might have said what I liked, however, for, having satisfied herself as to Kitty's dress, she had begun to give even closer attention to Kitty's partners, and they succeeded each other so rapidly that there was no keeping count.

"I like to watch her ways," she said, with a smile. "They amuse me. Such a child as she is—and yet she understands the game!"

I wondered whether Lucilla had understood it so well in days gone by. I thought not.

Presently her face clouded a little.

"She has danced too often with Charles I.—three times in succession. She will get herself talked about."

"She danced three times with the Nabob about twenty-four hours ago, if that is any comfort to you," I observed.

"You must be feeling very tired," Lucilla said, with sudden penitence. "Why will you not go home? I cannot bear to take her away just when she is enjoying herself so much," she added, apologetically.

A wave of the dance carried the child up to us.

She paused an instant to give her fan to Lucilla.

"Oh, Mr. Raph! don't go! Not yet," she cried.

Of course I stayed. I never meant to go. It amused me to watch Charles I. and the Nabob hating each other more and more. But Kitty was prudent as she was bold; she danced a fourth time with neither.

The sparrows were chirping when we drove away, and I saw the dawn as I had not seen it for many long years. It showed me that Lucilla looked more weary than I had ever seen her look before.

"It was a lovely evening. How I wish we were just going to start now!" Kitty said, unbuttoning her long glove regretfully. She looked as fresh as if she had spent the last six hours in rosy slumber, instead of in the arms of a dozen breathless young gentlemen, tearing round and round a hot, stuffy room with a slippery floor.

"Are you tired, Mr. Raph? It was good of you to stay all the time. I couldn't have had the heart to keep Auntie, if you had not taken care of her. Oh, Auntie dear, you are tired!"

"Not at all!" said Lucilla, bravely opening eyes that had closed already. "So you were happy, dear?"

"*Happy* is no word for it!" said Kitty. "I never was so happy in all my life." Lucilla smiled at me.

It is a satisfaction to a man getting on in years to think that he has had any hand in helping a girl to be happier than ever she was in all her life; and I recollected the words with pleasure whenever I was not falling heavily asleep in my employer's office, the whole of the next day.

VIII

I happened to be standing in the hall on the night after the dance when I heard a summoning, distressful cry from Kitty on the landing above.

As fast as my lame leg would let me, I hobbled upstairs.

"Is she ill?"

"No, but Auntie is so unhappy. Oh, Mr. Raph, do, *do* come in and comfort her! Persica is lost, and we can't find her, and Auntie is just as miserable as she can be."

Lucilla turned a mournful face towards me.

"Yes," she said trying to smile, "it is quite true. The poor thing is lost, and it is my fault. She was here after luncheon. She wanted to lie beside me on the sofa, and her hair is coming off, and I said, 'No, Persica, I can't do with you to-day.' It was very unkind when the creature was losing her fur. The door stood open, she walked straight out of the room, and now we can't find her anywhere."

Lucilla's voice "quivered ominously" as they say in English novels. I, as they say in French novels, experienced "a dumb rage." Such a fuss about silly old Katerfelto! I might have lost every hair on my head, I might have stayed out night after night, and no one would have cared about me. Did she expect me to go to the Cats' Home, to look for him?

"I hope she is dead," said Lucilla. "I should be much happier if I knew she were dead."

"I am quite sure she is dead!" I said, with determined cheerfulness.

Whereupon Lucilla turned away, not to let me see her—well, I did *not* see them! and Kitty behaved as if I had slain her precious pet with my own hands.

"How can you, Mr. Raph?" she said indignantly. "Don't believe him for a moment, Auntie dear. She will come back, I know she will."

"Perfectly certain to come back to-morrow morning," I chimed in, seeing that Kitty had the key of the situation, and it was best to follow her lead.

"Auntie has been tramping round all the streets in the neighbourhood, and ever so far along Brompton Road and towards Eaton Square," Kitty exclaimed, with a strong touch of drama, "and now she wants to go out again, right down to Chelsea, to take some brandy to a poor old woman who's not well! I don't know what to do with her. I would go myself, only she will not let me, because it's dark. Oh, Mr. Raph, do tell her not to go! She's much too tired, after last night."

Lucilla had on her little close bonnet, and her mantle was hanging over the arm of a chair. She was looking weary and worn, and most unfit for a night expedition.

"You must not think of it," I said, surprised into decision by Kitty's absolutely misplaced confidence in the power of "a man" to decide. "I'll take the brandy myself. Where does the horrid old woman live?"

Kitty shot arrows of reproach at me out of her gray eyes.

Lucilla was almost herself again in a moment.

"I could not let you go," she said, with the utmost seriousness, "if you spoke about her like that."

"Very well then!" I said, in desperation. "Where is that angel of an ancient lady? To what Heaven am I to turn my steps?"

Kitty, her folded arms along the head of the sofa, her head resting on them with an inscrutable air like that of a young and amiable Sphinx, nodded sagaciously.

"How very odd of you," she said. "Because, you know, the old woman really does live in Paradise! Paradise Row—No. 7—on the ground floor."

"I really cannot let you—" began Lucilla.

"Infirm of purpose, give me the bottle!" I said, again assuming the decision in which Kitty had the innocence to believe.

Smiling approval, she went to the cupboard at once.

Lucilla must have been very tired, for she yielded without more ado.

"You may as well take these too, Mr. Raph," went on Kitty, pulling a bunch of forget-me-nots out of the china vase in which they were blooming. "Auntie will only have to go back to-morrow, if you don't. She always takes a flower."

"Oh, very well," I said. "What else?"

I did not except the answer that I received.

"Would you—would you mind reading her a chapter out of the Bible?" Lucilla said.

I was fairly staggered. I had never read a chapter of the Bible to anyone. All that occurred to me at the moment was to say,

"Which?"

"Isaiah Sixty," Lucilla instantly rejoined.

I put the brandy bottle in my pocket—accepted the forget-me-nots, thoughtfully tied up by Kitty with a piece of silk which gave way the moment I reached the landing—and was preparing in the lowest spirits to depart, when Lucilla seemed to think that some explanation was necessary.

"I go to her on Wednesday nights because she is too lame to attend a Service at Chapel that she used to like. And she can't see to read to herself. She has a Bible—a Bible in large print, and she will be expecting—"

"Oh, very well," I said, "I can only trust that the magnitude of the transformation of the reader will not give her too great a shock; I never have killed anyone before, I daresay I shall to-night. But we must hope that, come what may, she will appreciate my first appearance as a District Visitor."

"She's not a district," said Kitty pleadingly, "she's only a very nice old woman, a Mrs. Trump, who used to work for Auntie before she grew too blind."

"I have no doubt she is charming," I said; "I daresay I shall be passionately in love with her by the time I return."

For some reason or other, the notion of this appealed to Kitty's sense of the ridiculous, and she began to laugh, and laughed so wildly that at last Lucilla was obliged to laugh too. I never felt less like laughing in my life.

"Oh, Mr. Raph," she cried. "You *must* come and tell us about it when you have seen her. Must he not, Auntie?"

Lucilla smiled, but she assented.

A vague idea of hiring Mahry for half a crown to go instead flitted through my mind as I made my way down the stairs. But it was dark. Lucilla would not have dreamed of letting Mahry do what she would not let Kitty do; I knew that well enough. She had a code of her own about servants, and she told me once that she considered herself just as much bound to look after Mahry if she had been her niece. As for the angelic old woman, she would evidently, in the opinion of all concerned, quit Paradise Row for Paradise, unless she got her brandy that very night. No, there was nothing for it but to go myself!

However, it was as Carlyle said of the only play that he was ever induced to witness, "not so bad as I expected."

Shyness is, I have sometimes thought, a form of conceit, and shy people are apt to exaggerate beforehand the unpleasant effect of their presence upon somebody else. Except on certain rare occasions, we all make less effect than we think we shall. Mrs. Trump had, it was clear, seen odder things than a small, shy, lame, middle-aged gentleman armed with a brandy bottle and a bunch of forget-me-nots—undergone experiences more strange than the sudden substitution of him as her chaplain in the place of a tall and gracious lady. I took to her at once. She was round and roundabout, had good, kind, straight blue eyes, wore an expression like a bowl of bread-and-milk, sweetened with sugar.

"The ladies is very good to me," she said, as I produced the medicine bottle. "My duty to Miss Z., sir, please, and tell her it'll do me well till she comes by again. I'm not a heavy hand on the drink."

There was little air in the room, because it was so very full of texts and china ornaments, but the lamp gave cheerful light, and showed a fern making a gallant struggle for existence in the window, and a bowl of glass wherein two gold fish swam round and round and round till I felt giddy.

Mrs. Trump explained to me that they only cost a penny a piece, that they ate nothing but ants' eggs, which are not, it appears, an expensive luxury, and that she had the glass bowl for ninepence "off of a friend." She seemed to fear lest I should think she had been extravagant in the matter of gold fish. Of course I did associate them chiefly with the gardens of palaces and with passages about a porphyry vase in "The Princess." All the more did I rejoice to see them adorn the unpalatial apartment of Mrs. Trump. As beheld from above, they were about the size of minnows; but the glass had a magical property, and if you looked at them from the side they were miniature whales. I do not think my cousin studies the ways of her Persian cat as Mrs. Trump studied those of gold fish. I learned much about the fern also—about the ways of ferns in general when they live in London. I have seen a fine conservatory full of them, that gave me less to think upon.

"I like a bit o' green," Mrs. Trump said. She could not walk further than the end of the street, but she seemed to possess the Park and Kensington Gardens that one flower-pot.

The interview passed off agreeably on both sides, and when I left, I was surprised to find that I had lingered in Paradise Row for nearly three-quarters of an hour.

If my walk thither had not been altogether an easy one, my walk thence was the best walk that I had taken for many a year. Not to my own dark, dingy room was I returning. I was going where I should find a welcome, where people would be pleased, amused to hear of my doings. How I liked passing my own threshold and the darkness within!

Kitty sprang to open the door as soon as she heard my step. Her cheeks were flushed because she had been kneeling by the fire, she was armed with a toasting fork, and a delicious smell of coffee filled the room. Lucilla, who was resting on the sofa, looked as if she were comforted, and smiled.

"You've been a very long while," said Kitty, with a martial flourish of the toasting fork, as though she were prepared to run me through if I contradicted her. "We were wondering and wondering when you would come. You must have ever so many stories to tell us. No, not now! Eat first and talk afterwards! Here is Auntie's coffee—here is a cup for you, nasty black stuff, that's what you like! and this is a piece of toast I made on purpose, just because I was tired of waiting!"

Kitty was in her element that night, Lucilla being too weary to interfere. She made much more stir about the little details than ever Lucilla did; but it was all as if she were playing a very important game; there was no room for any one to say a word till she had done.

"Would you mind holding a skein of silk for me while you are talking, Mr. Raph?" she said.

I was become a strangely useful member of society. Kitty was the kind of woman who always did something herself and caused everybody else to do something also. As I sat there, my hands caught in that silken chain, I thought how pleasant women made the night—the night that in my dingy room downstairs meant nothing but study or sleep.

"What's the silk going to turn into?" I enquired.

"Embroidery, of course!" she rejoined, holding up a ridiculously small volume of "Selections from Browning," ridiculously bound in white. "I've got a lovely piece of green serge. I'm going to work the 'C Major of life' in the middle."

"How absurd!" I said. "A book that is not a book at all, only a number of bits torn out, bound in white to begin with, and in green to go on with, when the very title shows that it never ought to be bound in anything except brown!"

"I don't care. I don't care in the least. I'm very glad it's white, not ugly brown, and I shall keep it clean and white as long as ever I can—all my life!"

"We have heard nothing yet about Mrs. Trump. Did you see the King and Queen in biscuit, on the mantelpiece?" asked Lucilla.

"Oh yes—and 'Little Samuel,' and 'The Huguenot,' and 'The Highlander' in the green kilt leaning against the pink china rock?" said Kitty.

We had not known that there was so much to see in Paradise Row until we came to talk about it. We had all seen different things, it appeared.

Another hour glided away before we came to the end of the discussion.

"What a delicious evening it has been!" observed Kitty, with a touch of regret, as she gave me her hand to say good-night. "Dances are awfully jolly, but after all, I would rather spend a quiet time like this, Auntie, with you and Mr. Raph."

"You would not think of going to a ball to-morrow if somebody asked you, oh, not you, would you now?" Lucilla said.

"You're very naughty indeed, Auntie. You have no business to ask questions like that! I shall go straight away back to my own house, this minute. Give me my cloak, please, Mr. Raph."

I put it round her shoulders; but even then she had so many last words to say to Lucilla,—whom she would see again the next morning,—that I went down before her.

As I opened the door of my own room, something darted past me up the staircase.

It was Katerfelto, who had been hiding under my table all the while. Then, indeed, was there such jubilation upon the Drawingroom floor that, once more summoned by Kitty, I was fain to repair thither. Mahry, grinning from ear to ear, brought back a jug of milk, Lucilla poured it into the Japanese bowl, Kitty sat on the floor and laughed.

"Well," I said, "I should think that cat will run away again! If it had saved the life of another cat, you could not make more fuss about it. Poor beast, how you are ruining its character! Not a chance for it to rise in the scale of being!"

The pleasantest evenings, however, must come to an end some time. The good-nights were said all over again, Kitty had gone home, the lights were out, the house had sunk into silence, and still I sat, below the statue of Gordon, reading the prophet Isaiah. Lucilla had not asked me any question about that part of my visit to Paradise Row. Even if I had seen her alone, I could not have told her. There was no need to do so, for I am sure she knew. The bitterness there had been in my heart about the poor—about the difference between one class and another—melted away as I read.

"*For brass I will bring gold, and for iron I will bring silver, and for wood brass, and for stones iron: I will also make thy officers peace, and thine exactors righteousness.*"

IX

An inexplicable shade of difference stole over our lives after that ball. Kitty was just the same, but Lucilla and I came to treat her as if she were more grown up. I do not think she noticed it, however.

The examinations were about to take place at the College of Music, and she went there oftener for lessons and worked rather more when at home. Nothing of that kind lay heavy on her soul; she was not in the least nervous. Her calmness of spirit amazed Lucilla, who was always more anxious for her than she was for herself. She never took the highest honours, perhaps because she did not seriously try for them; but she passed well and, so to speak, with a little feather in her cap, whenever she had the good luck to meet among the examiners any one who cared more for style than for technique.

As a consequence of the ball, the Nabob and Charles I., who had been on calling terms before with Lucilla, began to call very often, so often indeed that I used to ask Lucilla which of them intended to stay permanently.

She only laughed.

"Kitty amuses herself," said she, "but her heart is quite untouched. It is not, by a long way, the first flirtation of either of those young gentlemen. I have had broken hearts to mend before now. It will do no harm on either side. Besides, she is soon going home; that will put a stop to the whole thing."

"You will miss her," I said, with sudden fear—a sudden hope on top of it, that she might need the gentleman downstairs a little more.

The reply was different from that for which I looked.

"No," she said bravely, "I shall not miss her: I have always told myself that it would not be for long. I have been saying that to myself ever since she came. And by and by, when she is married, I will love her child."

But Lucilla's eyes glistened; and I believed her eyes rather than her lips. There was pain in my heart for her, and—stronger than the pain—the hope that she might need me more.

I cannot remember how it came to pass—the very vividness of certain moments annihilates those which precede them—but on a night of later July we were sitting, all three, by the piano, and an unwonted silence had fallen among us. Lucilla had but to listen as a rule—to listen as she always listened—and Kitty's tongue ran on; but that night she listened in vain. I thought perhaps the child might have some girlish confidence to make, and rose to go.

"No, Mr. Raph," said Kitty. "You are not going yet. You never go so soon as this. Auntie, we won't let him go!"

And I stayed, because, following the example of Lucilla, I always did what Kitty wanted.

"She is so sensible," Lucilla used to say.

As for being sensible, she was neither more nor less sensible than other people of her age, she was entirely capricious, but Lucilla liked to think she was sensible—liked to believe, I think, that she had made her so. Or else, being accustomed to command, it amused her for once to obey.

But although Lucilla asked me to stay—and though I meant to stay before she asked me and stayed accordingly—and though there were as many things in the world to talk about as ever, that uncomfortable silence fell again, and fell heavily.

Now Kitty in the part of the Silent Woman was Kitty in a part with which I was not familiar, and I did not know what to do with her. It was not the happy silence that Lucilla and I enjoyed so often. Girls under twenty are ignorant of that. When they are silent it is because they are shy or sad, or because they cannot find words—not because they have passed into a region where there is no need of them.

"How lovely the stars are to-night!" Lucilla said.

I have noticed that people will talk about the stars when they have nothing else to say. Strange presumption of human nature, to drag those vast worlds in, that we may escape a momentary embarrassment! If we saw things as they are, we should be afraid to speak of the stars. With Lucilla, however far afield she might roam, something practical was sure to follow. I waited, and it did.

"Let us draw our chairs up to the window! It seems a pity to shut them."

She signed to me to lift the sash higher, and the cool soft evening air crept into the little room and lightened the tension. A curious chequer-work of light and shadow, thrown from her own lamp and from somebody else's in another house, diversified the blank wall opposite. A bar of black roof stretched in a straight line above. Straight black lines of chimneys shot up from it. At right angles went a row of dusky houses, with windows like dim, veiled eyes, here and there faintly shining. An infant moon curled, feather-like, behind the chimneys. The stars shone thick and bright.

All at once Kitty began to speak.

"I wonder if there are people up there. Do you think there are, Mr. Raph?"

"Have you been reading 'The Story of the Heavens'?" I asked. It was a favourite book of Lucilla's.

"No. I can't read. What's the use of it? I never take in anything unless it's what I've thought before. Then I write *Glorious* all down the page. Then I think, 'How silly! when it's only my own thought stuck into words that I couldn't find.'"

"Have you thought all the thoughts that are in all the books, dear?"

"O Auntie, I didn't mean to be conceited! I only meant that, if I haven't thought the thought, it's no use reading the words; I can't understand."

"When you are older you will think differently. Books give me my thoughts."

"What is being older?" said Kitty, wrinkling her forehead. "It seems to me so funny to put people's ages on their tombstones. How can it possibly be true? One person has lived ever so long in five minutes. Another has never been alive at all for fifty years. Browning says, when we're happy there's nothing except *Now*. That's true, of course; I had to write *Glorious* all down the margin just before I came in to you.

"It is not true," Lucilla said. "There was always *Yesterday*; there will always be *To-morrow*."

"Not if you're living, Auntie—not if you're really alive, alive all the time. And if you've once been alive—really alive every bit of you—alive in some one else—it can't matter when they die, or when you do. It's all the same. It's not the house they live in that you care about. Why should you mind?"

"We *must* mind, dear!" Lucilla said, very tenderly, but as if she were alarmed. The subject went too near her heart for discussion, I could see that; and yet I had no wish to let it drop. Something in Kitty's earnest way of speech appealed to me. She seemed to be my own youth speaking, although, at her age, I could not have spoken. Just in that way I used to feel about the insignificance of death. The deceiver that we call Experience had taken away my early trust, but when I heard her speak I knew she came nearer the truth.

Besides, the power of death cannot be felt till it is known, and though the young think of it more often than we do, words cannot give them any idea of this. No, let their blessed ignorance remain! There is more faith in it than lies within the compass of our knowledge.

I tried a strain of thought which I knew that Lucilla would not follow.

"If we could remember that Time is an illusion—that it is only our way of thinking things, one after the other—"

"Yes"—Kitty caught me up eagerly—"then it wouldn't matter, would it, if one went away, and the other were left—if one died and the other were left?"

"It would always matter," Lucilla said in grave, distressed tones. "There's only one sorrow that can be worse."

"I think I've got no heart, Auntie. It's fast asleep in me. To-night I shall lie awake and think of all the dreadful things I've said to you and Mr. Raph. I don't know what to do now for thinking of them. I don't know why I've talked like this. I never do it to anybody else. It's something in the way you listen. Oh, I am very sorry! I know I am not old enough to talk. You and Mr. Raph never said a word—you only helped me along. O, will you both forget it, please? Will you promise me not to remember? Will you let it all go, the minute I've shut the door?"

Her words came hurrying out, vehement, eager, as if she had let some terrible secret fly, and were trying to catch it again.

I would have comforted her if I could, but my phrases were clumsy, they did not meet the winged need of the moment. Lucilla said nothing; she drew the girl down on to her knee as if she had been a little child, and held her fast.

The clock of a neighbouring church struck in, and reminded Kitty that, whatever her theories of eternity might happen to be, it was now, by mortal time, ten o'clock.

"Oh dear, I ought to go!" she cried. "I feel as if I can't—as if this talking would cling about the room when I'm gone. Why did I talk?" She rose to throw her cloak round her, protesting all the time. She turned to me, took both my hands in hers, looked in my face with something in her gray eyes that I had never seen there before—then flung her arms round Lucilla's neck, rested a moment against her, and went.

Lucilla followed.

The sweet voices were gone; there was no sound but the light rasping of a withered leaf against the rough brick wall. I was left alone in that room where I was never alone. Memory rose in her strength and took possession. She blinded and deafened me so that I did not heed Lucilla's return nor observe anything until I heard her sigh.

"What is the matter?" I said, awaking with an effort.

"I wish Kitty would not talk like that of things she knows nothing about."

"She is very humble, really."

"Do you think that? I am glad. I felt so much afraid that you should think her vain."

"No," I said. "You were right."

"What do you mean?"

It was her turn to look startled now.

"Do not you see what lay behind all that talk?" I said. "She cares for some-one. She is trying to face the thought of what it would be to her if he died. That's why she felt as if she had told a secret—as if she could not forgive herself."

Lucilla thought for several minutes.

"Yes," she said at last, with a dawning smile. "Yes. Perhaps it may be so. I believe you are right."

There was no pretext for staying any longer. I wished her good-night. I suppose she wished me the same; but notwithstanding, I spent a bad one.

X

When I came home from a business visit to the Record Office next day, I was met by the information that Miss Kitty had left that morning. It did not surprise me. No doubt she wanted to consult her own people.

There was a dismal sense of flatness about the house.

Mahry was going about with red eyes, she had evidently wept for several hours. I heard the landlady's shrill voice scolding away in the kitchen. The landlord looked more wistful, more resigned than before. Miss Kitty's box had come unlocked at the last minute, he explained, and no power on earth would induce it to lock. They had called him in next door, but he could do nothing. He seemed to imply that I could have done something if I had had the sense to be present. "Young ladies didn't know what they was going to encounter." In his opinion, it was tempting Providence to start with a box that would not lock.

After dinner, as I was sitting listlessly enough in the dusk, thinking how twenty-four hours may make another evening "Long ago," there was a tap at my door, and Lucilla entered.

She took my breath away.

It was the first time she ever came to my room—and the last. How I should have prepared for her, if I had known she was coming! But things are best as they are. At any rate I am not much of a smoker, and if there was no scent of flowers, there was no smell of tobacco. The kindly twilight would not let her see how different my room looked from her own.

I have honoured her coming since she went away, if I did not honour it before. In the chair that she occupied no one has sat since; though I dust nothing else, I dust that.

I could feel rather than see that she looked radiant. She held a telegram in her hand.

"News!" she said, a little breathlessly. "I was obliged to come and share it with you. You were right, Kitty is engaged."

"Which is it? Not Charles I., I hope? The Nabob would be better than that."

"Neither of them! An organist—a good serious young man—almost handsome. He has just passed out of College with the highest honours. He gave her the little white Browning that I admired so much. Don't you remember how she scolded you when you said Browning ought to be bound in brown?"

I did not choose to recollect.

"Has he anything else to give her?"

"O yes! He has been offered a very good post in Australia. They will have quite enough to live upon."

"A long way off," I said. "Why are you so much pleased?"

"Because she is happy," Lucilla said; and paused as if she had mentioned something sacred.

"I could not tell you before," she went on. "She only spoke to me this morning, just before the train started. She thought she ought to tell her mother first. I was not to say anything to you until I got the telegram to say she was with her mother. It came ten minutes ago.—She will make the dearest little wife, will she not?"

"Just like anybody else's," I said. "An enormous family of course, marrying so young—eleven or twelve children."

"That would not be in the least like Kitty," said Lucilla, very much hurt.

"O well," I said, "I daresay she will be more tiresome still about one or two."

Lucilla rose.

"I am sorry that I came," she said; "I did not know that you—that you were busy. I thought you really loved her. She sent you such a sweet message of goodbye. She wanted you to want her to be happy."

"I wish her every happiness," I said. "But she will never be so happy again as she was with you."

It vexed me that Lucilla should make such a tremendous point of some one else's getting married, when she was not married herself.

It vexed me that I should have appeared to her in my own hard, true colours.

I spent another bad night.

The next day I pretended that I had never behaved like that. And Lucilla pretended that I had not either. There are some occasions in life, when, between friends, this is the only way to ask—and to receive—forgiveness.

Everything turned out just as I knew it would.

A few months later, the giver of Browning endowed Kitty with all his worldly goods—there were not many of them,—and she went out with him to his new post in Australia.

Lucilla did not attend the wedding.

"I cannot trust myself," she said.

I knew then that she thought Australia a very long way off.

I was asked too, as a matter of form, but I could not feel sorry that the state of my finances made it impossible for me to accept the kind invitation.

In the long winter evenings that followed, Lucilla would often read aloud merry letters from the other side of the world. We laughed together as we made out, from Kitty's rough plans and sketches, where every bit of furniture stood in her tiny drawingroom, where every picture hung.

"It must be like a doll's house," Lucilla said, and smiled when she came to a passage describing how Kitty hung the Portrait of the Unknown, which I had given her at her own request, over the fireplace, to remind her of Mr. Raph.

One little letter came to my address, to thank me for the picture—but I did not keep nor did I answer it. There would be always a message for me, and I would send a message back. But she was gone out of my life.

For a short time I felt grievously the loss of the brightness, of the youth of the house. Then I became reconciled to such a point that I did not even desire her return.

Kitty had shown me what being young meant.

My own youth, after the first, had been rather like other people's old age. The accident that lamed me for life ruined my health for a time. I had spent many winters abroad, in frugal pensions, among maiden ladies and yet more maidenly widows, until I felt like a widow or an old maid myself. When I came back to England well and strong, no one believed it. My cousin shut every window as soon as I entered her drawingroom and was careful never, unless of course she really "wanted a man," to ask me out to dinner, "Because, poor fellow, he cannot stand the night air." It was the absence of the night air that I could not stand; I was careful not to enlighten her.

But, if Kitty had shown me what being young was like, she had also made me feel older than ever I felt before. She clearly thought Lucilla so very old; and if Lucilla were very old, I shrewdly suspected that I must be older still. For people like Lucilla—and like me—she knew, of course, that life was over. She took it for granted that I had lived—once upon a time—but I, who only once, for a moment had known what she called *life*, was silently cast down by the thought that she knew I could never live now. She turned the key in the lock for me as I had not yet turned it for myself.

When she was gone we resumed our former pleasant and peaceful ways. One habit Lucilla had not lost while Kitty was with us. She always continued to play for me on Sundays. I had gone rather more often of an evening too: she said it amused Kitty, and now she did not discourage my attendance. I had no feeling whatever that she needed me; but I was not in her way.

Still, that which had come and passed so quickly, did not leave us as it had found us. We were not quieter after Kitty went, we had been just as quiet before—but we were more conscious of tranquility. There was not the flutter of wings that I had always heard about the room when she was there—the sense of the strange unrest—the ever-varying charm of Spring.

If I had turned octogenarian, Lucilla seemed younger for the change, I thought. While Kitty was there she had taken her proper position as the experienced Aunt-like friend, the one who *knew* where youth was only guessing. It amused me to hear her wise, proverbial sayings when all the time I was aware, in secret, that the heart in her bosom beat with sympathy as keen and as unreasonable as that of the girl who sat perched on the arm of her chair. I never tried to be proverbial. Kitty shared her own youth with me in her joy; but speaking as she did on that last night, under the stars, she threw me back on old forgotten feelings, with such force that I shivered and hid my eyes. When we say, *It is good to be young*, we forget that at the same time it is terrible. I shook the recollection off as soon as I could but ever after I felt the older for it.

XI

"What a comfort it is, to be middle-aged!" Lucilla said, one day. "Some of the pleasure of being young is gone, not the happiness—and there is more freedom."

"I cannot imagine that you were ever in bondage to public opinion," I said, smiling. "Have you not always done just what you liked?"

"I suppose I have, more or less," she answered, as if she were amused. "But when I was young, I did what I liked, and it worried the aunt with whom I lived—she disliked it very much. Sometimes she worried me. And sometimes I liked things that were mere vanity. It seemed as if coloured veils hung between me and the true things that I wanted. Now I know what they are. One is happier really, reckoning it all up together—don't you think so?"

"I am happier than I have ever been," I said, as we say the truest things of all, without any intention to do so.

Lucilla made no response. She did not ask me why.

She was gazing into the fire. As I sat and looked at her, I thought again what happiness it was to see her, to be near her, to hear her voice. Othello's words came flashing to my mind:

> "If it were now to die,
> 'Twere now to be most happy; for, I fear
> My soul hath her content so absolute,
> That not another comfort like to this
> Succeeds in unknown fate."

Not that I had the slightest wish to die. I should have liked to go on living as we were living then, always.

Never without something of a shock, even now, do I recollect the minute that followed—the minute in which it first crossed my mind that Lucilla was hiding something from me. Had any one asked the question, I should have been puzzled to say what it was that she ever confided. I was wont to enter her thoughts as she entered mine, without any knocking at the door in set sentences. Suddenly—plainly—mysteriously—the door was shut. We were sitting by the fire together, just as we had sat many a week before; but in a moment she went her way, and I was left.

My way led, earlier than usual, down to my own room, where I sat and pondered.

Was she displeased?

Was she unhappy?

Was she—hateful thought!—thinking of some one else? For some want of reason or other, I could not get this last supposition out of my head. Such a strong sensation of hatred started up in me that it seemed ridiculous to have no object for the feeling. It must be a third, a shadowy third that had come between. Whatever, whoever it might be, he was hateful.

Why had I not stayed on, and affronted the question boldly?

What are you thinking of? Is there anything easier to say than those words? Why had not I said them? She was frank and candid as a child. Evasion, subterfuge, were things unknown to her. If she did not desire to speak upon a given subject, she told me so, and there was an end. It would have been easy to ask at once; and now it was impossible.

Perhaps I dreaded the answer. But would not any answer she could give be preferable to those which I was inventing for her?

What was it that had happened? What was it that, in a moment, divided her from me?

Could I have been mistaken? Was it some absurd fancy of mine?

I tried to think so, but I could not. Certain impressions of the mind are tangible as outward facts. If a wall had erected itself between me and my heart's friend, I could not have been more firmly convinced.

Well! Two days more, and Thursday would come round. I must learn something then.

Meantime I found an extraordinary interest in work. I went to see my cousin. I studied the questions of the day. I read books. It was all curiously stale, flat, and unprofitable. At every turn I thought of something that I wanted to say to Lucilla, of something that I wanted to hear her say. Politics were the only comfort. She was not a newspaper woman. *The Spectator* once a week more than satisfied her. Over the intricacies of a Bill I could sometimes forget her; she was tangled up with everything else.

On Wednesday night, however, Mahry brought me a note from the Lady on the Drawingroom floor. Lucilla begged to inform the gentleman downstairs that she was compelled to go out on Thursday.

Compelled! Who or what was compelling her?

I began to wish that I were very ill. If anything were ill, I had never known Lucilla deny herself the pleasure of taking care of it. If I were ill, she would hear from the landlady, and I knew, I felt sure, that she would come. But we are ill when we are ill—not when we should like to be ill.

Somebody else was ill perhaps. Who could it be?

Was it of this that she was thinking when the barriers rose up and remained?

If she chose to have another person there, some being whom I could not see, some creature whom she preferred to her visible guest, she might have him all to herself, I was resolved to share with none. I would not go again. Next time she asked me, I would refuse.

Thursday week, however, was a long way off. Was there nothing to be done in the meantime? I supposed she would play as usual on Sunday evening; it did not occur to me that she could fail there!

I composed a satirical appeal for a piece of music on a theme that I had never suggested before, *Souvent femme varie*, and I requested Mahry to take it up on Sunday evening; but she gave me no chance. For the first time in our long tenantry of the house in Back Street together, when I asked Mahry to take up the little note as usual, I was met by the announcement, "Miss Z. is out."

I am ashamed to say how late I sat up, waiting to hear Miss Z. let herself in.

I reproached myself. Perhaps I had let her see, when I left so early, that I felt annoyed. She had gone out, on purpose, to avoid playing. It was very good of her to play for me every Sunday; perhaps she was tired of it. Yet had I been no ungrateful listener. I had enjoyed this music far too much to think about the kindness. I imagined—was I wrong?—that she enjoyed it also. I had experienced little of the pleasure of intimate sympathy in my single life, and now I grew alarmed. What if it went? What if *I* had killed it? All the kindness in the world could not take the place of that. With every turn of the clock I grew more wretched.

Some deadly accident of course had happened—a judgment on me, because I had not valued this treasure while it was mine.

She had fallen from a 'bus.

She was imprisoned in the depths of an underground tunnel.

She was lying, desperately wounded, in some Hospital where nobody knew who she was.

London became the den of horrors that it really is. How did she dare to walk alone in it? How could I ever have let her go?

It fretted me past bearing, that neither the landlord, nor the landlady, nor Mahry, betrayed any anxiety whatsoever.

Called up and questioned as to whether she had left word that she should be away for the night, Mahry stared and said,

"Naow, sir!"

Called up and questioned, after Mahry had presumably gone to bed, as to the state of the weather, the landlord opined that the streets were like glass and there would be several people would have broke their legs in tomorrer morning's "Dyly Myle"; but when I said that ladies ought not to be out on such a night, he only remarked that Miss Z. went out in all weathers, and she was a real lady, she was, and it never seemed to do her no harm.

As for the landlady, I heard her going callously upstairs just as usual, after she had turned out the gas in the hall and left a candle and a box of matches on the bracket.

At length, just as I was preparing to start on a tour of inspection of St. George's, the Brompton Consumptive, the Workhouse Infirmary, &c., &c., I heard the key turn in the lock and knew Lucilla had come in. She came in just as if it were twelve o'clock in the middle of the day instead of midnight. I detected neither haste nor delay in the sound of her footsteps. I retired to bed in a state of virtuous indignation with her for being heartlessly unaware that she had caused me to spend hours of torment. She ought to have known—she, who always did know.

Next morning I thought again, very seriously, of the engagement that was to engage me that evening—or on Thursday—or whenever she condescended to ask me upstairs again. Certainly she deserved that. There was plenty of time before me. I need not invent it yet. The afternoon would do.

No note came down, however. I had never gone on Monday without a note. Of course I did not go.

Well, Wednesday would do for that invention!

And yet, when Wednesday came, my one dread was, lest Mahry should bring me another note; for on Thursday—it was the old arrangement—I went without one.

Wednesday came.

Wednesday passed.

The Ides of March were over. I forgot all about the engagement that was to engage me on the day following. I went to bed happier than I had been for a fortnight, and rose with a delicious sense of lightness.

A fortnight? It was a hundred years since I had seen her!

When I hobbled upstairs to the drawingroom floor at the accustomed hour, I felt like a schoolboy coming home for the holidays. I felt as if I had neither eaten nor drunk for several weeks. Yet was there a beating fear of difference, a shrinking in me lest that which had been so long, so happily, the same, should have changed. Better for me, if this were so, not to have left my dingy room again!

I had not crossed the threshold before all these fears vanished.

Katerfelto lay, fat and round, before the fire, and purred a little when I scratched his ear.

The parrot let down a skinny membrane half over his eye, which was his horrid way of winking, and said, as if he were making a confidential communication:

"How are you?"

Betsinda rose from her three-legged stool and made a curtsey—she had learned how from Kitty and was rather proud of it; and I made Betsinda a bow. She brought me my cup and saucer very carefully without spilling a drop, and was rewarded with a piece of cake, which she ate with the utmost decorum.

"Now, Betty," Lucilla said, "you may make us another curtsey and run away."

Betsinda vanished, regretfully but without demur, Mahry removed the tea-things, Katerfelto walked out of the room after her, the parrot went to sleep on his perch, and Lucilla and I were alone once more.

"Lucilla!" I said at once, not giving myself time to reflect, "what were you thinking of, this day fortnight?"

"I was thinking of some one whom I shall never see again," she answered quietly.

A feeling like remorse checked any answer that I might have made. I had been jealous of him. Poor fellow! and he was dead.

"It is wrong to forget," she said, after a pause. "If we are not true to those whom we cannot see, we are not true to those whom we can."

"He is—he is often with you?" I asked.

"He was always with me until this time last year," she replied, no tremor in her voice, but a seriousness of conviction as if she had made some statement against herself.

"You would never forget any one. You are constant by nature."

She shook her head sadly.

"I thought so once; but it is not like that. I did forget. When we talked about being happy the other night, something you said showed me that it was not like that."

I began to wish that she would forget again. After all, what was the use of remembering? It did the poor fellow himself no good, and it made me uncomfortable.

"If," I said sturdily, "if I were dead, I should not care to be remembered—much. Not if remembering had to be kept up, you know."

Lucilla's eyes flashed for a minute, but she said nothing.

I was concerned to defend her against herself. I really thought she was behaving with a singular lack of good sense.

"What is the use of pretending that you care more than you do?" I said. "It is not even sincere."

She changed the subject with a dignity that made me feel as much ashamed of myself as if I had broken all the Ten Commandments at once.

We talked on; but on my side, at any rate, there was a difference. It was better that not seeing Lucilla at all. How "like a winter" had her absence been! And I did not feel constrained to leave abruptly, as on the last occasion. Yet it was not so good as it had been before. Still the visionary third came between.

He had astonished me into surprise at myself as well as at Lucilla: and I was almost as much annoyed with him for the one cause as for the other.

After I had returned to my own apartment, I sat a long time, pondering over his antecedents.

A charming person, no doubt—otherwise Lucilla would not have cared for him.

Handsome of course, and all that. "A leg," like Sir Willoughby Patterne, a "balustrade leg!" Mine, I felt conscious, though I had never thought of it before, must distress Lucilla. She did not let me see; that was only part of her kindness.

He must have had a fine manner also—not *gauche* and awkward.

I wondered if he had ever sat alone with her. As I wondered, I hated him furiously; and, in a minute, all my anger turned to commiseration.

Poor fellow! He was dead.

It was this that had surprised me in the first instance. I am not wont to pity the dead. I never pitied one of them in all my life before. What! Pity those who are, beyond all power to think it, *free?* Not I!

The only men among the dead whom I dared to pity were those who died without having lived; and even those I pitied less than when they moved upon this lovely earth, not seeing it. Perhaps I was wrong there. Who shall say? I had known lives that were to me so piteous, that I was afraid to waste my pity on those who were—I could not but think it—better off.

Dying is bad, of course.

For myself I looked forward to dying—to the mere act of transition—sometimes with a sudden cold anguish of horror and surprise—at other times with such a high-wrought curiosity of interest that it was rapture—sometimes with complete indifference. If I die in a moment—or in my sleep—it can be no great matter. I have rehearsed it in a faint. The common lot involves greater suffering than that, and death, in whatever form it may draw near, is "violent death." I have often thought it strange that people should bestow more compassion on a murdered man than on one who has lain a-dying for years. Outwardly, man appears to be more merciful about this work, no torture that he invents can equal the pain of slow disease. But death, when it comes, causes the dead to forget even the terror of their dying. However they may have suffered, the look upon the face of the dead is the seal of the solution of all tragedy in divine peace.

"Poor Oliver!"

I used to think how my cousin, who will certainly live to be ninety, bar accidents, would say this over me, and would perhaps feel really very sorry as she did so. I should be far away, beyond her pity, no longer lame, no longer bound by all the chains of Illusion. I thought of it with deep humility, with trust in that Forgiveness which is Love, with hope. I thought also that I should see my friend again.

I did not care for funerals. Therein I incurred the reproach of my cousin.

"Every one should wish to pay the last tribute of respect," she said.

Funerals gave a neat finish to friendship in her opinion; but for me friendship did not end there.

I needed no other company than that of one dead man. Long ago I had smiled when my cousin said to me in a sympathetic voice, "You must feel so lonely in the evenings, Oliver!" Often I had refused to leave my room because, to leave it meant leaving him.

As I recalled these things, I seemed to creep into a strange sense of empti-ness. I found that it was long since he had come to me. Had I also begun to forget?

The dead are jealous; they will not come when there is any thought of others. Of late, as I sat in my rich solitude, I had thought of Lucilla.

My old fears of her returned upon me in full force. What was this that she had done to me? She had taken away the dead.

Not content with that, she had brought her own—a dead man whom I had never seen, to haunt me perpetually.

Why had she thought of him always "until this time last year?" It was eighteen months now since Kitty had left us. Why, this last year, had she ceased to remember?

This began to be worse than anything else. After all, the dead man was not my rival, but my fellow. She must have given him up for some one living.

With lightning swiftness the conviction struck me down, that this ex-plained her absence. She had gone out to meet the living man, whoever he might be. Why did he not come to her? Much as I should dislike his coming, it would be better than to know that she went to him. Perhaps he did come, though I knew it not. There were long hours of almost every day when I was out.

Yet, if this were her strange way of telling me, I did not know what she had told.

She had let me see that she was displeased with herself. It might be, after all, that she did not care—that the dead man was the stronger of the two.

Was this really so? Or did she only deceive herself?

She deceived herself, that was clear. She might forget for a moment—not for a year; and only now had she remembered her forgetfulness.

If I pitied even the enviable dead man because he was not alive to be loved by Lucilla, what were my feelings towards his successor?

There is considerable doubt as to what they should have been—and none at all as to what they were. I considered him very presumptuous.

What business had he to trouble a mind that had long ago ceased to be ruffled by the storms of youth? If he made her go to him, he was not showing her due respect. If he did not take the trouble to come himself, how could he be in earnest? I would have given the world to know whether he did come. I was frantic at the thought that Mahry must know perfectly well what it was life or death for me to know—and I could not. I went the length of propos-ing to myself to sit at home a whole day and watch. Fool! I might hear the hall door open, but could I rush out into the passage, or peep through the keyhole? Any one who would might come and go, and I be never the wiser. Besides, hot shame overtook me when I found that I was turning spy. Again, again, what had Lucilla done to me?

It was not Lucilla, it was the man. Did she then care for him, seeing she had forgotten the dead on his account? My sympathies were with the dead.

I began to feel a kind of friendship for that dead man. She had never neglected me for him as she did for the other. Now she had forgotten him, forgotten me. I also was numbered among the dead.

She had reposed great confidence in me when she spoke of him. In a few words the secret of much lay hidden.

It was for his sake that she lived unmarried in Back Street—that she who, whatever she might say about it, loved children, had no child of her own. It was perhaps for his sake that she had been kind to me—a lonely fellow with no one to care about him. But there I drew up. I hated that she should be kind to me for anybody's sake except my own. I could not but think that, after all, she was my friend—my own.

Well—what was my course to be henceforward?

If she cared for this other—had cared for him a year—she would marry him, I supposed. It was only natural to suppose that, once she was married, she would leave the house.

Leave the house!

I am ashamed of the turn that my reflections took at this point. Life, as people older than Kitty know, is made up of little things; that is the only excuse—and it is worse than none at all.

A nightmare vision of the house, as it had been before Lucilla came, rose up before me.

Mahry, I felt sure, would go with her. There would be another Mahry, like the first, her matted hair down her back, her shoes down at heel. The landlady would cook just as she used to cook.

There would be no Thursdays in the week, no Sundays—no music, not a note.

In the bitterness of my heart I wished that Lucilla had never come. Before she came I had not missed the harmony she brought, except with a vague sense of something absent. Now it was not a question of missing, but of definite and most serious loss.

My feeling towards the dead man grew more friendly than ever. He had been a good neighbour. So long as he remained alone with Lucilla, I was happy.

I must know whether she was going to be faithful to him.

I could not ask.

Clearly she was not. She had been unfaithful for the last year. She would not have told me this now, if she had not meant me to understand that she was going to give him up—with regret it might be—with self-reproach—for some one dearer.

Well! Had she not a right to do so? I had been on her side against herself. I had told her that fidelity to something remembered that you did not, of your own accord remember, was rubbish. People think that they can deceive the dead very easily. He could not speak for himself, and I had spoken for him. My sympathies were with the dead.

XII

On the Sunday following I asked Lucilla to play—not mentioning that this time it would be *in memory of a friend*—the movement following on Chopin's Funeral March—the Dead Leaf movement—where the dead boughs are whirled about the grave.

She might well consecrate as much remembrance as that to the memory of her own friend, I reflected. I wondered whether he had been a soldier, and fallen, like him I loved, in battle. Yes, that was it! That must be it. That was why, from the first, she had understood.

Again I caught myself thinking rather of her friend than of mine.

She played the March, however, and not the Dead Leaf movement. She played in the old, beautiful way, as if she were pouring out her heart, as she had seldom played while Kitty was with her—and not, I think, since Kitty left. There again, music is language, but it has no words; nor could I tell what was being spoken. Was it unutterable fidelity? or only unutterable regret that all things pass? She was making confidences, she was crying out from the depths of her soul, but I did not know what she said.

I was in a miserable ecstasy while it lasted. Afterwards the ecstasy went; and I was miserable and nothing else.

Why?

There was no reason at all.

I recollected fits of this absurd, aimless, disproportioned wretchedness, in the days of youth. In my freedom from that condition I had rejoiced for many years. Here I was, no better than twenty-five again!

I took myself to task finely, the next morning. It was all nonsense. It interfered with work, and with friendship. It was ridiculous of me to go on making myself unhappy because Lucilla was not unhappy enough about someone who had died—Heaven knew how many years ago—someone I had never seen!

Let me put away idle sentiment and every thought of the rivals, living and dead, who were contending for Lucilla's affection! Let them fight it out as they would! They were nothing to me. Let me make the most of what the gods had given! Let me "keep my pittance clear from poison of repining!" My part was to rejoice in her friendship so long as it remained—to help her if I could, if I dared, to be true to herself! Once before I had failed her at need, I had not entered into her unselfish happiness as she had trusted that I should. I would not fail her now in her distress.

From some undefined but very strong feeling I took her no flowers when Thursday came.

Did she notice? Was she too busy with another thought?

Other people often sent her flowers, but on that day my heart smote me when I saw that there were none. Her new friend, whoever he might be, was neglectful of his privileges.

"Why did you ask me to play that Chopin on Sunday?" she said, when we had finished tea. "I found it hard. You never gave me the name of any hero."

"Why should you always play it for a hero of mine?" I said. "Have you none of your own?"

"I have known very few soldiers in my life. The men whom I have known were mostly business men or scholars."

Here was the heroic death of the first admirer disposed of at a blow! I felt oddly disappointed. Had he died as other men die? That was not right.

"Every hero is not a soldier," I said; but without conviction, for in my heart I rather thought he was. It was because I thought he was a soldier that I had tolerated the idea of the man at all.

"Oh dear no!" she rejoined, with more alacrity than was desirable. "I have wondered sometimes why it was, that you gave only the names of soldiers."

"Would you have liked to play for a Bishop?"

I began to be afraid that her new friend was a heroic clergyman in the East End. That was why he sent her no flowers; he was too poor—he has conscientious scruples about spending a penny. She had gone to the East End to hear him preach—and that was why she came in so late the other night.

But her smile, at the thought of playing Chopin for a Bishop, dispelled my fears.

"No," she said. "I would play for a Missionary Bishop—they are heroes sometimes, from what I hear. Or I would have played for Westcott. You have only to look at his face to see that he was a hero. Not for any other Bishops.

I believe I have more heroes than you. But you have not told me why it is that you always give your hero the name of a soldier."

"Because I knew one."

She sat silent in the old, understanding way.

"It was a great thing for a lame dog like me," I said.

"The greatest—for anyone," she answered, low and reverently.

"Nothing else matters. In the end it is more real than anything."

"I wish I were sure of that," she said, the poignant note of self-reproach in her voice again. "One feels unworthy—unworthy afterwards, to have known. It is as if things went wrong that never need have gone wrong, if one had thought beforehand. I cannot understand it at all. I cannot understand myself."

I was in the awkward position of a man who hears a secret without in the least comprehending it. When women talk about *one*, they drive their auditors to distraction.

Lucilla—clear as light—Lucilla, who never got into difficulties because she always knew what she wanted—now spoke in riddles; she might, in fact, as well have played the piano so far as any definite impression, except that of sadness, was conveyed by her speech. Two people, who, as a rule, are independent of words, are in a bad way indeed when words become a necessity; they have got out of the habit of asking questions. I asked myself questions without end:

What had she done?

Why did she feel unworthy?

Why were things wrong that never need have gone wrong if one had known?

They were questions that I could not or would not ask her.

Yet I felt rather happy, happier than I had felt for some time. I had steeled myself to look upon her happiness. On the contrary, she was wretched; and she had told me so. I had always rebelled against the maxim of La Rochefoucauld, that there is something not displeasing to us in the misfortunes of our best friends; now, with an inward shiver at my own selfishness, I found it was true. I liked better that she should be miserable and tell me so, than that she should be happy and keep the reason to herself. What was become of all my fine resolutions?

I sat silent, hoping that she would speak further.

"We never ought to despise people, ought we?"

Here at last the next move was an easy one.

"Most certainly!" I replied. "Despise anybody who does not think as you do. It is the only weapon you have against him. He is not worth anger, and clearly he is not worth sorrow."

I was feeling, with scorn and self-contempt at the moment, how differently Lucilla would have acted, had I confided to her that I was troubled in mind.

"I mean," Lucilla said, humbly but not much as if she had been attending, "there is a friend—no, not a friend—an acquaintance of mine, who lost her husband. She married again—and on her wedding day she laid a wreath on the grave of her first husband. I used to laugh at that."

Good heavens! Had Lucilla been married before?

"And now you wish to do the same?" I inquired.

She laughed outright this time, and I was reassured in a moment. No widow ever laughed like that.

"I ought not to be amused," she said, as soon as she could speak. "If I had married, I dare say I should have done just the same."

"Perhaps you would. You remember the words of the French diviner, '*Il ne faut jamais dire, Fontaine, je ne boirai jamais de ton eau.*'?"

"I do not *think* I am faithless," she said, with a touch of something like defiance.

"I warn you that I do not care whether you are or not," I replied, catching something of her tone. "You recollect how Kitty said that *Now* was everything?" More and more I felt as if I could not trust myself to use my own words. "It is. But—" here I spoke out because I could not help it—"I think you have some faith. I think you will not quite forget even so late a friend as I am, when the time comes for you to go away."

A look of utter amazement crossed her features.

"To go away?" she repeated.

"You are going, are you not?"

I stopped breathing until I had her answer.

"Yes."

It seemed as hard as if I had never expected it, never made up my mind to it, never known that it must be so. I felt as if she had taken a pistol, and fired it point blank into my breast.

"How did you know? I have not told any one."

"You forget that I hear your thoughts."

"Not thoughts like that!" she said, as if bewildered. "They don't go deep enough."

It was foolish of me to have held my breath. Now, for some reason or other, I could not let it loose again. It only came in long gasps. I was gaping in an odd way. Everything in the room was first extremely clear and then invisible. Everything out of it was first acutely noisy, and then it turned into a sound like the waves of the sea. I stood up, meaning to move towards the door. But I had not gone one step when my conscious life ceased altogether.

It came back with a stinging taste of *sal volatile*—a sense of shame at having fainted in somebody else's room—a powerful disinclination to get up and see whose room it was.

"Lie still!" said Lucilla.

Oh yes, I would! I would lie still there for the rest of life, if I could look at her. It was not lying still that was difficult. Outside were the storms and the strangers.

She smiled, held up her finger when I tried to speak, laid it on her lips, took a book from the table, and seated herself at the end of the sofa, where I could see her well.

It was very pleasant to lie and look at her.

She had drawn a screen between me and the light so that it might not hurt my eyes. There was something restful in the fact that I saw only the grand outline of her figure, and not the details of her face. She seemed to be busy with that book, for she never once raised her eyes from it. But I did not want to talk, nor even to think, although my mind was clear.

I was weak. Now that I come to think about it, I believe that I had not eaten much that day. I had been rather busier than usual, and had not recollected. Every 'bus was full when I started for home, and being too impatient to wait, I had taken the unusual course of walking.

There came over me the gentle ecstasy of a mystic after a long fast, I had reached the end of all effort; there was nothing left for which to fight or to struggle. I lay still, as she bade me, and looked at her.

I remembered a great many incidents of which I had not thought for years, and I remembered them in the right succession. Underneath it all ran the current that runs when we are dreaming—know that we are dreaming—are resolved not to awake. If I could only lie still there, could only go on dreaming, Lucilla would not drive me away. She would let me lie still there till I had done. So I began to exist over again.

In some strange manner, without the slightest exertion of memory,—I cannot explain it—my past life seemed to have risen to the same level as the present—to be, as the objects are in a Japanese picture, on the same plane. It was as if I lived through all that was gone by once more, yet without losing consciousness of the actual moment, of Lucilla, seated there with her book.

I cannot omit what happened, for it seemed as much a part of the continuity of life as if it had never happened before; but I must fail to give the true impression, because I am compelled by the terms of language to relate it in the past tense. Really it all went on in the same room, at the same time.

XIII

Lucilla's room was yet Lucilla's room, and still I was a lame man lying on a sofa; she sat beside me still—I felt the comfort of her presence—and yet I was again a little child.

It began with the sound of a voice singing "Bonny Dundee."

I knew this by some inner sense more subtle than that of hearing—knew that it was my nurse who sang as she moved about, airing the linen before the nursery fire. How merrily it danced upon the bare, familiar walls! Down below in the street the lamps were lighting.

> "To the Lords of Convention 'twas Claver'se who spoke,
>   'Ere the King's crown shall fall there are crowns to be
>   broke,
>   So let each Cavalier who loves honour and me,
>   Come follow the bonnet of Bonny Dundee!"

Into my nursery they rode, these jolly riders, out at the window, and I after them. I felt so very happy, so very safe! How I galloped down "the sanctified bends of the Bow" and over the Causeway! How I "spurred to the foot of the proud Castle rock!"

I was holding my breath when—

> "The Gordon demands of him which way he goes—
>   'Where'er shall direct me the shade of Montrose!'"

On we went, on we went, flouting the Whig, racing over "the hills beyond Pentland and lands beyond Forth," rousing "the wild Duniewassals three thousand times three!" We were about to "couch with the fox," when there was an end of all this.

A footstep on the stairs.

The singing left off suddenly.

The scene shifts.

This time Lucilla's room is the diningroom at the bottom of the tall house in Bayswater—a room to which I rarely go, because, unless I am sitting under the table, I do not feel safe there; and I never feel happy. It is Friday afternoon, however, and on Fridays I am tempted down to see the man who—as my nurse says—"has the time," and puts it into the great big clock in the corner. (I used to wish that he would take out some of the afternoon time, which was long and dull, and put in more of the evening, for that was short and full of romance and ended up too soon with bed.) We call him, between ourselves, Man Friday, for "Robinson Crusoe" is one of the few books in the nursery, and I like to play at being Robinson Crusoe. Man Friday is a kind, sociable, friendly fellow. He is laughing and showing me how the clock works when again that footstep is heard outside the door. He stops laughing at once, he does not even finish what he is telling me, but slinks away as if he had done something wrong.

Again the scene shifts.

This time it is the library that rises within Lucilla's walls.

Into that room I never go, for there my father sits. But on that day I thought that he was out. The door was standing open, and I ventured in, lured by the bookshelves. Up in the nursery there were no books at all except the Bible, and "Robinson Crusoe," and "The Pilgrim's Progress." Here there were rows upon rows of books from floor to ceiling, books of all sizes and colours. I took out one, the nearest and the gayest, bound in scarlet, and opened straight on the stag-like eyes of my beloved Dundee, on the account of his death at Killiecrankie, slain by the silver bullet. Safe in my happiness, I had begun to read when I heard the footstep outside. I put the book back on the shelf, and slunk out of the room like Man Friday.

It was like that always.

Wherever my father came, there also came fear and silence. Wherever he came I shrank away from him.

I was not fond of that solid square house, even as a child; but then I was indifferent—its dreariness did not afflict me as in later years, and there were certain portions of it, certain oases in the desert that seemed to me to be inhabitable. One was the floor under the diningroom table—one the triangular space behind the grand piano in the drawingroom. From these coigns of vantage I would peep out upon my father. The rest belonged to him; but these, like the nursery which he did not enter, belonged indisputably to me; they were my home.

There was always, even in these dim days, a consciousness that I wanted some one.

When I was taken out to walk in the Square, when I heard the cries, the shrieks of laughter of the other children, as they raced and romped together, I thought it was another child that I wanted. I used to give them names of my own as I watched them shyly, longing that they would ask me to play with them.

They never did.

Sometimes, if they were not there (but they were almost always there) I could be very happy by myself. I remember making a nest of dried leaves once, and sitting in the midst of it, persuaded that I was a bird. But I could not play at that kind of thing if they were there. The shouts, the laughter, gave me the feeling of an exile upon a desert island.

Often, of course, I played at Desert Islands. It is a very good game when you are all alone.

But still, I wanted some one, I always wanted some one.

So, like a long, slow dream—not happy, not unhappy—childhood went by.

As time passed on, a tutor was engaged for me, a good and conscientious man, who taught me a great deal more than he was paid to teach.

I did not like him at first. I was very backward, never having learnt the lessons that other children learn as a matter of course. I was slow, as children are who live alone. I was not good at games. Outwardly submissive, I rebelled in my heart against the drudgery alike of school work and of the solemn cricket, that my tutor wisely compelled me to play with him in the Square. It filled me with an inarticulate sense of outrage, to find that books—my one delight—were now a burden; to have to waste precious hours (I had not known before how precious freedom was) adding up the bills, or measuring the walks, the drain-pipes, the wall-papers, of utterly uninteresting, impersonal people called A, B, and C. Claverhouse and the Jacobites had not accustomed me to that kind of thing.

Furthermore, my kind nurse was sent away. I was not told that she was going, until, in a burst of tears, she revealed the dreadful secret on the morning of her departure. I rushed downstairs to the library. Weeping, I besought my father that she might stay. He told me not to be a baby. She left the house that afternoon.

When she was gone, however, I attached myself to my tutor. The first and the worst hours were over, and I began to like Latin and Greek, and, indeed, every other lesson that was not arithmetic.

I owe it to him that I gained admission to the library. He promised my father that I would not hurt the books.

Hitherto, ever since my unlucky intrusion, they had been forbidden fruit. I was not allowed to touch them. This prohibition added to—perhaps I should rather say it created—the interest that I felt. My eager eyes were familiar with half their titles long before my fingers grasped them. What wealth it seemed after those years of envious gazing through the half-open door!

Except for the moment during which I held "Dundee" in my hands, I do not think they had been touched since my grandfather's time; it was he who collected them, for he was a great lover of books.

He was my mother's father, and it seemed to me that, if he had been there, he would have liked me and I should have cared for him. I used to sit devouring those old books of his, what time my own father wrote his letters or studied the papers, with the curious concentration of the practical mind upon financial issues.

The backs were variously bound, according to the subject. To this day I always think of Theology in inky black—of Geography and books of travel in brown, the colour of the Earth—of History in purple like the robe of an Emperor—of Shakespeare and Milton (there were no other poets) in the hue of an evergreen. In all that great drab house there was only one patch of red—the shelf that held the Lives of Soldiers.

These last awoke in me passionate admiration of the British Army. It was a grand collection of Memoirs; the old business man must have made it his chief recreation to read about the high-handed deeds of the Redcoats. Here and there a faint line of pencil in the margin attested his love of them. When I saw this line—when I felt my heart stirred as his had been at the sound of a trumpet, I met him—I knew, for all the intervening walls of space and time, that he was nearer to me than the figure in the armchair at the writing-table, adding and adding empty cyphers that stood for nothing but little bits of gold.

These books did much to save me from the oppression of the house that was their prison as it was mine. The library was the only room that seemed to be alive. As I sat there and read, I recovered something of the old sense of freedom, of property of my own, that I had enjoyed when I lived under the piano or between the legs of the dining-room table. Yet even here the many-coloured bindings were so solid that I felt sometimes as though I could not get at the contents for the cover. Among a hundred, no handwriting adorned the flyleaf of any one book. There was a plate, stuck correctly right in the middle of the first leaf of each, a dagger, and the words *Once and for all*. Not one had been a gift; they were bought and paid for. Except the faint pencil line, no token existed of any human sympathy. These books of peril and adventure opened a new life for me, showed me there was a world elsewhere. They made of my existence a different matter—but in one way they made it worse.

The impersonal heaviness and stiffness of the place weighed on my spirits as if it were the perpetual assertion of a thing that I knew *not* to be true. The cliff-like mantelpieces of dull, impenetrable marble—the tables, immovable as rock—the ponderous chairs that mocked each fugitive desire to change the look of even so much as a single corner of one of the symmetrical square gloomy rooms—these bits of wood and stone had no humanity, and they de-humanized those whose business it was to dust and polish them. The servants were stony persons that "knew their place." At stated times and seasons they appeared—did their work—vanished again. In between they were neither seen nor heard. For all their fear they had a certain esteem of my father, who possessed an irritable temper and would fly out at them on occasion in a manner to make anyone belonging to him red with shame. Me they did not like. I was always polite, more from dread of the loss of personal dignity and from a weak-kneed love of peace than from any higher motive. A feeble, timorous habit of this kind causes a gulf to open between people who live under the same roof. My father, in his outbursts of passion, leapt across, and those whom he flew upon did not resent his conduct: but I remained for ever upon the other side.

My nurse had long ago gone back to Scotland, and no one sang now. Once, while I was still a child, I had found the key of the drawingroom piano in the lock.

I had opened it.

I had picked out the tune of "Dundee."

Just as I was about to repeat this—to me—extremely beautiful performance, my father came in.

"Father!" I said, "I want to learn to play."

The look of utter astonishment on my father's face alarmed me even more than the frown that I had looked instinctively to see.

"What for?" he said.

I could not give a reason.

I daresay Rubinstein, if he had been asked, at that age, why he wanted to learn to play, could not have given a reason either.

In those days I still felt younger than my father; but now that I had grown up, we presented an odd contrast. Spite of his iron-gray hair and the many lines on his narrow forehead, his was the youthfulness, the stir, the bustle, the excitement of life in a crowd, the eager interest in affairs of the day. I—a recluse by nature and never more of a recluse than during those first years of consciousness—lived like a student of sixty, absorbed in books, careful of my latter end, taking no risks because nothing tempted me to do so.

Religion moved me secretly and strongly, but only after a personal manner, not with any view to public reform, to evangelization, to work amongst the poor. The simple lessons of my good nurse remained with me. The example of the good man who was my tutor bore fruit. I was no Gallio. I cared about these things. I read the inky volumes through and through. At that time I existed but to read—to study languages, for which I have always entertained a ridiculous affection, considering the difficulty that I find in expressing myself in my own—to dream—to brood upon the transitoriness of this world. The thought was a refuge to me when quite bowed down by the material force of it. I was little affected by the chance that I might yet remain in it forty or fifty years. I prepared for death in short, not for life. I could not face the immediate future. It meant that I should be condemned to enter the business, to adopt the kind of occupation that resulted in furniture and servants and a house and ways of going on like ours. I looked beyond.

The earth was cold about me: but never having known the warmth of sympathy I was not conscious that I lacked it, and I supposed the deep dissatisfaction, the loneliness that I experienced, the need of some one, to be the common lot of every man. Soldiers appeared to enjoy certain moments; but all the writers of sermons assured me that life was a poor business, and I was quite disposed to believe them. I had hopes and aspirations that nothing outside me justified. I drew the conclusion that they pointed on, to another scene altogether.

<h1 style="text-align:center">XIV</h1>

As I grew to manhood I became aware of a new atmosphere of consideration that surrounded me.

It was because I was going to be—so every one said—*very rich*.

My cousin was, apparently, the first to discover it.

She was then a newly married woman, just come to town, with a younger sister à *marier*. Casting about for an eligible partner, she decided on me. Her husband was a City magnate, and my father had been, for many years, well-known in the City. It was a shame, she declared, that a young man with prospects like mine should not be given every advantage. Neither my father nor my tutor had realized that I was grown up.

She spoke to me about it, and I felt grateful to her for her sympathy, and expressed perfect willingness to make the most of any and every advantage that she could prevail upon my father to afford me. I might not have been as wax in her hands if I had gauged her power or suspected her motive; for though I liked her well, I had no desire to become her brother-in-law. Secretly, I entertained little hope of her success.

The right expression in the mouth of the right person goes a long way, however. She did it all with two words—*very rich*.

Because I was going to be *very rich*, she spoke to my tutor, she compelled him to think it was his duty to take steps in the matter. She left him no rest until he made urgent representations to my father, to the effect that I ought to be allowed to complete my education by attending lectures at University College.

"A man who has not been at one of the Universities is nowhere," she said. "Your father will have nothing to say to Oxford or Cambridge. Very well. University College *sounds* like a University! University College is the next best thing."

It was because I was going to be *very rich* that she persuaded my father to have me taught riding and dancing, "exercises" which as she said, "befitted my station."

I was nothing loth. At University College I did well; I loved the place where people could be found who cared for books; and active exercise was of great benefit to my health, which had began to flag in the close air of the library. At her instigation and with her approval also, I became a volunteer.

"It makes a man hold himself straight like nothing else," she said.

Sacred enthusiasm filled my heart when, in the company of two other youthful patriots, on a wet, muddy afternoon, attired in stiff, uncomfortable uniform, the buttons of which were always coming off, I heard the raucous voice of the drill sergeant exclaim, "Fifty-fifth Middlesex, prepare to receive cavalry!"

A little later, when my cousin had had time to make her own way in society, and to assure herself that her pains were not entirely wasted on me, it was because I was going to be *very rich* that numerous invitations to the houses of people, who were all very rich themselves, began to pour in on me. Every one of these I declined by return of post, feeling very proud and grand as I did so. These were the children whom I had wanted so much long ago. They would not play with me then; now they wanted to play with me. No! It was too late! I had learned to do without them. I had "put away childish things." I preferred books,—books, and the prospect of Eternity.

I laugh now as I think of the airs that I gave myself, but then I felt extremely contemptuous. Had they no idea, these people, of the extreme stupidity of being *very rich?* If I had the misfortune to become *very rich*—I did not think it possible, I might have expected the fall of a pyramid sooner than the death of any one so much more solidly than myself as my father—I had made up my mind what to do. I would give away everything except the few hundred pounds that would save me from dependence in case of accident. I did not want to part with my substance from generosity, but because I hated to be responsible and disliked the close attention that money requires. I did not know at the time, that very little requires even closer attention than very much. I was a prudent young man. I had a horror of becoming even more dull than I was, but a still greater horror of existing on benefits. It is the curse of families who have lived by careful thrift for two or three generations, that their young people are born old. My admiration of the life of daring and adventure was keen as ever. I could not see a regiment pass down the street but I longed to run away, to take the Queen's shilling, to trudge along the road beside those fine fellows who were all for death and glory. But in my heart I knew that life was not for me.

God gave me all of it that could be mine in a friend.

Lucilla, of him I cannot speak! He only, of all those called by remembrance to your little room, was not there. He only, when—on the sudden failure of that life which had been granted me for the last few years—I questioned all the rest for its meaning, I lived it through again to cry:—*What was the meaning, if not this friendship with you?*—he only was not there.

I met him first about the time of which I have been speaking. He was but an acquaintance then. Conscious that he had everything—I nothing—to offer, I shrank from forcing myself upon him.

It was not till afterwards that I became his friend, but he was mine from the first.

Even apart from this, I was beginning to feel keener interest in life. Certain powers of imagination awoke, and fed by the sweet air of encouragement and approval at College, they grew like the gourd that sprang up in a night.

Once more the Jacobite gentry came to my aid. The College authorities proposed an essay on the great Scotch leaders in the cause of the Stuarts.

I dreamed of it by day and thought of it by night. I devoted every spare moment to the study of the scarlet shelf in the library. I became as Stevenson says, "a great friend to paper-makers." Many waste-paper baskets stand behind the scenes of even the very slightest success in letters. I fulfilled this primary condition; waste-paper basket after waste-paper basket I filled; and in the end my essay was the best. I cannot say that I felt surprised. I had known that it must be. The other students were writing as a task. I was writing to prove there was something in me beyond the power of addition and subtraction. I was writing to justify myself in an attempt to escape from everything that made life not worth living. I was writing for love of the heroes of childhood. It was a more vital affair to me than it was to the others. I was not surprised therefore, but I was much elated.

It was my twenty-first birthday.

I read my name at the top of the Class List, and then I walked home through the busy streets, eager, happy, my heart full of humility and thanksgiving.

I would go, flushed with success, to my father. He would see that there was something in me, that I was not fit for office work, that he must set me free to follow my own bent. I remember how brightly the lamps were shining on that winter night, with what a friendly air the stars looked down.

At home I found my cousin in the library. She had looked in to remonstrate with me about an invitation to a dance, which I had just declined. I took her hand and told her of my good luck.

"I am so glad, Oliver," she said blandly. "About the Jacobites? Oh yes, delightful! I never thought Cromwell was a gentleman. What's that? Your father coming in?"

It was the footstep in the hall. For the first time—so happy and safe I was,—my heart did not sink as I heard it.

"Father!" I said, going up to him as he entered. "I've come out first at College for an essay on the Jacobites."

And suddenly the words froze on my lips just as they had frozen long ago when I asked to learn music, at the look of gray bewilderment on his face.

"Indeed," he said. "That shows it is waste of time and money to keep you there."

I was taken away from College at the end of the term and set to work as a clerk.

XV

"Leaving a perpetual remembrance, thou art gone; in thy death thou wert even such as in thy life: wealth to the poor, hope to the desponding, support to the weak. Thou couldst meet desperate troubles with a spirit that knew not despair, and breathe might into the trembling."

"The Lord of China owes thee thanks for thy benefits: the throne of his ancient kingdom hath not been cast down.

"And where the Nile unites the divided strength of his streams, a city saw thee long-suffering. A multitude dwelt therein, but thine alone was the valour that guarded it through all that year, when by day and by night thou didst keep watch against the host of the Arabians, who went around it to devour it, with spears thirsting for blood.

"Thy death was not wrought by the God of War, but by the frailties of thy friends. For thy country and for all men God blessed the work of thy hand. Hail, stainless warrior! Hail, thrice victorious hero! Thou livest, and shalt teach after-times to reverence the counsel of the Everlasting Father."

So things went on until the year of the War in the Soudan.

Crushed, weary, overworked, ill, sick at heart because of ceaseless drudgery, my transitory interest in the life of this world was fading out by that time. The overwhelming interest of another grew every day more strong.

It is the tendency of each one of us to think himself alone and singular in suffering. Doubtless there was many another in my case. I suppose there are living now thousands of middle-aged men and women who remember what that year was to them. I suppose there stands on many a shelf a little black Thomas à Kempis with a date scrawled at the beginning, a resolution to read it in memory of that strange warrior who found his tactics in its pages.

At last there stood on earth a man whom saints disputed for with heroes. The reign of Heaven on earth was, in one man, begun.

He had been offered the contents of a room packed from floor to ceiling with gold, and had refused it as if it were dross.

I heard all the people who were *very rich* saying how wonderful this was. I felt glad that he had done it, of course, but to me that was his least title to honour.

He had put by the crown of Fame as if it were made of paper. There I bent my knee to him.

He fought for nothing in Time, but for the Lord. Had he been cruel as Dundee, cold as Wellington, I had adored him; but he was on fire with mercy and pity.

When Charles George Gordon went to Khartoum, he carried me with him. I followed his course from day to day. I saw the dusty figure on the tall camel, jogging through the desert. I saw the Bible and the gleaming sword. I saw the entrance into the city—the stern blue eyes, bright when they rested on a child. I stood in the crowded market, to watch the posting of the proclamation. I heard the cheers, the murmurs, the tales told there of wise and happy ruling in the past—of his ride, unprotected, into the midst of the enemy's camp, to bring back peace.

When Gordon asked for the great Slave-driver, my brain reeled with astonishment for a moment; I had enough of the theologian in me for that, but I did not waver. If he wanted Zebehr, if he wanted the tyrant he had done his utmost to destroy, if he wanted the Devil for that matter, the Devil was the person to go. I lived in white and silent rage for days after Zebehr was refused. I had thought that I was a Liberal: Gladstone fell from his place in my esteem like a stone.

After that, I beheld, my own heart tightening, the lines drawn close and closer—the digging of the trenches—the entanglements of barbed wire—the arming of the steamers—the cannon on the roof of the Palace—the defence growing every day bolder and more imaginative as Hope, by inches, died. Still, Hope was absolute in me, I did not admit the possibility of defeat; but I could not sleep.

The night to which I now go back in thought—the night on which the kindled torches of grief and joy flashed on the deadness of my mortal nature, and kindled that also into life, is the night on which London learnt the Fall of Khartoum.

In stupefied rebellion, in a dim wild agony of revolt I sat, my eyes glued to the paper.

I doubted the existence of God.

"Ah well!" my father had said when I came in, speechless, and pointed to the news. "Gordon was mad, of course."

I thought I, at that moment, became a murderer. I would have killed my father if I could.

I do not know how long I had sat in an intensity of passion that crowded years into hours when the door opened.

Something was said that I did not hear nor heed; and two ladies entered.

"May I ask the favour of a few minutes in private with you?" the elder of the two inquired.

If it had not been for the utter bewilderment of my senses, I should have noticed my father's unusual politeness. Few visitors came to our house, and when they did they received little encouragement. He begged the younger lady to be seated, and left the room with her companion. I remained dully sitting were I was. I had not even the good manners to rise. I suppose she saw the paper in my hand.

"Is there any news to-night?" she said, turning to me as soon as the door had closed.

I had almost said *No:* but first I looked at her, as she sat by my father's writing-table. The tall lamp stood behind her, and she was wearing a dark hat so that I scarcely saw her face at all, only two great dark eyes looking straight into mine.

"Yes!" I said, slowly. "Khartoum has fallen."

It was a curious relief to my heart to say the words. Madness passed from it as I spoke.

She clutched her hands together.

"Gordon?" she said in a kind of cry.

"Gordon is dead."

The light of the stars went out. She hid her face, I saw her whole frame shaken with weeping. By her weeping she saved two worlds for me; and yet I could not endure to see it.

"Listen!" I said fiercely. *"There is God."*

She did not speak. She could not; but she held out her hand. . . .

Voices out in the hall; and my one thought, to screen her!

I came forward, spoke rapidly to my father to distract his attention. What nonsense I repeated, I do not know.

They stayed only a few minutes longer. There was one more word for me. The elder lady passed out first, and, as my father busied himself helping her on with her mantle, I touched the girl on the shoulder.

"We cannot meet here! Will you wait for me? Will you write?" I whispered low in her ear.

Once more the stars shone.

"I will wait," she said. "Yes, I will write."

She touched my hand—turned—hurried from me.

She was going out at the door, and the door was the door of Lucilla's room and yet the door of the library in the old house at Bayswater, when Lucilla raised her eyes from the book and looked at me.

"Do you remember what day this is?" she asked.

I shook my head. Yet her question fitted my thoughts in some way. There was no interruption.

"It is the 26th of January," she said, "the day of the Fall of Khartoum."

I signed to her that I wanted music, and she went to the piano and began to play.

She could not see me as she sat; and before the sweet notes ceased I rose from my couch and stole away.

There was more remembering for me yet, but not of that which, in the room with her, I dared to recollect.

XVI

Scarcely upon the night of its occurrence, on the first 26th of January, had that scene in the library appeared more real than it was to me, though I had not suspected the anniversary as I lay on the sofa in Lucilla's room.

I was shaking with fright as I hobbled downstairs again.

I felt myself still too weak to be in the clutches of Memory, when Memory was not the sweet-scented dead-roseleaf affair that she is at most times, but rather the vulture of Prometheus. I shuddered at the thought of going through again anything like the tortures of longing—of the doing to death of hope slowly, little by little—that brought me, in the months which followed that night, to the edge of despair.

Whether I was too much exhausted in body for my mind to work any more—whether Lucilla had played the vulture to sleep—I know not; but certain it is that I went to rest and rested, and that I rose up next morning, refreshed and strong.

Mahry brought me down a note with an inquiry as to how I had passed the night, and a friendly invitation to come upstairs to tea again that very afternoon, if I felt able. I added it to the collection that I already possessed, with a sigh. I smiled to myself a little sadly as I wrote the only possible answer. Women are always so anxious that two should not make four.

When she had satisfied herself that the music of the night before had charmed away my weakness—when she had professed her eager willingness to play to me again whatever I preferred to hear,

"Lucilla," I said, "do you never play for a dead woman?"

"Do you wish me to play for one?" she inquired, an unusual expression on her face. I could not, for the life of me, tell whether she wanted the answer to be *Yes* or *No*.

"Yes," I said, "I should like you to play for a girl who died long ago."

"Are you sure she is dead?" said Lucilla, turning round abruptly. She spoke for once just as most people speak, and I felt annoyed.

"She is dead to me."

"I will not play for her," said Lucilla, "I do not believe she is dead at all. You cared for her. You care for her still."

"Yes," I said, "I care for her so much that, from the day I saw her, I have never spoken of her till now. I shall always care for her. She saved my life once."

For the first time when I spoke of a matter that seriously interested me, Lucilla showed no interest whatever.

She kept silence.

"I know nothing about your life," she observed, rather wilfully.

"There is little enough to know."

I suppose I glanced down at my lame leg, for she said, with more tenderness, "You were not lame always. What was it that made you lame?"

"Admiration of a hero; and one of those results of fixed laws which we call accident."

"Never mind the fixed laws! Tell me about the hero and the accident."

"You can imagine who the hero was," I said, glancing at the statuette on the mantelpiece.

"Gordon?"

"It was at the Service in memory him—outside the Abbey. A rough knocked down a woman in the crowd. I fought him. You cannot think what fun it was, at such close quarters. Don't be admiring, please! I should never have done it, if I had known what the result would be. And the woman was drunk. I daresay the rough turned out, after all, the better specimen of the two. It only lasted a minute. The ground was slippery, I fell against a lamp post, and the bone of my leg snapped."

"*She* came and nursed you, I suppose?" asked Lucilla, still as if she were inquiring into the character of a dressmaker who had cheated her.

"If she had done that, I might perhaps have walked again like any one else."

"How long is it since you saw her last?"

"Nineteen years to a day."

The statement affected her in some way, for her manner changed. She left the piano and came over to her usual seat beside the fire.

"That's a very long time ago."

"It did not seem long to me last night."

"You saw her very often?"

"Once only."

"Why only once?" she cried, fire kindling in her dark eyes.

I hesitated.

Unwittingly, she who so seldom asked questions had asked me one, the answer to which involved such pain in the rousing of old sorrow, that I could not choose but hesitate.

"You need not tell me unless you like," she said. "I'm sure I do not want to know."

I wished Lucilla would leave off being like other people. It suited her ill.

I tried speaking the truth. If the refuge of silence were interdicted, the plain, dull, naked truth was my only resource. "Something happened which made it impossible for me to think of marriage," I said stupidly.

"The accident? You could not believe that she would mind that?" Lucilla said, with a thin tremble in her voice. "If she had anything at all in her, she would have cared for you the more because you were lame. She could have done things for you: it would have made her happier."

"Would it really have added so much to her happiness?" I said, smiling. "Perhaps it would. I have been told that women are like that—some women. I never had the chance of testing it. The accident happened too long after."

"After what?"

"Must I tell you?"

"Good gracious!" Lucilla said, and she was cold and sharp as steel again. "You speak as if you had committed a crime."

"My father did commit a crime."

She started so violently that a pang shot through me. Was I about to risk her friendship by telling her of my father's disgrace? Surely it could not be. That was not like Lucilla. But it made me resolve to tell her at once.

"My father committed forgery," I said.

"She gave you up because of *that?*" Lucilla asked.

Once more I felt relieved. Lucilla did not intend to give me up because of *that*—so much was clear. She spoke as if it were the merest trifle.

"I did what any man would have done under the circumstances. My name was dishonoured; I had not a penny left. I made no attempt to see her again.

"And your father?"

"I could do nothing for him. He had run away from it all."

"Do not speak—if you cannot," she said again, in her own voice.

"I would rather tell you now that I have begun. It was on the morning after the Fall of Khartoum. My father was found dead in his chair. He had learnt, the night before, that exposure was inevitable."

"You had money of your own, money that was yours by right, through your mother—you gave it up to save his credit, left yourself penniless?"

"You knew, all the time?"

"I only guessed. I heard a story something like it, a long while ago. Besides, I always thought you must be living here, somehow or other, by your own choice."

"I had no choice in the matter. Would you have felt that you had any?"

"No," said Lucilla reluctantly, after a long pause.

She is given to admire in others actions that she herself would perform as a matter of course. I experienced a momentary triumph at having brought her to bay.

"Now *you*?" I said, "you really chose to come to this house. You need not have done so?"

She smiled—a smile with depths in it, like the smile of Mona Lisa.

"I had to come."

"Why?"

"The money that my aunt left me had cost life. I could not have borne to touch it. I gave it to a Hospital, that it might bring back life again. I had a little of my own; and I made more by teaching, and reading aloud, and painting. So things were never very difficult."

"It does not matter much where you live. You would make it home always."

"I think I could—if I were free. Freedom is the one thing that matters. After the first—of course that was terrible—I daresay you were glad to be free from all the heavy responsibilities, from the enormous gloomy house that very rich London people always live in?"

She spoke as if she had seen it.

"I should have been glad, only then, you see, I fell lame."

"O," she said, looking ready to cry. "I forgot that."

"Do not mind! It was then that I found a friend. When he saw me tumble down, he picked me up. Every day while I lay ill he came to see me, and cared for me as tenderly as any woman. I had thought that I could not bear to be at once poor and dependent. He never let me feel that I was."

"And does he never come to see you now?"

I did not answer.

"I see," she said softly. "He too is among the dead."

"He died at the Atbara."

She honoured silently with me all those who had fallen. I wonder if there is any monument that a man need covet so greatly as the pause that follows after his name if he has died well.

"And what became of you? How did you live?"

"After he went away to Egypt? I hardly recollect. I was condemned by a Doctor to live abroad for two or three winters. If you know the way to do it, you can starve in a Swiss *pension* without much personal discomfort. In fact it quite restored my health. I scribbled for the Press—I translated books that nobody cared to read—when I came home I looked up authorities in the British Museum—I read and copied manuscripts. At last an old uncle died, and left me enough to enter a solicitor's office. I live very well now, and have more than enough."

"You have been cruel to her, I think," Lucilla said slowly.

"Cruel to *her?*"

"Yes; you asked her to wait. How could she tell why it was that you never came near her?"

"She must have known what happened. It was in all the papers."

"She wrote to you.

"Not a word."

"I am quite sure she wrote to you."

I began to feel annoyed with Lucilla again. What business had she to be so certain when she knew nothing about the matter?

"She never wrote," I said. "Why should she have written?"

A thousand times in the year of my misery I had asked myself this question, as I sat waiting, waiting, in the great bare library from which my well loved books were gone, and all day long, and half the night, post after post came in without the letter that it should have brought. I had answered myself so many times, "There is no reason why she should," that at last I believed it. Now, nineteen years after, came Lucilla, to make me doubt again!

"Why should she have written?" I repeated.

"She was bound to write. Besides, she could not have helped it."

I sat silent.

Her voice expressed something that had spoken long ago in my own heart.

"Well," I said, with deliberation, "at any rate I know more of her than you do. The fact remains, that she did not write. I daresay she married someone else after a year or two. She is, you may be sure, a happy wife and mother. And now you understand perhaps why I said she was dead to me."

"But I *know* she wrote," said Lucilla. "The letter was lost—that's why you never heard. The house must have been all in confusion after a dreadful thing like that. The servants mislaid it."

I shook my head. The servants never mislaid anything in our house.

Lucilla's eyes, when she turned and looked at me, were soft with tears. I had not seen such a thing before. It distressed, and at the same time it pleased me.

"Dear friend," I said, "do not trouble yourself. It is better as it is. I should have hated to drag her down—and then my lameness!"

"I cannot bear it," said Lucilla. "All these years she might have been helping you."

"The memory of her has helped me always—when things were at the worst."

"You must find her," Lucilla said. "You will find her still."

I rode, bade her good-night, and went downstairs to my room.

I was miserably agitated. When first we stir with words dark depths of consciousness that have lain silent for many years, we hardly know what it is that comes to the surface.

XVII

Women are terribly practical. My friendship with Lucilla had taught me that much. I began to regret what I had done. I feared to see her again lest she should say, that I must, without delay, set forth on a pilgrimage in quest of a lady, whom, after the lapse of nineteen years, it was more than probable that I should not even recognise if I saw her.

Lucilla said nothing of the kind, however.

She was too wise to fall into the error of many sympathetic women who go on expressing their sympathy, time after time, until the exhausted receiver grows weary. She made no allusion to what had passed. She talked of this and that—our tiny household politics—my cousin, Mrs. Hopgood, and her anxiety about Frida, who had just begun to assert herself, and wanted go to the Royal College of Music, like Kitty—the last news from Australia.

"Kitty is happier than ever."

She lingered lovingly over the words, but she did not offer to read me the letter that had come for her by the last mail.

Great as my relief was, I felt surprised. Is it so easy to be back on the old terms? What had happened to restore her serenity since the day when she announced that she had not been faithful? Quickly and mysteriously as she had gone away, she had come back again; but why?

My eyes fell by chance on the old mirror, on the words engraved beneath, "*Hier c'est demain.*" Whoever wrote them knew a woman like this, one who kept faith. There might be hours of night between, but yesterday would be to-morrow; after all, *why* matters very little.

I had not then committed an indiscretion in telling her so much. I was not to be made to pay for it. Our gentle, familiar intimacy would go on as before, untroubled by her deeper knowledge. The hidden life, which I had dragged forward with such pain, sank back into the depths. Every trifling commonplace act, every single word reassured me. She would never make me repent of my confidence. It was all well. Nay, it was better than before, because she knew.

"By the way," she said, when I rose to bid her good-night, "where is the book that you promised to lend me? You promised it, three weeks ago."

Three weeks ago! How could I be expected to know what I had promised in those prehistoric ages?

"What was it? I am afraid I have forgotten."

"It was a Life of Somebody, by Somebody," Lucilla said, slightly frowning. "You must remember; you said every one ought to read it. I daresay I shall not get through. I do not care for Lives, as a rule."

"You lose much," I observed, not unwilling to prolong my stay by a friendly argument. We held very different notions concerning books.

She took the ball, but rather as one who did not want the game to stop, than as one who cared greatly about winning.

"What do I lose, except a little trumpery gossip? If I want to know what men have done, I read history. If I want to know what they ought to have done, I read romance."

Lucilla's attitude in this matter was not unknown to me, and I regretted it. I thought she deprived herself (and me) of much innocent pleasure, through her scorn of biography. In her eyes, as in those of many women, it was but so much raw material, out of which, given the proper craftsman, a good novel might be constructed. In person I find it, as a rule, easier to read a bad Life than a good Novel, so weak is my imagination, so strong my interest in my fellow-creatures. And as she could not read Lives, and I could not read Novels, we both read much that it was impossible for us to discuss.

Lucilla, of course, read more for what books suggested than for what they could tell her. She read so much of herself into them, that I had been woefully disappointed sometimes when I essayed to follow in her steps.

She would tell me a glowing tale, full of mysterious perils, of wit, of courage, of characters original as those of Fancy out for a holiday.

Enchanted with the brilliancy of her description, I would take the rash step of going to the Library in search of this treasure of a novel, believing that now at last the longed for successor of R. L. Stevenson was really come.

I got it easily enough. I carried it home, full of triumph. In the chill solitude of my den I sat down to peruse it. Alas, what was gold to her was only dead leaves to me! Where she saw all the myriad forms of life, I saw nothing but flat incompetence.

She had that singleness of aim which is peculiar to feminine readers. If the book fired her imagination, that was all she demanded. The author might violate nature and truth at every turn, and she cared nothing. She had a magnificent disregard of style—even of grammar—in the interests of "the story." Nothing annoyed her more than what she was pleased to call "correcting the press." She had not the remotest feeling for that fine age of accuracy when scholars took each other's lives, because they held divergent views as to the position of a comma.

The real reason of her neglect of biography was, perhaps, that it told her too much, that it hemmed her in with facts when fancy was all that she wanted. She liked to dress the doll herself, not to have it dressed for her.

"One good character in a Novel is worth fifty Lives," she observed carelessly, as I sat silent, pondering on this idiosyncrasy of her disposition.

"Not always! Dr. Johnson is much better fun in Boswell than he is in 'The Virginians'."

"*Boswell's Life of Johnson!* That was it," she exclaimed. "You said everybody ought to read that."

"A general proposition that there is no disputing!"

"Will you lend it to me now?"

"Gladly. Mine is an old edition in ten volumes."

Lucilla's face fell.

"Have you read them all?"

"I have read the first nine till I know them almost by heart; but I have never gone further than the middle of the tenth."

"Then, the next time you come," said Lucilla, ("mind, I am in no hurry for it!) bring me the tenth volume. The tenth volume of *Boswell's Life of Johnson*. I will begin where you left off. If I can read the tenth, then I will read all the rest."

A most fantastic reason; but I knew her too well to attempt remonstrance. I bowed to her decision, and went downstairs.

It occurred to me to wonder a little, that she should have asked so urgently for a book, whose very title she had forgotten.

In the beginning of our acquaintance, when I often recommended volumes that, later on, I knew she never could have cared to read, I noticed that she graciously let their names drop. She had not time just then—she was busy with something else. She never wounded me, but she held her own, and by degrees I came to understand that her reading was as free as every other action of hers, and that no one influenced, or ever could aspire to influence her choice.

Why was she going to read Boswell?

For the first time I doubted Bozzy. I felt myself uncertain of his power to amuse.

She was going to read him to please me—that we might have some recognized subject to talk about. She was going to read Dr. Johnson's *Life* in order that I might not be afraid that she meant to speak again of my own.

A week later I dug out volume ten from his fellows, and carried it up to her. I wished that she had not desired to see that volume. As I touched the cover, a host of painful and bitter thoughts rushed back upon me.

"It is very dusty," she said, with disapproval. "I can see that you have not read it for a long time."

"No," I said, "I do not recollect a word."

"And yet you know the others by heart?"

"Yes."

"Why did you treat this one so badly? Did you not care about the end?"

"Too many other things came to an end for me when I was reading that."

"Ah, forgive me!" she cried quickly, "you were reading it when—when your father died?"

I stood as in a dream. The whole day came back to me.

"Yes," I said. "It was the 27th of January, 1885, the day after the Fall of Khartoum,—the day after that night. They came and told me about my father. I went to see. There were hours, long hours—it was the only time when they left me alone. They pulled the blinds down. It was quiet and dark. No one knew yet. I thought about the night before. I felt as if it must have been I, I myself, that had killed my father.

The book was lying on the table, where I had laid it down the night before, when I went out to buy that paper. I read and read as if I were taking opium; I read till I could scarcely see. It grew dark then, quite dark. Some one came in with an ugly, absurd, long face to say, 'Would I come and give directions about the coffin?' I put a mark in the book, I remember, because it gave me a minute's respite. I know I meant to come back to it. Somehow I never could."

"Of course you could not."

She was sitting by the fire, and I heard her sigh gently as she turned over the dusty leaves.

All at once she drew a quick, sharp breath.

I looked up.

"Nothing!" she said, in the voice of one repressing some strong excitement. "I happened to open the book just where you must have stopped reading. Look! Here is the mark! You must have thrust it in—forgotten it. You never broke the seal. Look!"

There between the pages, the ink dry and faded, lay an old letter. The writing bore an odd likeness to her own, I noticed that at once, but the hand was very young and unformed.

"Her letter—her letter to you!" Lucilla said. "I told you that she wrote."

As in a dream I took the letter from her and sat silent, gazing at that old Bayswater address.

"Open it!" she said imperiously. "It deserves to be read now, any way."

I obeyed.

She seemed to know by intuition when I had done.

"Well?"

Her eyes were fixed on me with a look between triumph and suspense.

"Yes," I said, "you are right. If I had read this nineteen years ago, it would have made a great difference."

"Can it make no difference now?" she enquired.

"I am not going to look for her, if that is what you mean," I said, doggedly.

"You never really cared about her then?"

I made no answer.

"Would you do anything that I asked you to do?" she said quickly.

"Yes."

"Would you burn that letter?"

I hesitated. I grew indignant. I thought she had no right to ask that.

"I cannot. Think how long I have waited for it. Nineteen years!"

"Mere sentiment!" she said. "If you will not burn it, will you let me see it?"

I was beyond measure astonished. Still—if she could ask such a thing—I held it out.

I did not like doing so; but Man is the fool of consistency, and it seemed odd to say I would do anything she liked, and then refuse her twice. Besides, I had the words by heart:

> "Dear Friend (it ran).
>   I grieve for everything that grieves you Remember what you said There was light yesterday There will be light to-morrow Remember that I will always wait for you
>   Your Friend"

"No name! No address!" Lucilla said. "Perhaps she did not mean to wait for you, after all."

I wondered why Lucilla smiled so brightly as she said this. It was unreasonable to feel vexed—but the reasons of our vexation are seldom reasonable.

"She was very unpractical if she did."

I could not deny it.

"Girls *are* unpractical," Lucilla said. "You never tried to find out her name?"

"Never. When, to the best of my belief, no letter came, I thought quite naturally that she felt shocked at what had happened, at my father's conduct—that she would have nothing more to do with me."

"Tell me the rest!" Lucilla said gently.

"The lady who came with her—her mother or her aunt, I suppose—had insisted that my father should give back at once a large sum of money that he owed. He had lived all those years under a false name to avoid paying. He had forged the signature of her husband at the time that he borrowed it. *Borrowing* is the word, you know, if you happen to be what is called a gentleman. Gentlemen never *steal*.—Mrs. Hopgood? Oh yes, she was my mother's cousin, our only near relation on this side of the water!—How was she taken in? My father made her think that he had changed his name on account of a legacy. At first he had been really unable to pay, you understand. Afterwards, the love of money grew. Yet I believe he always meant to pay in the end; they always do mean that. At the moment when this lady found him out—tracked him down—very properly claimed her due—he was involved in some heavy speculation. Payment—exposure—whichever alternative he faced, meant ruin. He gave her a cheque, but he knew that it could not be honoured; that as soon as it was refused, the world would know everything. I believe that he appealed to her mercy in vain. I do not wonder. She had had to wait many years."

"She could not have guessed what would happen."

"Of course not. It was in all the papers directly after, though. She must have known then; any one who lived with her must have known. As soon as I had done what I could—as soon as I felt sure there was going to be no letter for me—I took my mother's name, for that was stainless; and went abroad."

"Did you tell no one?"

"My friend knew, of course. My cousin rather added to the difficulties of life in those days, and I did not try to keep up with her. She was very kind, but she held that I had no right to dispose of what was my own—that I ought not to let it go out of the family."

"Ah!" said Lucilla, smiling, "I can imagine."

"'I thought we should be better friends if we had no opportunity of contradicting each other for a time. I was right, as things turned out. She lost sight of me so completely that she thought I was dead. When she saw me again, she did not know me at first. I suppose I was greatly changed. However, I explained that I was only the same thing under another title. She has been very kind to me since."

"Did you forget?" Lucilla said, "that there was some one else—some one whom you had asked to wait?"

"No, but I had no right to expect that she would remember."

"Is it not strange to think," Lucilla said, "that perhaps, while we are sitting here over the fire, perhaps this very night, she is waiting? She is an old maid by this time. She has little set ways of her own, and her hair has grown gray."

"No, no," I said, "not that! Nineteen. I do not think she can have been a day older. I myself was only just twenty-one. For me she will be nineteen always."

"What colour *was* her hair?" said Lucilla.

"I do not know. I saw herself, not her hair."

"If you could see her again at this moment, simply because you wished it, would you wish?"

"No, not if she is some one else's wife; and probably she is."

"She may be dead."

"I think not."

"I think with you," Lucilla said, "I think she is still alive, waiting. I think she lives in a little room like mine. I think she keeps a bright fire burning; and she has friends. But she is always waiting."

Strange, how feebly the idea of this other little room appealed to me! I did not want to see it.

"Well, then, she must wait!" I said. "I don't know where her little room is, and I am quite happy in this one."

Again Lucilla smiled.

"Give me back my letter please!"

She gave it back to me without a word.

XVIII

It was an odd thing that, having got this letter, I did not know what to do with it. I had a vague idea of never being parted from it, of having it buried with me in my grave.

Just to try how it would feel there, I laid it under my pillow when I went to bed; but it made me as uncomfortable as if it were alive. I could not sleep a wink for it, and, being prosaically anxious to go to work again as usual next morning, I had to put it away.

Every day it troubled me more. It was like a cry out of the past, the cry of an unknown something for something unknown. It is harassing to keep a perpetual cry out of the past in your waistcoat pocket.

What if Lucilla were right? What if this young lady—now no longer young—should be really waiting? I dismissed the thought as absurd; but thought is a servant that, however often dismissed, always returns, demanding higher wages than before.

I forgot it, however, when the time came for me to go upstairs to the drawingroom floor.

Serenity and peace I had always found there, until the night when I told Lucilla that I was happier than I had ever been. There was more than peace and serenity now. There was a force of joyfulness about her that nothing could withstand. Every doubt, every grief, every fear vanished in her presence.

She was looking forward eagerly to the next mail from Australia, she told me.

Of course she was, but I did not feel, this time, as if her steady happiness were all for Kitty. I knew it was her own. I knew it to be so solid that I risked giving it a little shake. Why were confidences to be all on my side?

"What an odd thing memory is!" I said. "The shadow comes to be more than the substance. The shadow grows so strong that people are afraid to free themselves from it, even to clasp the substance. I wish I could feel that I had set myself free, as you have done. It is not so long ago since you could not be happy with me, nor let me be happy with you, on account of some one whom you would never see again."

"I ought not to have said that," observed Lucilla thoughtfully. "Never is too long a word. I did see him again!" And she glanced up at *The Unknown*.

At once those jealous fears rushed back upon my heart.

"Was it the night you were out so long?"

"Ah no!" she said, half pityingly, half as if she were amused. "That was the night dear old Mrs. Trump was so ill—before she had to go to the Infirmary. I was sitting up with her. That was why I did not get home till late. There was no one else who could come before eleven."

The agonies I had gone through! And all the time Lucilla was sitting peacefully by dear old Mrs. Trump, watching the goldfish swim round and round in their bowl. What a waste of good emotion! I went back to my other agony.

"Shall you see him when you go away? You are going away, you know. You told me so on the 26th January."

"Quite true!" she said musingly. "I was going away because of him. I had determined to pay a little visit to Kitty's father and mother. One can think more clearly away from home; but now I know he does not want me in the least, and I am not going."

There was not a shadow of regret in her tone.

"Will he never want you to go away?"

"Never."

"Heaven's blessing on him!" said I.

Again her radiant smile shone out.

It was March now. The wild winds blustered. The bare boughs strained and budded. Wild showers of rain swept, like a lyre, across blue sky.

One evening, as I sat reading for the thousandth time my little brown old letter, wondering for the thousandth time where the writer of it could be, I heard the piano above stairs begin to play, very softly, *Les Adieux*.

The next night Lucilla played *L'Absence*, and broke off.

On the third night she ought, of course, to have played *Le Retour*, but she did not. She played *Les Adieux* and *L'Absence*, one after the other; and stopped short.

I think now that there came to her, in mercy, a warning, a presentiment.

Casting about at the time for something to explain her mood, I said to myself:

"The Australian mail is late because of the winds. That is why she feels anxious; but it will come with the last post."

The next day was Thursday.

As soon as I crossed the threshold, I knew that something had happened. A darkness hung about Lucilla's eyes, a grave and gentle tenderness was in her manner, that boded ill from the first. Yet I had not courage to ask; and she, brave as she was in everything, had no courage to speak.

There was a bright fire on the hearth.

We ate and drank almost in silence, conscious that we were only delaying the moment that must come for both at last.

"Why have you been going away and never coming back again these last three nights?" I asked, forcing myself to speak as if I had remarked nothing unusual. "You made me feel so wretched that I could have howled like a dog."

"I have had a letter," she said. It means that I must go away."

"What is the matter?" I asked, bending my head, for there was in her voice that heralding of sorrow which, at the moment, seems worse than definite grief.

"It's Kitty. Kitty is dead."

I looked up, dazed and stupid, and she met my gaze with clear, tearless eyes.

I only felt that I felt nothing.

Here had we been going on just as usual—eating, drinking, sleeping, talking, reading, writing—and Kitty, little Kitty, was dead.

"I can't understand."

"Nor I," Lucilla said, with a heavy sigh. "Such a child herself! And so happy!"

We sat a long time silent.

On her pale, wan brow, there were traces of that misery which cannot sleep and cannot weep.

"You have had a bad night," I said at last.

A silly thing to say!

She gave me a scrap of foreign paper, on which two or three words were written in pencil.

"Auntie dear, will you bring Baby home?—K."

"He sent me that, poor man!" she said. "The last words that she wrote!"

I looked into the mounting flames, and thought how absurd it was that we should be there—we so much older—speaking about a scrap of Kitty's writing as if it were a relic.

I looked into the mounting flames, and thought how it would be with me when the fire on that hearth was cold.

I looked at the reflection of them in the smooth shining surface of the piano, and thought how it would be with me when that casket of sweet sounds stood locked and silent.

I looked at the little picture of the sea.

"You must not go!" I said, thinking aloud.

"I have sent a telegram to say that I am coming," she replied, quietly. "I start at once—to-morrow."

I tried to pull myself together, to say something that would help her, and all that I could think of was:

"Have you the money?"

"Yes," she said, "I have always kept a reserve at the Bank, in case of illness. I am drawing on that. I shall put it back by and by."

"It is a wild-goose chase. You will lose what you have hardly earned. You will never even see the child, it will be dead before you get there."

"Perhaps!" Lucilla said; and something in the way she said it made me ashamed.

"I will come and see you off. When do you start?"

She shook her head.

"I do not want that. I would rather go by myself. I would rather say good-bye to you here. We need not say it yet. I have done all that I had to do. There is plenty of time."

"Plenty of time"—and she was going the next day! "Plenty of time"—and in an hour I must leave her. It seemed to me as if I might as well depart then and there. "Plenty of time"—how could she say the words?

"I suppose you are going third-class—or in the steerage?"

"No, not that. It is not necessary."

The daring offer to lend her money froze on my lips.

"When shall you come back?" I asked. Not that I felt as if she would.

"I am keeping on my rooms," she said. "You will see that they are not let over my head? Our landlord would do anything for me, I know, but I do not trust his wife in the same way."

"Any one who enters this room enters it over my dead body."

"You will be kind to Persica?"

"I will do my best to be a mother to Persica," I said, stretching out my hand to the cat. But Persica made eyes that were rounder and greener than ever, and stared at me with the utmost want of confidence over a rim of blue-lined basket.

These were the only remarks in the testamentary line with which Lucilla favoured me, and I felt grateful to her, for I could not have borne more. I was afraid she was going to leave me Tricksy Wee.

I do not know how the long moments went. Every single one as it passed, seemed to be the longest in life, and yet I grudged its passing.

"Will you write to me?" I said at last.

And suddenly I recollected something that I could do for her, the only thing that she had asked me to do, and I had left undone.

"Do not answer yet!" I said hurriedly.

I took the old faded letter from my waistcoat pocket.

"There!" I said. "Burn that!"

And I put it into her hand, and I turned away.

There was a long silence.

When I looked round again, Lucilla, a soft pink colour flushing her cheeks, the letter still in her hand, her eyes most marvelously bright, sat gazing at me.

She held it up; I could see that her hand trembled.

"Listen!" she said, and indeed it was necessary, for my eyes were making my ears deaf, "I have written to you before. This is the first letter that I wrote you."

The years had fallen away. The veil that Time had dropped was lifted. She let the writing go. She covered her glowing face with her hands. The girl of nineteen summers stood before me; (but O, more beautiful!)

I have the letter still.

She would not see me again. She was inexorable as to the next morning.

"No, no!" she whispered. "Not again, I cannot. Say once again to me those three words that you said long ago, in the library! Say nothing more! Keep me as I am, and I will come back to you. We have waited all these years, you for me, I for you, we can wait half a year longer."

And I am waiting.

And to beguile the days—and for my wife when she is married—I have written out what my most weak and stumbling words could not make clear to her.

Parting, in middle age, is not the anguish of youthful parting; but the risks are increased, the insurance money is higher. I watch the winds, ever before my eyes I see the restless waves. Stronger than winds and waves is my faith that she will return to me. Her life upon the treacherous water is not a whit more guarded than mine in the little dingy street where we dwelt together.

It may be—I do not think it will—it may be that, before she returns, I shall have started on a longer voyage over that unknown sea whither we are all bound. If this should happen, I would leave behind me something that would recall to her the days of my unconscious wooing, something that should tell her, however faintly, that through all my life, from the day on which Khartoum fell, and the door of that dreary house in Bayswater shut behind the bright-eyed girl, to the day when I set forth on death with hope undying, and see again before me the same bright eyes, there has been nothing, there will be nothing in my heart of hearts but this one word,

LUCILLA.

~

SELECTED POETRY
BY *ANODOS*

A Clever Woman

You thought I had the strength of men,
Because with men I dared to speak,
And courted Science now and then,
And studied Latin for a week;
But woman's woman, even when
She reads her Ethics in the Greek.

You thought me wiser than my kind;
You thought me 'more than common tall ;'
You thought because I had a mind,
That I could have no heart at all;
But woman's woman you will find,
Whether she be great or small.

And then you needs must die—ah, well!
I knew you not, you loved not me.
'Twas not because that darkness fell,
You saw not what there was to see.
But I that saw and could not tell—
O evil Angel, set me free!

The Other Side of a Mirror

I sat before my glass one day,
And conjured up a vision bare,
Unlike the aspects glad and gay,
That erst were found reflected there—
The vision of a woman, wild
With more than womanly despair.

Her hair stood back on either side
A face bereft of loveliness.
It had no envy now to hide
What once no man on earth could guess.
It formed the thorny aureole
Of hard, unsanctified distress.

Her lips were open—not a sound
Came though the parted lines of red,
Whate'er it was, the hideous wound
In silence and secret bled.
No sigh relieved her speechless woe,
She had no voice to speak her dread.

And in her lurid eyes there shone
The dying flame of life's desire,
Made mad because its hope was gone,
And kindled at the leaping fire

Of jealousy and fierce revenge,
And strength that could not change nor tire.

Shade of a shadow in the glass,
O set the crystal surface free!
Pass—as the fairer visions pass—
Nor ever more return, to be
The ghost of a distracted hour,
That heard me whisper:—'I am she!'

The Witch

I have walked a great while over the snow,
And I am not tall nor strong.
My clothes are wet, and my teeth are set,
And the way was hard and long.
I have wandered over the fruitful earth,
But I never came here before.
O lift me over the threshold, and let me in at the door!

The cutting wind is a cruel foe.
I dare not stand in the blast.
My hands are stone, and my voice a groan,
And the worst of death is past.
I am but a little maiden still,
My little white feet are sore.
Oh, lift me over the threshold, and let me in at the door!

Her voice was the voice that women have,
Who plead for their heart's desire.
She came—she came—and the quivering flame
Sunk and died in the fire.
It never was lit again on my hearth
Since I hurried across the floor,
To lift her over the threshold, and let her in at the door.

We Never Said Farewell

We never said farewell, nor even looked
Our last upon each other, for no sign
Was made when we the linkèd chain unhooked
And broke the level line.

 And here we dwell together, side by side,
Our places fixed for life upon the chart.
Two islands that the roaring seas divide
Are not more far apart.

Doubt

Two forms of darkness are there. One is Night,
When I have been an animal, and feared
I knew not what, and lost my soul, nor dared
Feel aught save hungry longing for the light.
And one is Blindness. Absolute and bright,
The Sun's rays smote me till they masked the Sun;
The Light itself was by the light undone;
The day was filled with terrors and affright.

Then did I weep, compassionate of those
Who see no friend in God—in Satan's host no foes.

Shadow

Child of my love! though thou be bright as day,
Though all the sons of joy laugh and adore thee,
Thou canst not throw thy shadow self away.
Where thou dost come, the earth is darker for thee.

When thou dost pass, a flower that saw the sun
Sees him no longer.
The hosts of darkness are, thou radiant one,
Through thee made stronger!

The Deserted House

There's no smoke in the chimney,
And the rain beats on the floor;
There's no glass in the window,
There's no wood in the door;
The heather grows behind the house,
And the sand lies before.

No hand hath trained the ivy,
The walls are grey and bare;
The boats upon the sea sail by,
Nor ever tarry there.
No beast of the field comes nigh,
Nor any bird of the air

To Memory

Strange Power, I know not what thou art,
Murderer or mistress of my heart.
I know I'd rather meet the blow
Of my most unrelenting foe
Than live—as now I live—to be
Slain twenty times a day by thee.

Yet, when I would command thee hence,
Thou mockest at the vain pretence,
Murmuring in mine ear a song
Once loved, alas! forgotten long;
And on my brow I feel a kiss
That I would rather die than miss.

Two Songs

The blossoming of love I sang.
The streams adown the mountain sprang,
And all the world with music rang.

A cloud has darkened Heaven above,
I only hear a moaning dove.
I singe the withering of love.

Horror

Thy body is no more thy house,
It is become thy sepulchre.
I cannot any more arouse
The spirit that did inhabit there.

The brain's asleep before its time.
I would that thou hadst died outright,
And I had seen thee, in thy prime,
Go half to darkness, half to light!

Mortal Combat

It is because you were my friend,
I fought you as the Devil fights.
Whatever fortune God may send,
For once I set the world to rights.

And that was when I thrust you down,
And stabbed you twice and twice again,
Because you dared take off your crown,
And be a man like other men.

Marriage

No more alone sleeping, no more alone waking,
Thy dreams divided, thy prayers in twain;
Thy merry sisters tonight forsaking,
Never shall we see, maiden, again.

Never shall we see thee, thine eyes glancing.
Flashing with laughter and wild in glee,
Under the mistletoe kissing and dancing,
Wantonly free.

There shall come a matron walking sedately,
Low-voiced, gentle, wise in reply.
Tell me, O tell me, can I love her greatly?
All for her sake must the maiden die!

Unwelcome

We were young, we were merry, we were very very wise,
And the door stood open at our feast,
When there passed us a woman with the West in her eyes,
And a man with his back to the East.

O, still grew the hearts that were beating so fast,
The loudest voice was still.
The jest died away on our lips as they passed,
And the rays of July struck chill.

The cups of red wine turned pale on the board,
The white bread black as soot.
The hound forgot the hand of her lord,
She fell down at his foot.

Low let me lie, where the dead dog lies,
Ere I sit me down again at a feast,
When there passes a woman with the West in her eyes,
And a man with his back to the East.

Master and Guest

There came a man across the moor,
Fell and foul of face was he.
He left the path by the cross-roads three,
And stood in the shadow of the door.

I asked him in to bed and board.
I never hated any man so.
He said he could not say me No.
He sat in the seat of my own dear lord.

'Now sit you by my side!' he said,
'Else may I neither eat nor drink.
You would not have me starve, I think.'
He ate the offerings of the dead.

'I'll light you to your bed,' quoth I.
'My bed is yours—but light the way!'
I might not turn aside nor stay;
I showed him where we twain did lie.

The cock was trumpeting the morn.
He said: 'Sweet love, a long farewell!
You have kissed a citizen of Hell,
And a soul was doomed when you were born.

Mourn, mourn no longer for your dear!
Him may you never meet above.
The gifts that Love hath given to Love,
Love gives away again to Fear.'

Regina

My Queen her sceptre did lay down,
She took from her head the golden crown
Worn by right of her royal birth.
Her purple robe she cast aside,
And the scarlet vestures of her pride,
That was the pride of the earth.
In her nakedness was she
Queen of the world, herself and me.

My Queen took up her sceptre bright,
Her crown more radiant than the light,
The rubies gleaming out of the gold.
She donned her robe of purple rare,
And did a deed that none may dare,
That makes the blood run cold.
And in her bravery is she
Queen of herself, the world and me.

Self-Question

Is this wide world not large enough to fill thee,
Nor Nature, nor that deep man's Nature, Art?
Are they too thin, too weak and poor to still thee,
            Thou little heart?

Dust art thou, and to dust again returnest,
A spark of fire within a beating clod.
Should that be infinite for which thou burnest?
            Must it be God?

~

True to Myself am I,
and False to All

"To thine own self be true;
And it must follow, as the night the day
Thou canst not then be false to any man."

—Hamlet, I.iii. 55–57

True to myself am I, and false to all.
Fear, sorrow, love, constrain us till we die.
But when the lips betray the spirit's cry,
The will, that should be sovereign, is a thrall.
Therefore let terror slay me, ere I call
For aid of men. Let grief begrudge a sigh.
'Are you afraid?'—'unhappy?' 'No!' The lie
About the shrinking truth stands like a wall.
'And have you loved?' 'No, never.' All the while,
The heart within my flesh is turned to stone.
Yea, none the less that I account it vile,
The heart within my heart makes speechless moan,
And when they see one face, one face alone,
The stern eyes of the soul are moved to smile

Go

Go at the deepest, darkest dead of night,
When no foot shall be stirring save thine own.
Go forth, unlighted, to his couch, alone,
And break his slumber with thy kisses light.
Go, while the deeds and characters of day
Are but as dreams and fleeting visions vain.
Go take him to thy beating heart again,
Ere all the world awake and find the way!

~

Gone

About the little chambers of my heart
Friends have been coming—going—many a year.
The doors stand open there.
Some, lightly stepping, enter; some depart.

Freely they come and freely go, at will.
The walls give back their laughter; all day long
They fill the house with song.
One door alone is shut, one chamber still.

Lines*

Stay with me, happy Day!
Fly not away!
Dost thou think, when thou art fled,
I shall but love thee better, being dead?
Not so, not so!
To-morrow I shall say,
' 'Twas long ago!—
He lies, for ever shorn of rainbow wings,
Among forgotten things.'

~

Grief and Death*

Deep joy was mine, I owned a fountain fair
That watered with its soft refreshing dew
The plants and flowers that in my garden grew
And made them spring and bud and blossom there.

And boasting of the world without, I spake,
'Come sit within my honeysuckle bowers,
And breathe the sweet scent of my lily flowers,
And listen to the song the waters make.'

Strong grief was mine, I gat me forth alone,
Into my garden dry and bare I stept,
And laid me down upon the grass and wept.
No ear, divine or human, heard my moan,
For joy bids welcome all the guests that come,
But sorrow hath no voice—Despair is dumb.

~

To One Who Was
Nursing a Blind Father[*]

The other day
I thought and thought and ever thought again,
How, while I sat in joy, apart from men,
In perfect joy of sun and sea and air,
You sat within the reach of nothing fair,
In darkness with the darkened. Then and there
Intolerable pity broke in prayer
Hushed by a whisper those wild words above:
'How dar'st thou pity whom I greatly love.'

To an Old Friend*

Now when the sweet sunny weather
Quickens all that once was dead
I remember how we two,
You and I, I and you,
Wandered about the streets together,
Reading the books that had to be read,
Saying the things that cannot be said.

The world was young, and we were younger
In those bright forgotten days,
I remember how we two,
You and I, I and you,
Read and read for the spirit's hunger,
Walked in the old familiar ways,
Talked and talked for each other's praise.

The world is young, but we are older,
Many a book we shall read no more—
I remember how we two,
You and I, I and you,
Vowed that love should not grow colder,
That we would love as we loved before,
And the years should make us love the more.

~

To Time the Comforter*

Dumb Comforter of woes!
The depths of whose deep comfort no one knows;
Whose consolations on the spirit steal
More gently than Love's gentlest word; and heal
Where Love falls back affrighted; only life
Proves Thee the Comforter of mortal strife,
Of all that doth begin and end—that He
May speak in thy dread silence endlessly!

*Unpublished Poems from *Gathered Leaves*

~

ESSAYS AND
OTHER WRITINGS

~

"Words, Words, Words!"

Aids to Reflection is written so large over everything that makes the furniture of the House of Life, that a person by nature disinclined to reflect may not escape if he would. How can he avoid thinking, so long as he has a fire in his room when he sits at home,—so long as the sky is over him when he walks out? He cannot help himself. We think all day. The Art of finished thought we may never learn. We are not all—Heaven save the mark!—professional thinkers; but each one of us is, at the least, an amateur of some experience.

It is because they cannot think that infants are happy, despite internal sufferings and coercive treatment from without which would cause a person of riper years to commit suicide. It is because in sleep we cannot think, or only think distortedly, that in sleep we are happy. Distorted thinking is sometimes (not always) less wearisome than that unceasing rush of trivial images through the brain which, for want of a saner word, we call *thinking* when awake. In certain moods the thought of thought eternal will even drive us to curse our immortality; we should be ready to sell that inalienable and oppressive birthright for the condition of a stone. More grateful to our ears than *There shall be no night there* is *The night cometh.* We wish that death would indeed come not as a new dawn, but like the end of day, bringing with it the same exquisite sense of freedom from the endless spinning and weaving of the intellect. To some this remedy of the quiet fall of darkness may appear more soothing than sleep itself inasmuch as we are more conscious of happy influence. It gives us over to the life of feeling. It mesmerises the brain, yet leaves the rest of the man awake.

Sleep then is one specific against reflection, and darkness is another; but do what we will we cannot spend more than half our lives in bed, and the sun is accustomed to shine so many hours daily. If we cannot but think, we must speak. We did not make the thoughts ourselves, but we make the sentences that express them, and by so much do we reduce the vague, intangible, bewildering whirl that is within us.

The strange part of it is that somehow or other we all become the hero of *Frankenstein* in the process; our own creations obtain a monstrous power over us. They get wings, and fly whither we know not. Instead of ruling the words that we have made, we let the words rule us. We consider ourselves and others chained by a promise that has been spoken. The silent vows that lie below the faculty of expression we can forgive ourselves for breaking; we are, as we say, "bound by a word." Any one would think we must owe great things to words, to feel that we are thus beholden to them. We do indeed. They are the keys with which we enter other hearts, with which we open the doors of our own. Yet, when we most need these keys, they are nowhere to be found. They are not good enough, it seems. Since I can find for the one whom most I love no other words to tell it than those which have been everywhere profaned, I leave them unspoken. I dare not change my admiration into so many letters of the alphabet; it would break the sentence to pieces, and leave me foolish and ashamed. I let the hero go unpraised. Adam was the only man that could ever have proposed to a woman,—and he was above the necessity.

Perhaps it is this reiterated failure of speech at need that makes people distrust it altogether. Goethe never mentioned beforehand any plan on which he had set his heart, having a superstition that if he once allowed himself to be limited by a form of words, he could not carry it into effect. "I cannot trust myself to speak" is a common phrase. On the other hand, this very dread has an affirmative side to it, and shows by implication the power of words,—a power which is practically unbounded. What will not a man do for such a word as Honour—Fame—Love? He may never have got below the word, he may not have the faintest conception of the thing signified, but for this alone he will live, for this alone he will, if need be, die. Many a creature whose whole life is untrue would extinguish it, if he foresaw the possibility of being called *Liar*. The word *Coward* has slain its thousands, the word *Ungentlemanly* its tens of thousands. In one of the most interesting chapters of his *Souvenirs* Tolstoi describes the tyranny exercised over him in early youth by the expression *comme il faut*.

Over against this overwhelming power there must be set the charm of words. Generals, admirals, politicians know the value of a good signal, how the mere repetition of it will kindle zeal and inflame courage. Orators are apt to be led astray. They are deceived by their own mastery. How often have not the burning words of a preacher made a red bonfire of his thoughts? Poets are the musicians that play upon the various combinations of letters as on the instruments that make up an orchestra,—now and then with the same rousing effect. "I never read the old song of Percie and Douglas, that I found not my heart moved more than with a trumpet." Critics are, for the most part, the doctors of language. They assist at the birth of new words, they cure the old of wrong meanings, they restore health and vigour to the weak.

The longing for expression is almost universal. Because we cannot express ourselves we rush to hear the words of one who can. It does not calm the restlessness of the wish to know that we shall be soon beyond the dominion of words. Nay, of all others, it is the dying who are commonly most eager to speak, most eager to listen.

"There was near *Athens* a town called *Megara*. The nearer they are the more do cities quarrel. The enmity between the Athenians and Megarians was for some years so great that, if any Megarian came across the frontier, he was put to death by the Athenians.

"A few days after the war between these cities began, Socrates was sitting at night on the bank of the *Ilyssus*, near the plane which used to give him shade by day. Hearing a noise he raised his head, breaking off his meditation. Then he saw a lad stretched before his feet, panting. He recognised a pupil called Apodemus of *Megara*.

The lad said, 'Oh, master, be quick; converse with me; tell me what you did not plainly tell when you talked with the others. The watchmen of your people are pursuing me; the laws of your people condemn me to death for daring to come hither. Teach me what you know about the soul of man.'

"Then did the master clear up that which he had left doubtful about the second life."

~

Recollections of
Mrs. Fanny Kemble

Is it ever worth while to have a quarrel? When one is in the right, one thinks it is. I was in the wrong in a quarrel that I had with Mrs. Fanny Kemble. And yet I think it was worth while.

The quarrel came about in this way.

I went to see her one January day, about three weeks after my first introduction. She was sitting on a sofa by the window, dressed in black velvet, busy with the most hideous bit of worsted work in the world. I do not remember any of the colours in it, except that the worst and the most prevalent was violet. She looked as if she were going to cry—very sad—very old.

She had met —— in a cab, the other day, she said, and promised him that she would urge me to show her something that I had written.

I was flustered, lost my head, said I could not do it because, if I could never write even to satisfy myself, &c. &c.

"Oh, that's conceit! Don't think I want to see it because it will turn out to be anything. I only urge you because I have promised. When I had written anything myself, for the first three days I thought it not ridiculous but sublime. I was full of conceit. I would have read it to any one I met in the street. I wrote to express myself, as the birds sing. After that I didn't care about it—never thought any more of it. I fell back upon conceit again. I wrote to my publisher and said: 'Take these things and print them if you like, but don't alter one line—one word—for I won't stand it.' He replied saying he meant to alter this, that, and the other, and signed himself *Your abject publisher*. I never gave away my things, but I took whatever my publishers chose to give me for them. I would have taken a penny."

"I do not want to weary people," I said. "If I were to show you what I have written, I should have to show it to others also."

"You mean to those who have more claim on you than I?"

"Yes."

"And that manuscript is difficult to read?"

"Yes."

"There is a kind of modesty that comes dangerously near self-love. I think it would be more modest to say, 'Well, I don't care! If anybody wants to see my things, here they are.'"

"May I say what I really think?"

"Say what you really think! Of course you ought never to say anything else. Then you admit you've been telling lies. It is true you may have said nothing."

"I have a strong feeling against it."

"Then I have nothing more to say. Tell —— I have discharged my duty and fulfilled my promise. I shall never speak to you on this subject again. I love Power [the word had a capital] wherever I find it. I do not recognise the right of any one human being, not even a parent, to interfere with another. I have not done so with my own children.—How do you mean to get your things published, if you never allow a publisher to read them?"

"It is quite a different matter. It is the publisher's business."

"You would allow a publisher to look at them because it is his business, and you would not yield to the request of a friend?"

Here I cried out. I thought she was cruel. She did not press the point. She said that "a good and right-thinking person," such as she felt sure I was, never acted without consideration! And on a sudden her wrath flamed out scathingly.

"My dear, you are either very untidy, or your maid deserves to have her ears boxed."

Down came the hawk's eyes upon my crumpled brown silk, which had been lying in a drawer for months. We were in mourning, and I had taken it out in haste, for a special occasion.

"I have just come from a wedding ——"

"I don't care whose wedding you've been at. You deserve to be called *a scribbling woman*. You are that thing men call *a blue*. I like the colour—I could not wear a thing like that. I have a passion for dress. That's because I am French. I remember in my youth old hags shockingly dressed; they should have dressed for the sake of others, if not for their own. You don't know how good it is of me to dress up like this and come down and sit here. I had ever so much rather be in bed."

"There is one dress of yours about which I have always longed to ask you," I said, seeing a chance of escape and taking that chance. "You talked about it in the *Records*."

"Yes," she said. "I was staying with friends near *Manchester*. It was in the part of *Isabella*. It was not crimson—it was blue satin and velvet. The wretched poky little holes of dressing-rooms we actors had, made it pleas-anter for me to dress before going to the Theatre. A lady who happened to be staying there told me afterwards how strange it was when the folding-doors opened and I appeared."

Here the maid brought in Mrs. Kemble's tea, and a big white dog. She of-fered me some tea, but I declined; and the white dog was languid.

"I like you because you are clean," she said to him. "He loves water as I do. But I won't say what I think of dogs that refuse brown bread and butter while there are little children starving in the streets. He likes being petted better than bread and butter."

My mind was running still upon dress.

"The *Isabella* vision reminds me of a story I heard in *Warwickshire* about a man who saw the picture of a ghost there, and then recognised her dancing opposite him at a fancy ball in *Florence*," I said.

"Have you read Grillparzer's *Ahnfrau?* There is one thing I remember—a scene in which the heroine, looking at herself in a mirror, sees her face re-flected, but with the arms clasped in despair above her head."

In the twinkling of an eye Grillparzer's heroine was there before me.

"That is something like a scene in *St. Ronan's Well*."

"I have forgotten it. I have been reading *Waverley* again with great plea-sure—*Waverley* and *The Vicar of Wakefield*. I bought them as Christmas presents for my maid, and I asked her to lend them to me before I passed them on to her."

"Which is your favourite *Waverley?*"

"I have so many favourites," she said, with some impatience.

"*Rob Roy* is mine, I think. Why is Di Vernon so different from all his other heroines?"

"She was French. Lady Scott was a silly woman, but she had that French vivacity; Scott showed it in Di Vernon. My favourite is *Guy Mannering*, but then it was the first I read, and I think that may have something to do with it. I saw Scott when I was in Edinburgh. The first thing he said was, 'You are a good horsewoman, Miss Kemble, and that is a great recommendation in the eyes of an old Borderer like myself.' My father and I were asked to stay for a week at Abbotsford. We were play-actors; our engagements would not allow us to accept the invitation. I have never ceased to regret it. *I would have made him talk to me.* Shakespeare was a great poet, but he wrote with the coarseness of his age. Scott never wrote one word that now—in Heaven—he need wish unwritten. Some hostile criticisms of my acting appeared in Ballantyne's magazine. Ballantyne sent me a note of his in which he said: 'I think you are hard upon Miss Kemble. I have seen nothing so good since her aunt, Mrs. Siddons!' I gave it away to some one who wanted an autograph. What should I do with it? I acted badly."

"But if Scott said you acted well?"

"He did not say I acted well. He said he had seen nothing so good since my aunt. How can I tell what he had seen since my aunt? He may have seen nothing but what was bad. I hated acting. I enjoyed reading, and I read very well. I have a devilish spirit of pride in me. My first curtsey to my audience was a disclaimer of their presence, but when I began to read I forgot myself."

"There is a description of your reading in *The Life of Longfellow*, is there not?"

Her face grew soft.

"Dear Longfellow! He was a friend of mine. I will tell you a story about that. I was staying with him at Cambridge once, and I was going to read. One of the learnèd gentlemen there, Dr. Webster, offered to give me his arm that night, to conduct me to my desk. I said that I was staying with Mr. Longfellow, and he had offered to do me this service. It was an accident that saved me from *laying my hand in the hand of a murderer.*"

The room was growing dark. I felt myself start bolt upright. And she went on.

"There was a Mr. Parkman who had lent Dr. Webster money. He disappeared. In a little place like that every one knows every one, and it was noticed. After some time there was found in the place—what do you call it?—where Dr. Webster made his chemical experiments, the fragment of a jaw with teeth, which Mr. Parkman's friends recognised. Dr. Webster was accused—tried—condemned. I was reading *Macbeth* at the time. His Counsel, and all the people engaged in the trial, were among my audience. One of them told me afterwards, the effect of the murder scene had never been so fine. Their minds were full of horror at the crime. The man destroyed himself in prison. You have heard of Charles Sumner? He was a friend of Dr. Webster's. He was allowed into the prison, and it was generally thought that he had conveyed prussic acid to him, that the public disgrace of the execution might be avoided. In that country, though there is a nominal executioner, the sheriff has to carry out the sentence. The sheriff was a friend of Dr. Webster's.

"Another time I read that poem of Longfellow's—not *The Making of the Bell*, but something like that—what is it?"

"*The Ship?*" I suggested.

"Yes—*The Building of the Ship*. Longfellow sat opposite, gazing at me; he had a friend beside him, but the friend covered his eyes. Dear Fanny Longfellow (I was very fond of her—she was very like me) sat just below, her beautiful brown eyes streaming with tears. I tell you she was like me—and then I say she had beautiful brown eyes!"

A few indifferent words; a little pause; and I rose to go.

She took my hand, or rather she kept it.

"If you come to another mind, I desire that you will let me know."

I promised.

"Ring yourself out."

. . .

I waited about three weeks; and then I went again. Nothing could have been kinder or more gracious.

"Well—what have you been reading *and writing?*"

"I am reading Dante. I wonder why Goethe said he was bad for young people."

"I cannot think why. Old heathen that Goethe was! (in some respects I am quite as much of a heathen myself.) Unless he thought it would tend to persuade young people to be Roman Catholics. I think I recollect another passage in his Works, where he says that he would never entrust Government to Roman Catholics. I do not cling to forms. I think we are permitted to choose the form of religion that suits us best. But I have two objections to Roman Catholicism. Confession is one. The conscience of any man should be in his own hands; or, if it be a woman, in the hands of her husband. And the other is—that they have not the same standard of truth as we have. Protestants tell just as many lies as they do; but we don't think it right. I have told many lies in my life, but I do not think I did well to tell them—I think I sinned. They are differently brought up. In a *Child's Catechism* that I was looking over, I found this question, *When is a lie not right?* And then the answer, *When it is for your own advantage.* I knew a saint, Madame Craven—she was the *fine fleur* of Catholicism. I had been engaged to the man she married. His father would not allow the match. He said, very sensibly, that however charming I might be, we were two paupers, and nothing added to nothing made nothing. So, at the end of a year, I sent back his letters to Mr. Craven. After that, I went to America—fell in love with a gentleman there—and returned to England a married woman."

"One night, when we were at the Theatre, I saw a most beautiful person in the box opposite ours, and raised my opera-glass to look at her.

"'Don't look at that lady!' my brother said.

"'Why not? If you give me any reason why I should not, I will leave off; but if you don't, I won't.'

"'Don't you see Augustus Craven at the back of the box?'

"The beautiful woman was his wife.

"She called on me, and we became great friends. She brought me the manuscript of her *Récit d'une Sœur*.

"'Don't read it,' my sister Adelaide said to me. 'You will only distress yourself and her. You will not like it; and she thinks it is all right and good.'

"I carried it back to her, and she lent me *Eugénie de Guérin* instead. Presently I came upon a passage in which I found that Miss Eugénie's father did not approve of her keeping a journal, and therefore she had it bound exactly like another book, so as to deceive him. Do you remember?"

"No. It is a long while since I read the book."

"It is a long while since *I* read the book, but *I* remember. I took it to Madame Craven.

"'Surely you do not approve of this?'

"'Ah!' she said, '*ça vous fait cet effet-là?*'

"My father and my uncle John were educated at Douay. It was thought they might become priests. My uncle John, I am sure, was not a Roman Catholic. My father, when he was dying, went back to the old Catholic prayers that he had heard at Douay. But we were all brought up Protestants."

"I feel as if I could not breathe in a Convent."

"Yet many people have breathed there. Do you remember Milton in the *Penseroso?*

'But let my due feet never fail
To walk the studious cloister's pale.'

That was pretty strong for an old Puritan."

"Wordsworth has it too," I said.

'The holy time is quiet as a nun.'"

"But they were not quiet."

She began to quote her favourite Dante, repeating various passages, as one seemed to awake another in her mind. But when she came to

"All hope abandon, ye that enter here!"

her memory failed her.

And she said,

"This is tragedy!"

~

The Drawing-Room

I sometimes wonder how the room I sit in looks to other eyes.

"Do you live in *London* all the year round?" people say; and then, even if they are too civil to condole, their eyes take a compassionate expression. Alas, how that good thing, pity, is wasted! Who would be so lavish of love or of money? Once—once only I think—it happened to me to be envied. "You people who live in *London* do not know how glorious it is. You cannot!" said a British Resident in Foreign Parts, whose drawing-room was a jungle.

To have lived in one place ever since memory began is to have seen that place change as you change yourself; but more perceptibly. Our own faces and figures in a glass are strange to us as the forms of those with whom we are not acquainted. I do not know after what fashion the little girl who played battledore and shuttlecock here differed from the big girl who came after her, and the woman who now sits in her place. But I know that long ago the drawing-room was much larger than it is now, all the chairs and tables much higher, and the piano unaccountably higher still. It was a vast space of country in those days. I owned a little of it here and there—a dusty cabinet in the backwoods where my story-books lived—and everything underneath the piano. The rest had nothing to do with me. The beautiful brick towers almost as high as myself that I built upon that alien territory were doomed to fall, a few minutes after they were finished. I grieved for them. It seemed to me that they adorned the drawing-room.

In the firelight, of a winter's evening, my possessions expanded. As I danced in and out of the wreaths of white roses on the faded crimson ground of the carpet, I thought those also were mine. And if I had a cold, the sofa belonged to me.

After that came a dreadful time, when I was shut out of the drawing-room almost entirely. An exile feels as I used to feel when I passed the door. Within there was quiet, peace, music, and books to read that were never dull. Without—sums, scales, French verbs, and everything to make existence dreary. Even if I did get in, I was turned out remorselessly when a particular clock struck, and whenever people began to say something I should like to have heard.

By-and-by, when there were parties, I was brought down to sit with a book behind the piano. Thus I made the acquaintance of *King Lear* and was not greatly horrified. Thence I witnessed a love-scene for the first time. My Aunt called me away, afraid lest my too evident sympathy should interrupt it.

A little later on, I came to view the drawing-room in the light of a Theatre. There did I appear, first as the Beast in a black mask, then as the radiant red velvet Prince, wedding his Beauty—I did enact Theseus—I was a wandering Duchess—I was a Puritan in red ancestral boots. The drawing-room was musical with sweet voices then—full of people coming and going. Once I remember that we danced there.

As I sit alone, I wonder who will come when I also have gone.

I should like to think of another child—merrier—not so much afraid of the dark on the stairs outside—and that her mother would play and sing. I should like to think of another girl—as gay, as full of bold ambition and not so shy—not so shy—acting and dancing where I danced and acted. I hope she will see the greatest man in the world come in, as I saw Robert Browning come through the door one evening, his hat under his arm. I wonder whether she will train the creeper over the balcony to the West and plant geranium and mignonette, and sit there in summer to watch the gold of sunset over the roofs. Bright be her pictures in that shining window, and may she sometimes love a book that I loved!

~

Gifts

There are gifts that are no gifts, just as there are books that are no books. A donation is not a gift.

A portrait painted—a teapot presented—by subscription, is not a gift. The giving is divided among too many. The true gift is from one to one. Furthermore, tea, sugar, and flannel petticoats are not gifts. If I bestow these conveniences on one old woman, she may regard them in that aspect; but if I bestow them on eleven others at the same time, she looks upon them as her right. By giving more I have given less. The dole is no more like the gift than charity is like love. A £50 cheque on the occasion of a marriage between Blank and Blank is not a gift; it is a transfer of property.

And why is it *de rigueur* that if somebody I like goes into partnership with somebody she likes, I must give her an enormous silver buttonhook when she has six already? The pleasure I confer on her by doing so is not worth the value of the penny stamp which she must, equally *de rigueur*, waste on informing me that she is pleased. It is not within the bounds of possibility that a human being can appreciate more than—say fifty presents at a time, when she has to write notes for them all. The line should be drawn at fifty—for large and generous natures at seventy; and all friends who have not sent in their buttonhooks before a certain date should be requested to distribute them over the coming years instead. As a lily in winter, so is the unexpected gift. But the gift that arrives by tens and tens of tens is a nightmare and an oppression.

Again, the periodical gift is never refreshing; it is too much of the nature of tribute. A present on Midsummer Day would be worth two at Christmas.

"The free gift only cometh of the free."

The articles of furniture—lamps, matchboxes, footstools, and so on—duly exchanged between members of the same family, at certain seasons, are not gifts. They are a kind of tax levied by duty on liking, and duty claims the credit of them. Liking responds with what is called gratitude—a doubtful virtue at best, impossible between true friends—too near obsequiousness in the poor, too hollow for sincerity in the rich. There is no element of surprise about these presents. The spirit of giving is killed by regularity. How can I care—except in a material way—for what is part of my annual income? The heart is not interested. I get these things because my name is down on a piece of paper, not because some one is possessed with an impatient desire to please or to share pleasure.

Rarely, among the many things that are passed from hand to hand, is one a gift; and the giver is not so common as he was. System has attacked and ruined him even in the nursery. Santa Claus no longer comes down the chimney on Christmas Eve as he (or she) did when the child was never sure what might be in his stocking. As soon as he can write at all—or sooner—the child writes a list of "Christmas wishes," and these are conscientiously fulfilled by his father and mother, who know a great deal more than his grandfather and grandmother knew, only they do not know—unless he tells them—what it is that he wants. A feeling of depressed amazement stole over me one day when I heard a little girl enumerating the items on her list:—

A Writing-desk.

A Muff.

A Prayer-book.

A Whole Family of Giraffes.

What sort of mother could that have been who was not aware that her daughter wanted A Whole Family of Giraffes unless she saw it in black and white? And as for the Writing-desks and Muffs and Prayer-books, the child ought to have had them anyhow. We should never have thought such things were presents at all when we were young; the bare necessities of life!

No. A gift—to be a gift—must not be asked for. Dante laid down this rule, with many others, which lead one to reflect that it must have been difficult to give him a present. The request is payment; he who receives in this case buys, though he who gives cannot be accused of selling. The poet also decrees that a gift which is not so valuable to the recipient as it would be to the giver is no true gift. Romantic generosity would have been spared many a pang, had she considered this precept. *The Falcon* would not have been cooked for dinner; the life of *The Kentucky Cardinal* might have been saved. People who have pearls are curiously fond of stringing them together and offering them to pigs. It makes the pig unhappy in the end.

There is a third saying of Dante, which is a counsel of perfection; the face of the gift should resemble the face of him to whom the gift is given. If this be so, only those who understand each other's appearance should venture to give. My friend, who has an expression like a beautiful sermon, must not present me with a volume of Lightfoot when French novels are written all over my speaking countenance. Neither must I inflict on her the works of "Gyp."

It is a complicated business altogether. Three minutes of serious thinking make it impossible for anyone to give anyone anything. Yet the deed is done every year boldly and openly, and few are sensible that they have undertaken a more delicate transaction than the robbery of a Bank in broad daylight.

When Rosalind, at a moment's notice, gave Orlando the chain from her neck, the action was perfect on her side and on his. Any man a little lower than Shakespeare would have made Orlando show it and talk about it in the forest; he would not have let it pass without a single further allusion. Celia remembers, she teases Rosalind; but the two lovers will never speak of it again. There was no merit in Rosalind; she gave because she could not help herself. How could Orlando thank her except in silence? Like another young gentleman in the same circumstances, he had been little happy could he have said how much.

There is in some natures a high intolerance of the airy fetters cast round the heart by the constant memory of beneficence. They give freely, but freely they do not receive. They must send something by return of post, like the two friends in *Elizabeth and her German Garden*, who regularly transmitted to each other the same candlestick and the same note-book turn about, as each anniversary chimed the hour on their clocks—whereby they saved an incalculable amount of time, money, and emotion. One sweet lady goes so far as to say that all presents should be of perishable character—a basket of fruit, a bunch of flowers—that they may be at once forgotten.

Yet, if the truth were known, it might be found that the smaller, the more insignificant the gift, the longer it is remembered. There may be many motives for keeping the Golden Rose; there can be only one for keeping a rose-leaf. Thus was it said by a man of old time who knew what a woman liked and gave her a distaff: "Great grace goes with a little gift, and all the offerings of friends are precious.

~

The Making of Heroines
[From *The Reflector*, March 1888]

I believe I am quite capable of being a hero: but so far as I know, I am not one; and I want to have some good way suggested to me of occupying that desirable position. After all, this, if any, is the age when Sancho Panza (or Mrs. Panza for that matter) seems to have a good chance of enjoying, at all events for a time, the position and reputation which even Don Quixote found so hard to obtain in days when chivalry had already gone out, and interviewers had not yet come in. Everybody must have noticed that celebrated people nowadays, especially celebrated ladies, have nearly as many lives as a Kilkenny cat. They are born, they are married, they die over and over again, in the columns of newspapers and in the pages of biographers. Even before their natural decease, they very often live in a world of looking-glass, which reflects all their most important actions—or their least important, as the case may be—for the benefit of the outside world.

It was not always so. Mrs. William Shakespeare's sufferings may, in her different sphere, have equalled Mrs. Carlyle's, and she may have been just as cross and just as clever, but no one of her husband's friends was entrusted with the unpleasant duty of describing her conjugal adventures for the edification of posterity. We know next to nothing of those much-to-be-pitied young women, the daughters of Milton, and what little we do know does not redound to their credit. Had they but lived a couple of hundred years later, we should, no doubt, have possessed an interesting work entitled 'The Real John Milton,' of which they were the suffering heroines. Let all downtrodden wives and daughters of the *genus irritabile vatum* take courage! Their day was long in coming, but it has come at last. A strong character must that be indeed which can stand the glare of light thus flung on it from all sides. The results of different treatment are sometimes as perceptible as those in varying portraits of the same person. One artist is perfectly convinced that the eyes were pale blue; another would go to the stake for the opinion that they were dark brown. It is a rare thing when the subject is too striking to admit of any mistake. Mrs. Gaskell, Mr. Reid, and Mr. Birrell are three very different people, but Charlotte Brontë is much the same in all their pictures. It has been wittily said, that every individual stands really for three—himself, the self he thinks himself, and the self somebody else thinks him. She seems to have been one of the very few who cherish no illusions on their own account and permit none to be cherished by others. She had one good strong self, and she stuck to it, and stamped it indelibly upon her every word and action.

What befalls celebrated people invariably after their death, and frequently during their life, befalls commonplace people only at rare intervals and at certain crises. Few of us have strength of mind enough to make heroes of ourselves, but once or twice at least, in the course of our existence, events make heroes of us in our own despite. The first Mrs. Dombey, had she 'made an effort,' would never have been the first Mrs. Dombey. Circumstances, we know, rendered it impossible, and those circumstances made her immortal; but she is only cited as an extreme case. Woman is, as a rule, quicker to take advantage of her life than man; she is less passive. Man at a crisis—unless it be a crisis of war—is a stupid thing. He either makes a fool of himself, or allows the world to make a fool of him, from which fate woman is preserved by her innate self-respect, and by a certain capacity which she possesses for making the most of emotion. A bridegroom is either the silliest or the most miserable of mortals, but marriage can always make a heroine out of the least heroic of women. She is the centre of attraction, for the time being. Everything is forgiven her, on account of the ordeal through which she has to pass. Her married friends pity her. Her unmarried friends envy either her or the bridegroom, as the case may be. Her will is law. Her prospects and her presents are the subject of conversation among all her acquaintance. She is obliged to take the opinion of the whole household, from Grandmamma down to the lady's maid, as to the fit of her wedding-gown. No one spares her blushes about the ring. Every one says 'Poor thing!'—if the height of the bride does not absolutely forbid it, 'Poor little thing!' The borderland between Miss and Mrs., especially the extreme verge of the borderland, has an odd fascination. Some people, like Racine, always cry at a wedding. Sir Thomas Browne, we know, thought it a far more solemn thing than death.

It is, at any rate, a crisis, whether from the lady's maid's point of view or Racine's.

Some are made heroes of (most unwillingly) by a fire, a burglary, a mad dog, or the small-pox. It is a mistake to suppose that success ever makes heroes. A certain element of melancholy is almost always needful. The Archbishop of Canterbury is not a hero, unless he has to go to prison. The Chancellor of the Exchequer is not a hero, unless he is compelled to offer up his lofty position on the altar of his country.

It is appalling to think how full the world is of intermittent, involuntary, nameless and numberless heroes and heroines. I know at least nineteen, and my acquaintance is limited. I have never yet been a hero in my own person, but I comfort myself with the old saying, 'While there is life, there is hope.'

Her Grace, the Duchess
[From *The Theatre*, September 1884]

The world is getting daily more democratic, and it is possible that we may soon arrive at that golden age of Socialists and Quakers which is to turn us all into Citizen this, and Friend the other. Still there are certain members of the aristocracy who will never even then be asked to don the *bonnet-rouge*, who will still exist to remind a free, equal, and fraternal world that there were once such things as kings and princes, and such-like futile distinctions between man and man. Their crowns will be as fresh then as on the day they wore them first, their courts as noble as before; for they cannot be got to talk the vulgar tongue, and they shall live for ever and ever, these grand aristocrats, most of whom never lived at all.

Strange that a prince who can make dukes by the dozen for the five years of his lifetime, should after that be at the mercy of a king-maker, whose style is generally plain Mr., and who can make nothing, not even money! Yet so it is, and the poet king-makers are very tyrannical in their choice of candidates.

Who is Shakespeare's ideal monarch? Not Alfred the Good, who first taught England how to read; not Edward I., who made her feel that the strength of her strength was unity, but that expensive hero who plunged her into one of the most unjustifiable and, in the end, most fatal wars she ever undertook, to satisfy his own hungry ambition.

Queens in all ages and amongst all classes have been popular; as theirs will probably be the last of all titles to die out in the actual world, so theirs is the first in the world of poetry and plays. By the grace of William Shakespeare,

Esq. (and others), they are, and always will be, Queens, Defenders of the Faith, within their dominions supreme.

Others there are too, not less noble, ladies in the great sense of the word, on whom their two hundred years and odd sit lightly, who claim the homage due to them as justly now as in the days of old, and prominent among these is the wonderful lady, whom Webster imaged to himself somewhere about the year 1612, and whom he called, in default of any Christian name that could properly express her, simply the Duchess—'The Duchess of Malfi.'

The age of ugly heroines had not set in when she was born. We see her first as a young and beautiful widow, hated by her grasping and envious brothers, Prince Ferdinand and the Cardinal, distrusted by her mean, suspicious courtiers, loved only by the very few who knew her well. As to her relations with her dead husband, Webster observes a significant silence. Shakespeare would almost certainly have noticed them, and shown how they re-acted on the true crisis of her life, just as he touched on Romeo's sentimental love for Rosaline, before he saw Juliet; but Webster leaves us to draw our own conclusions from the bare fact that he says nothing—good, bad, or indifferent. It is often so with him; he leads us to infer whatever it does not suit him to express, and his principal figures stand out all the more clearly for their dark background. He is reticent even about his hero, the steward, unwilling to put him forward, lest the Duchess should suffer so much as a momentary eclipse. Excepting for his beautiful description of her in Act I., Antonio speaks seldom and briefly; enough to show us that he is a perfect gentleman, and not enough to show us much more, but for certain wonderfully fine little touches, in which the love that he keeps under lock and key peeps forth and will not be hidden. We can fancy the eloquent silence of such a man, how he would throw himself heart and soul into the Duchess's accounts, and keep her books as they were never kept before; how she, a sensitive, highly strung woman, could not fail to note this dumb devotion, and rate it at its true value. All this is matter of long standing, when the play begins. Webster had no business with the soft uncertain hints of early love; his passions are all grown-up, like his characters. Young though she be in years, the Duchess is old in prudence, and in that absence of girlish coquetry, which leads her, knowing that Antonio will never woo her of his own accord, to place the ring herself upon his finger. It is one of the most ungrateful tasks in the world to depict a woman making the first advances to a man; even Shakespeare achieved a very doubtful triumph with such a character as Helena in *All's Well that Ends Well*.

There is something absolutely repugnant to good taste about the leap-year lady. All the more wonderful for its refinement is the scene in which the Duchess of Malfi declares her love. All the struggles that it cost her, all the womanly shame which almost chokes her utterance at the last moment, are in those few words, spoken to her maid, Cariola, before Antonio enters.

> 'Good dear soul,
> Leave me; but place thyself behind the arras,
> Where thou mayst overhear us. Wish me good speed,
> For I am going into a wilderness
> Where I shall find nor path nor friendly clue
> To be my guide.'

She had told no one what she meant to do, driven to do it by the intolerable loneliness of her position, knowing that even Cariola would not dare to approve her—but do it she must and would. Pretending that she wants to make a will, she questions Antonio (rather vaguely) about the state of her finances.

> 'ANT. I'll fetch your grace the particulars of your
> Revenue and expenses.
> DUCH. Oh, you're an upright treasurer; but you mistook,
> For when I said I meant to make inquiry
> What's laid up for to-morrow, I did mean
> What's laid up yonder for me.
> ANT.   Where?
> DUCH.   In Heaven.
> I'm making my will (as 'tis fit princes should)
> In perfect memory; and I pray, Sir, tell me
> Were not one better make it smiling thus,
> Than in deep groans and terrible ghastly looks,
> As if the gifts we parted with procured
> That violent distraction?
> ANT.   Oh, much better.
> DUCH. If I had a husband now, this care were quit.'

Here after the Elizabethan manner, they fence a little with puns on the word 'will,' Antonio counselling her to marry again, and to give her husband all, even her 'excellent self.'

> 'DUCH. St. Winifred, that were a strange will.
> ANT. 'Twere stranger if there were no will in you
> To marry again.
> DUCH.   What do you think of marriage?

ANT. I take it as those that deny purgatory;
It locally contains or heaven or hell.
There's no third place in 't.
DUCH.   How do you affect it?
ANT. My banishment, feeding my melancholy,
Would often reason thus.
DUCH.   Pray let us hear it.
ANT. Say a man never marry, nor have children,
What takes that from him? Only the bare name
Of being a father, or the weak delight
To see the little wanton ride a cock-horse
Upon a painted stick, or hear him chatter
Like a taught starling.
DUCH.   Fie, fie, what's all this?
One of your eyes is blood-shot; use my ring to 't.
They say 'tis very sovran; 'twas my wedding ring,
And I did vow never to part with it
But to my second husband.
ANT.   You have parted with it now.
DUCH. Yes, to help your eyesight.
ANT.   You have made me stark blind.
DUCH.   How?
ANT. There is a saucy and ambitious devil,
Is dancing in this circle.
DUCH.   Remove him.
ANT.   How?
DUCH. There needs small conjuration when your finger
May do it; thus: is it fit?
[She puts the ring on his finger.
He Kneels.]
ANT.   What said you?
DUCH.   Sir!
This goodly roof of yours is too low built!
I cannot stand upright in't, nor discourse
Without I raise it higher. Raise yourself
Or, if you please, my hand to help you; so.
ANT. Ambition, madam, is a great man's madness
That is not kept in chains and close-pent room,
But in fair lightsome lodgings, and is girt
With the wild noise of prattling visitants,
Which makes it lunatic beyond all cure.
Conceive not I'm so stupid, but I aim
Whereto your favours tend; but he's a fool

> That, being a-cold, would thrust his hands in the fire
> To warm them.

So long as she leaves him room to doubt for an instant whether she can live without him, he will not take advantage of her confession. In generosity, at least, he is her equal. As he says himself:—

> Were there not heaven nor hell,
> I should be honest; I have long served virtue,
> And never ta'en wages of her.

But his grave and noble rejoinder only fires her still more, and, with an outburst of magnificent, appealing scorn, she flings all vain equivocation to the winds:—

> The misery of us that are born great!
> We are forc'd to woo, because none dare woo us:
> And as a tyrant doubles with his words,
> And fearfully equivocates, so we
> Are forced to express our violent passions
> In riddles, and in dreams, and leave the path
> Of simple virtue, which was never made
> To seem the thing it is not. Go, go, brag
> You have left me heartless: mine is in your bosom;
> I hope 'twill multiply love there: you do tremble.
> Make not your heart so dead a piece of flesh,
> To fear more than to love me; Sir, be confident.
> What is it distracts you? This is flesh and blood, sir;
> 'Tis not the figure cut in alabaster
> Kneels at my husband's tomb. Awake, awake, man,
> I do here put off all vain ceremony,
> And only do appear to you a young widow.
> I used but half a blush in 't.
> Bless Heaven this sacred Gordian, which let violence
> Never untwine.
> ANT. And may our sweet affections, like the spheres,
> Be still in motion.
> DUCH.   Quickening, and make
> The like soft music.

It would be difficult anywhere to surpass this scene, beginning with deli-cate raillery, half feigned to hide the passion underneath, ending in words that leave us doubtful with Cariola, 'whether the spirit of greatness, or of woman, reign most in her.'

The second act is the weakest and least interesting in the play. The sudden illness of the Duchess, accompanied by other untoward circumstances, raises suspicion at Court, and on the night of the child's birth a treacherous courtier, Bosola, who has sold himself to Prince Ferdinand and the Cardinal, picks up a scheme of its nativity which Antonio had carelessly dropped. By this clumsy expedient the brothers are made aware of their sister's condition, though still ignorant of the child's father. It seems as if the genius of Webster, overpowering when at its height, lost itself in the petty details of an intrigue which many inferior men might have rendered less cumbersome. His very wealth of imagination stifles him. The simplest and most apparent things cannot be discovered without an altogether disproportionate outlay of time, tricks and trouble. It is like cracking a walnut with the proverbial sledge-hammer. Nor does he sufficiently explain the envy of the brothers, since, even had their sister died a widow, her son by her first husband (whose existence seems to have been conveniently forgotten further on), must, one would think, have succeeded to the dukedom. Of course it may be said that Webster wrote in the first place for the stage, and that on the stage effect is everything and causes matter little; but it is certainly strange that he took no pains to correct this and other inaccuracies of the same kind, when 'The perfect and exact Copy, with diverse things printed, that the length of the Play would not beare in the Presentment,' was afterwards given to the public.

A few years of happiness behind the curtain, and the tragedy begins again. The Duchess is now the mother of three children; strange rumours are rife about her in the Court, but nothing certain has yet been discovered, and no one suspects the cold, discreet Antonio. A charming scene of light, graceful banter, while Cariola is brushing her lady's hair, shows us how free they are from any sense of peril. While she is still speaking, Antonio steals away unnoticed into an inner chamber, taking Cariola with him, for the fun of making her angry.

> DUCH. Doth not the colour of my hair 'gin to change?
> When I wax grey, I shall have all the Court
> Powder their hair with arras to be like me.
> You have cause to love me; I entered you into my heart
> Before you would vouchsafe to call for the keys . . . .
> For know, whether I am doomed to live or die,
> I can do both like a prince.

Suddenly Ferdinand bursts upon her, dagger in hand. She meets his frantic and violent abuse with a quiet declaration that, as she is married already, it does not and cannot apply to her, and when his fury rather increases than subsides, she tries to reason with him in the gentle persuasive tones that would naturally befit a sister pleading with an angry brother. He is her twin brother, her old playfellow; surely to him she may speak as she would deign to speak to no one else. She herself gets a little angry, only a little, that he should insult her, as if she had committed some great crime by following the dictates of her nature:

> Why should only I,
> Of all the other princes of the world,
> Be cased up like an holy relic?
> I have youth and a little beauty.

It is difficult to explain Ferdinand's excessive brutality excepting on the ground that he is rather mad already, and the audience must be nearly as glad as the Duchess when at length he rushes from the room, bidding her expiate her dishonour by killing herself with the dagger that he leaves behind him. Her one thought is how to shield Antonio. She will dismiss him instantly and roughly from her service, following him afterwards in secret as soon as the coast is clear. She has just time to warn him before Bosola enters the room, and she begins to act—unfortunately to over-act—her part. Antonio, taking the cue, submits with well-assumed dignity, but the practised courtier, comprehending the whole situation at a glance, only allows him to escape that he may win the heart of the Duchess by his pretended indignation at the way in which she dismisses her old servant. What could be more straightforward and uncourtierlike than his sharp reproof?—

> For know an honest statesman to a prince
> Is like a cedar planted by a spring.
> The spring bathes the tree's root, the grateful tree
> Rewards it with his shadow; you have not done so.

It gains the Duchess in a moment. With the royal generosity of a nature that can do nothing by halves, she at once confides to him everything, and yields to his treacherous counsel that she should go on pilgrimage to Loretto, the better to colour her flight. There is a cunning little touch of character in Cariola's objection:—

> In my opinion
> She were better progress to the baths at Lucca,

Or go visit the Spa in Germany, for, if you will believe me,
I do not like this jesting with religion,
This feigned pilgrimage.

The maid is an excellent foil for the mistress everywhere; timid and conventional, where she is bold and independent; distrustful, when she is confident; able to hope, when she despairs; faithful and loving always, the very type of an ordinary nature desperately bound to follow a much higher one, which it cannot understand.

Of the many strange things in this play, nearly as original in its faults as in its beauty, the scene at Loretto is one of the strangest—being indeed no scene at all, but merely an elaborate dumb-show, by which the Cardinal and various other people decree the banishment of the Duchess and her family to the accompaniment of 'a ditty,' the authorship of which is modestly disclaimed by Mr. John Webster in the margin. As it is not a very striking ditty, we are not surprised at this: but the marvellous pathos of the scene which follows can only heighten our wonder that he should have turned what might have been the central point of his drama into a mere bit of pantomime. Of course Bosola overtakes the fugitives, and the Duchess is made to accompany him back with two of her children, while Antonio and the eldest are suffered to escape.

DUCH. I know not which is best,
To see you dead or part with you. Farewell, boy,
Thou art happy that thou hast not understanding
To know thy misery; for all our wit
And reading brings us to a truer sense
Of sorrow. In the Eternal Church, sir,
I do hope we shall not part thus.
ANT.   Oh, be of comfort.
Make patience a noble fortitude.
And think not how unkindly we are us'd,
Man (like to cassia) is prov'd best being bruis'd.
DUCH. Must I, like to a slave-born Russian,
Account it praise to suffer tyranny?
And yet, O Heaven! thy heavy hand is in 't.
I have seen my little boy oft scourge his top,
And compar'd myself to 't: nought made me e'er go right,
But Heaven's scourge-stick.
ANT.   Do not weep.
Heaven fashion'd us of nothing, and we strive

> To bring ourselves to nothing. Farewell, Cariola,
> And thy sweet armful. If I do never see thee more,
> Be a good mother to your little ones,
> And save them from the tiger. Fare you well.
> DUCH. Let me look upon you once more, for that speech
> Came from a dying father. Your kiss is colder
> Than that I have known an holy anchorite
> Give to a dead man's skull.
> ANT. My heart is turned to a heavy lump of lead,
> With which I sound my danger. Fare you well.
> DUCH. My laurel is all withered.

Can we not hear the very tones in which they speak, *les larmes dans la voix*, she with her books and flowers and little children, he with his masculine dislike of tears, and dim, heavy foreboding of worse evils to come? Surely the fable about a salmon and a dog-fish with which the act concludes must have been one of those things which were omitted during 'the presentment.' What actress would ever risk marring the effect of an intensely pathetic scene by such a queer bit of humour as this?—

> A salmon, as she swain unto the sea,
> Met with a dog-fish, who encounters her
> With his rough language: Why art thou so bold
> To mix thyself with our high state of floods?
> Being no eminent courtier, but one
> That for the calmest and fresh time of the year
> Dost live in shallow rivers, rank'st thyself
> With silly smelts and shrimps, and darest thou
> Pass by our dog-ship without reverence?
> O (Quoth the salmon) sister, be at peace,
> Thank Jupiter we both have passed the net.
> Our value never can be truly known
> Till in the fisher's basket we be shown:
> In the market then my price may be the higher,
> Even when I am nearest to the cook and fire.
> So to great men the moral may be stretched:
> Men oft are valued high when they are most wretched.

We cannot imagine that the gifted Mrs. Betterton, who played the part in 1678, ever allowed herself to go so far, though perhaps Master R. Sharpe, the first Duchess on record, may have managed it.

But now the plot thickens, the stage grows dark, the voices sink to a whisper, as the numbered hours pass quickly on to doom. Still the Duchess bears her imprisonment nobly, still her brother's cruelty has not availed to break her spirit. If she will not die naturally, she must be tortured to death; so much the better. Ferdinand comes to visit her in the darkness (having sworn never to see her face), and holds out, for her lips to kiss, a dead hand, which he feigns to be that of her husband. Bosola shows her 'behind a traverse' the bodies of Antonio and her children ('fram'd in wax, by the curious master in that quality, Vincentio Lauriola'). No cry, no lamentation does she utter. The sight freezes the blood in her veins, she cannot faint, nor weep away her ice-bound anguish; nothing but death can help her:—

> BOS. Come, you must live. . . .
> DUCH.   Good comfortable fellow,
> Persuade a wretch that's broke upon the wheel
> To have all his bones new set, intreat him live
> To be executed again. Who must despatch me?
> I account this world a tedious theatre,
> For I do play a part in 't 'gainst my will.
> BOS. Come, be of comfort, 1 will save your life.
> DUCH. Indeed I have not leisure to attend
> So small a business.
> I will go pray. No: I'll go curse.

She speaks wildly, yet with a certain restraint that never lets us forget she is 'Duchess of Malfi still.' Once before, when she was helping her husband to escape, she quoted Tasso, now she remembers Portia. In her old artificial life alone in the Court, books had been her only reality; now in the tremendous realities of her own life they came back to her. Wonderful indeed is this picture of a mind hovering on the edge of madness, yet still intact:—

> DUCH. What hideous noise was that?
> CAR.   'Tis the wild concert
> Of madmen, lady, which your tyrant brother
> Hath placed about your lodging: this tyranny
> I think was never practised till this hour.
> DUCH. Indeed I thank him; nothing but noise and folly
> Can keep me in my right wits, whereas reason
> And silence make me stark mad; sit down,
> Discourse to me some dismal tragedy.
> CAR. O 'twill increase your melancholy.

DUCH.   Thou art deceived,
To hear of greater grief would lessen mine.
This is a prison?
CAR.   Yes: but thou shalt live
To shake this durance off.
DUCH.   Thou art a fool.
The robin red-breast and the nightingale
Never live long in cages.
CAR.   Pray dry your eyes.
What think you of, madam?
DUCH.   Of nothing.
When I muse thus, I sleep.
CAR. Like a madman, with your eyes open?
DUCH. Dost thou think we shall know one another
In the other world?
CAR.   Yes, out of question.
DUCH. O that it were possible we might
But hold some two days' conference with the dead,
From them I should learn somewhat I am sure
I never shall know here. I'll tell thee a miracle;
I am not mad yet, to my cause of sorrow.
Th' heaven o'er my head seems made of molten brass,
The earth of flaming sulphur, yet I am not mad:
I am acquainted with sad misery,
As the tanned galley-slave is with his oar;
Necessity makes me suffer constantly,
And custom makes it easy. Who do I look like now?
CAR. Like to your picture in the gallery;
A deal of life in show, but none in practice:
Or rather like some reverend monument
Whose ruins are even pitied.

Even yet she has not suffered enough. The madmen are let loose into the room to play their horrid gambols before her sleepless eyes, and deafen her with their wild songs and shrieks. As they are retiring, Bosola, disguised as an old man, enters to dig her grave. Apparently she recognises him after the first moment, for her dignified

Am I not thy duchess?

would seem to recall the former passages between them. She has lost all sense of fear—nay, even of that solemn awe which sometimes takes the place of fear at the last hour. Nothing shows the intensity of her grief more than her complete indifference:—

> DUCH. And thou comest to make my tomb?
> BOS.   Yes.
> DUCH. Let me be a little merry.
> Of what stuff wilt thou make it?
> BOS. Nay, resolve me first, of what fashion?
> DUCH. What! do we grow fantastical in our death-bed?
> Do we affect fashion in the grave?
> BOS. Most ambitiously; princes' images on their tombs do not lie as they were wont, seeming to pray up to heaven; but with their hands under their cheeks (as if they died of the toothache). They are not carved with their eyes fixed upon the stars; but as their minds were wholly bent upon the world, the self-same way they seem to turn their faces. . . .
> *[A coffin, cords, and a bell, produced.]*
> Here is a present from your princely brother,
> And may it arrive welcome, for it brings
> Last benefit, last sorrow.
> DUCH.   Let me see it.
> I have so much obedience in my blood,
> I wish it in their veins to do them good.
> BOS. This is your last presence chamber.
> CAR. O my sweet lady.
> DUCH. Peace; it affrights not me.

It is the 'nothing can hurt me now' of Marie Antoinette. Calmly she listens to her dirge, assisting at her own funeral before she dies. The naïve horror of it strikes chill, like a deep expression on the lips of a child:—

> DIRGE
> 'Hark, now everything is still;
> This screech-owl and the whistler shrill,
> Call upon our dame aloud,
> And bid her quickly don her shroud.
> Much you had of land and rent;
> Your length in clay's now competent.
> A long war disturb'd your mind,
> Here your perfect peace is sign'd.
> Of what is 't fools make such vain keeping?
> Sin, their conception; their birth, weeping.
> Their life a general mist of error.

Their death a hideous storm of terror.
Strew your hair with powders sweet,
Don clean linen, bathe your feet;
And (the foul fiend more to check)
A crucifix let bless your neck.
'Tis now full tide 'tween night and day;
End your groan, and come away.
CAR. Hence, villains, tyrants, murderers: alas!
What will you do with my lady? Call for help.
DUCH. To whom? to our next neighbours? They are mad folks!
Farewell, Cariola.
I pray thee look thou giv'st my little boy
Some syrup for his cold; and let the girl
Say her pray'rs ere she sleep. Now what you please?
What death?
BOS. Strangling. Here are your executioners.
DUCH.   I forgive them.
The apoplexy, catarrh, or cough o' the lungs,
Would do as much as they do.
BOS. Doth not death fright you?
DUCH. Who would be afraid on 't,
Knowing to meet such excellent company
In th' other world?
BOS.   Yet methinks
The manner of your death should much afflict you;
This cord should terrify you.
DUCH.   Not a whit.
What would it pleasure me to have my throat cut
With diamonds? or to be smothered
With cassia? or to be shot to death with pearls?
I know death hath ten thousand several doors
For men to take their exits; and 'tis found
They go on such strange geometrical hinges
You may open them both ways: any way (for Heaven's sake)
So I were out of your whispering. Tell my brothers
That I perceive death—now I'm well awake—
Best gift is they can give or I can take.
I would fain put off my last woman's fault;
I'd not be tedious to you.
Pull, and pull strongly, for your able strength
Must pull down heaven upon me.
Yet stay, heaven's gates are not so highly arched
As princes' palaces; they that enter there

Must go upon their knees. Come, violent death,
Serve for mandragora to make me sleep.
Go tell my brothers, when I am laid out,
They then may feed in quiet.
[They strangle her kneeling. Ferdinand enters.]
FERD.   Is she dead?
BOS. She is what you would have her.
Fix your eye here.
FERD.   Constantly.
BOS.   Do you not weep?
Other sins only speak, murder shrieks out.
The element of water moistens the earth,
But blood flies upwards and bedews the heavens.
FERD. Cover her face—mine eyes dazzle—she died young.

She was beyond fear, but her woman's nerves remained to her; she felt they must give way if the strain lasted much longer. She had borne the cries of the madmen, but she could not bear this 'whispering' about her; it made her nervously eager for the last horrible moment. Rest, rest was all she wanted; let them give it her quickly.

A modern writer would have had the play end here in the silence and darkness of the chamber of death, but Webster and Co. were not artists in the modern sense of the word. Their villains were not mere bits of wickedness contrived to throw into relief the virtues of the innocent and then sink back into the nothingness from which they came, but flesh and blood, and as such to be punished, at the risk of outraging the moral feelings of the audience. Furthermore, they saw that after any dreadful deed the world went on its way very much as usual; that a curtain did not fall for ever on the perpetrators of it; that the vacant place was filled up somehow; and it was this great truth of continuity which they sought to impress by leading our thoughts on to the future. It shows a change in the temper of the English people that the last scene of *Hamlet* should never be acted now. In those old days the fall of a monarch was nothing compared to the fall of monarchy, which would have thrown too deep a shadow even for tragedy. At any cost there must be a successor to the throne. *The Duchess of Malfi* fulfils both these conditions. It would be tedious to follow the web of plot within plot which gradually brings about the mutual murder and assassination of the Cardinal's mistress, of Antonio, of the Cardinal himself, of Ferdinand, and of Bosola, but there is one exquisite scene in which Antonio, walking unconsciously near to his wife's grave, is made to hear the echo taking her voice:—

> DEL. Hark, the dead stones seem to have pity on you,
> And give you good counsel.
> ANT. Echo, I will not talk with thee,
> For thou art a dead thing.
> ECHO. Thou art a dead thing.
> ANT. My Duchess is asleep now.
> And her little ones, I hope, sweetly. O Heaven,
> Shall I never see her more?
> ECHO. Never see her more.
> ANT. I marked not one repetition of the Echo
> But that; and on a sudden a clear light
> Presented me a face folded in sorrow!
> DEL. Your fancy merely.

How well the old playwrights understood that sense of foreboding, the very existence of which many people in a less robust age are willing to call in question!

The Cardinal's last soliloquy over his Dante has a touch of grimly irresistible humour that reminds one of the fantastic devils of some ancient German artist:—

> I am puzzled in a question about hell.
> He says in hell there's one material fire,
> And yet it shall not burn all men alike.
> Lay him by. How tedious is a guilty conscience!
> When I look into the fishponds in my garden
> Methinks I see a thing armed with a rake
> That seems to strike at me.

On the whole, my Lord Ferdinand, with his laugh, 'like a deadly cannon that lightens ere it smokes,' is excelled in wickedness by my Lord Cardinal, who never laughs at all. Ferdinand had the grace to go mad after his sister's death at any rate, but the Cardinal seems to have felt no ill effects whatever, except the trifling little vision afore said.

Quiet and brief are the closing words of this great tragedy. No sentimental moralising, no weak appeal to pity, no feeble buttressing about of virtue with pasteboard-angels; by her own right she stands.

> MAL. Oh, sir, you come too late.
> DEL.   I heard so, and
> Was arm'd for 't ere I came. Let us make noble use
> Of this great ruin, and join all our force

To establish this young hopeful gentleman
In 's mother's right. These wretched eminent things
Leave no more fame behind 'em than should one
Fall in a frost, and leave his print in snow;
As soon as the sun shines, it ever melts
Both form and matter; I have ever thought
Nature doth nothing so great for great men
As when she 's pleas'd to make them lords of truth.
Integrity of life is fame's best friend,
Which nobly (beyond death) shall crown the end.

We know almost nothing of the life and death of John Webster. No monument, however humble, rises over his tomb, no *hic jacet* points to his last resting-place. It was Thomas Middleton who, with a true prescience of the things that pass away and the things that endure, wrote over his friend's 'maisterpeece':—

Thy Epitaph only the Title bee,
Write Dutchesse, that will fetch a teare for thee.

~

Mrs. Gaskell
[From the *Times Literary Supplement*, 14 September 1906]

Almost a hundred years have passed away since Mrs. Gaskell was born, and the lustre of her fame is yet undimmed. She was no wild poet of love among the moors like Charlotte Brontë, no learned professor of the analytical arts and sciences like George Eliot; but the special graces of womanhood are hers rather than theirs, and it was not without reason that Dickens called her his 'Scheherazade,' for the innate gift of storytelling is greater in her than in her sisters. Charlotte Brontë swept the world away in the storm of her passion; George Eliot conquered it with the power of understanding; Mrs. Gaskell forced it to weep for pity, charmed it with the sunny wit of a lady who was never in all her life mistaken for a man, even when she signed herself Cotton Mather Mills, Esq. She did not write at first because she must, but because she would. The sufferings of the poor had entered into her soul like iron. She felt them as Dickens and Kingsley felt them; she threw her strength into a mighty effort for peace—not on compulsion—for Christianity, not for compromise. The fairness and sweetness of *Mary Barton* make it the noble thing it is. She never for an instant would admit that bitterness could be right. She did not justify the bitterness of the poor, though she pointed out to the rich what had caused that bitterness. It is not only by taking a gun and shooting some one that a man breaks the commandment, 'Thou shalt do no murder': yet, if he breaks it thus, he makes himself the equal of the man who has let another starve, and both alike must pay in blood the awful penalty of hatred, both alike must be brought to acknowledge that love is the only power that can rule the world. A strange subject, this of 'forgiveness.' With one sternly ironical reference, 'Oh, Orestes! you would have made a very tolerable Christian of the nineteenth century!' Mrs. Gaskell takes us back to the dead-alive conviction of the ancient world, still walking ghost-like in the midst of us, that justice is vengeance; in the light of her own unquenchable faith she leads us on to see that justice is forgiveness. She never imagined anything more true to human nature at its highest than this bending of the spirit of one heart-broken father to the spirit of another, in stricken, reverent submission to the Father of all.

Perhaps it was reserved for a woman to show that, in women guiding their conduct by the Bible, forgiveness may become, as it rarely becomes in men, an instinct. Electra, in the old world, urged on Orestes; the idea of forgiving her mother never entered her heart. Desdemona not only forgave the Moor her death, but tried, with her last breath, to take the guilt of it upon herself. Shakespeare clearly held that, when a woman loves, forgiveness is involuntary, she does not even think of it; but what would Desdemona have felt towards any one who had killed Othello? Isabella's forgiveness of Angelo, the would-be murderer of her brother, in *Measure for Measure*, is the result of thought, of pity for his betrothed, of resolution—it is not instinctive.

'They'll know it sooner or later, and repent sore if they've hanged him for what he never did,' replied Job.

'Ay, that they will. Poor soul! May God have mercy on them when they find out their mistake!'

So says Jane Wilson, mother of the accused Jem in *Mary Barton*, without any consciousness of the sublimity of her words. Mrs. Gaskell might have taken for her motto the name of one of Tolstoy's most delicate short stories, 'Where love is, there is God also!' In her unending compassion, in her love of the gentleness of the frail and the old, in her clear condemnation of violence as a remedy, her scorn of military prowess, she resembles the great Russian more closely than any of her countrymen. But he was still to come; and, though she afterwards withdrew them—it may be from a sensitive feeling that they revealed too much of her inmost heart—she found in Uhland's words a link to fasten to her work the memory of two spirits.

Mary Barton was begun, by her husband's earnest desire, to relieve her own mental sufferings after the death of her little son. Terrible indeed must have been the thoughts from which the thoughts that gave it birth were a relief! The men and women who were writing about the dreadful year of '48 had great courage. They did not fly from the most agonising problems of life and conduct. They stood up and faced them—not with the indifferent calm of the student, careful only to note and compare, but with the enthusiasm of the Church militant. They recognised the fact that these problems, although so troublesome, are for the most part expressed in simple terms. They were not so much concerned about the form of religion a man ought to belong to, or which woman he ought to have married, as they were about whether he did or did not understand the words of Christ—whether he was or was not doing his duty in that state of life unto which it had pleased God to call him. Humour—imagination—eloquence—they did not use these gifts for their own solace, they pressed them into the service of those who had none. 'To my thinking, them that is strong in any of God's gifts is meant to help the weak!' Job Legh expresses the thought of all the leading writers of that time. As the sonnet, which had been as a lute for lovers, became in Milton's hands a trumpet, so the novel, which had been once (and was to be again) a toy, became in theirs a sword with which to fight in the cause of the oppressed. Away—but only for a time—went the dashing, splashing fellow with the white plume, that we are all so fond of! Thackeray wrote a novel without a hero; Dickens took a child for his; Charlotte Brontë made a heroine out of a poor little plain governess; George Eliot showed how much more gentlemanly than a gentleman a carpenter might be. Mrs. Gaskell, more daring than any of them, rivalling Victor Hugo's choice of a convict, as she lay sick and sad upon her sofa, took an assassin. She called the book at first 'John Barton'; and of the living, moving characters on that wonderful canvas he is the first to arrest our attention, the last that we could forget. Small wonder is it that an Oldham labourer should have taken his children regularly to look at the house where she lived who thus could read the heart of the working man, who thus could turn all hearts towards him! From the moment when we meet him at the stile and he takes Jane Wilson's baby, to the moment when he dies, forgiven, in the arms of the man whose only son he has murdered, loving and pitying sympathy follows him step by step. Some of his words strike on the conscience now like hammers:—

'When I was a little chap they taught me to read, and then they never gave no books.'

'It 's not much I can say for myself in t' other world. God forgive me; but I can say this, I would fain have gone after the Bible rules, if I 'd seen folk credit it.'

'I would go through hell fire, if I could but get free from sin at last.'

'It was not long I tried to live Gospel-wise, but it was liker heaven than any other bit of earth has been.'

Apart from its own intrinsic interest, the first considerable work of a great novelist awakens our curiosity for the hints it may contain of future excellence. Jem's first sight of John Barton after his disappearance, going to the pump to fetch a jug of water—that vision of the murdering, not the murdered man, haunts memory like the spectre that it really is. The woman who wrote this could not have found any great difficulty in writing, as she afterwards did, one of the best ghost stories in existence, the 'Old Nurse's Story,' and the finer parts of that unequal study, 'The Poor Clare.' We might have known, too, that no hero of hers could be really base. She held a brief for the heroism of everybody as against the heroism of a favoured few. We might have known that her heroines would be, for the most part, maidenly, pretty, wayward creatures, with their hearts in the right place. 'It is but a day sin I were young,' says the old woman, trying to comfort the heartbroken girl in 'Half a Life-time Ago' with the reflection that life is short; and the poetry of this, and of many other faithful servants, may be, to some slight extent, foreshadowed by the old nurse in *Mary Barton*. But we could never have foreseen the great ladies of the old *régime*, the doctors, the ministers, the enchanting spinsterhood presided over by Miss Galindo and Miss Deborah Jenkyns, who were to charm us in *Cranford*, in the far less popular but just as perfect picture, *My Lady Ludlow*, and once again in *Wives and Daughters*. Mr. Gray, in the second of these three works, meets and beats Amos Barton, Mr. Gilfil, and Mr. Tryan on their own ground. We say it with hesitation—we are not unaware of the indignant protest likely to follow—but still we assert that we should greatly have preferred his ministrations. And if, for ourselves, we had the joy and privilege of calling in a doctor from the realms of fiction whenever we are not quite well, it would be Dr. Gibson, and not the husband of Rosamund Lydgate, for whom we sent. There is barely the shadow of a doctor, there are no clergy at all, in *Mary Barton*. Perhaps the symmetrical scheme of the work, the strong, sharp contrast of employers and employed, did not admit of people in an intermediary position. The *grande dame*, naturally, did not exist in Manchester.

It might be, if we had to choose our favourite character from this long gallery, My Lady Ludlow whom we should select. There are no such ladies now. You might search England through, from end to end, and never find the like of this lovely, beneficent little old despot. What need of heroes, or of heroines either, if she be there? There are certain words that never must be mentioned in the ancient house where she lives, with the five 'young gentlewomen' who are to her instead of her dead daughters, and the twenty old servants to do the work of the twenty other old servants who are too old to do any work at all. 'Musk' is one of these words.

She cannot abide such a vulgar and common odour. Lavender and woodroffe are her favourite perfumes—lavender and woodroffe and the scent of decaying strawberry leaves in the autumn, noted by Bacon for its fragrance, and cherished by her because only a nose of gentle birth can detect it. What would she have done in these days of Board Schools and of cheap literature, she who had sheltered the victims of the French Revolution and believed that it would happen over again in England if the children of her tenants were taught to read! How beautiful she is in her gracious tyranny, in her courtly, determined opposition, in the rigid reserve of her strong feelings, in the endless outgoing of her generous heart to those who are in distress! Etiquette itself becomes a kind of worship with such a centre. The sorrow that plunged the village into mourning comes to us like a personal sorrow when Mr. Gray goes up to her to break to her the death of her only son—'and she had been the joyful mother of nine!' The sky is darkened because she sits, a whole month long, in a black room, with lamps and candles, seeing no one except her maid, reading nothing except the names of all her children on the first page of the family Bible. We breathe again as soon as she comes back to rule her little kingdom. When she conferred a favour it was always as though she asked it; and she 'never forgave by halves.' When she sends for a destitute, one-legged sailor to manage her property we tremble for her justification, we feel she must be right, we trust her as she trusts herself and him, through all the mistakes of the first year. Certainly it was hard upon her that a Baptist baker, a person of no social standing whatever, should so contrive that his fields were in much better condition than hers. Even Miss Galindo only partially softened her heart towards this person.

'I daresay,' said Miss Galindo, 'he would have been born a Hanbury, or a lord, if he could. . . . It was his misfortune, not his fault, that he was not a person of quality by birth.'

'That's very true,' said my lady, after a pause for consideration, 'but, although he was a baker, he might have been a Churchman.'

Dear Miss Galindo! She 'often thought of the postman's bringing her a letter as one of the pleasures she should miss in heaven'—a reflection which occurred to Dr. Johnson also, when he was talking to Bozzy. But it will never do to begin about Mrs. Gaskell's old maids. They are as inexhaustible as Rembrandt's Jews. Let us end rather with a friendly counsel to every one who does not already own these 'unappropriated blessings' to purchase them at once.

~

Queen Elizabeth
[A lecture given to some working-girls]

Queen Elizabeth, when first she saw the light of day, was a great disappointment. She was a girl—she ought to have been a boy.

Why ought she to have been a boy? To fight Scotland on one side and Ireland on the other—France and Spain over the water. Why ever all these countries were the enemies of England, it would take me too long to tell. But you must remember, please, that they were—four strong enemies, Ireland, Scotland, France and Spain.

We are every one of us made up of a great many different people. Elizabeth was made up of her grandfather, who was cautious and prudent, of her father, who was impetuous and charming, of her mother, who was vain, had a high temper, and never cared what she did, so that she got her own way. The impetuous and charming father very soon grew tired of the vain, light-minded mother, and cut off her head. If four stepmothers can make up for one real mother, then the baby Elizabeth was not to be pitied; but can they? At first she was so badly off that she had not even clothes enough to wear. In later life she more than made up for this deficiency, for she wore a new dress every day, 365 dresses in a year. She liked to be painted as a goddess. When she appeared as a 'mere woman' it was in a dress all over eyes and ears to show that she could see and hear everywhere—which, after all, was not quite like a mere woman. There were always two opinions about her. People who admired her called her Gloriana, Oriana, The Virgin Queen, The Maiden Queen, Great Elizabeth, and Good Queen Bess. People who did not admire her called her a serpent and a viper.

At the time when she was young, it was quite a new idea that little girls ought to be taught as well as little boys, and her impetuous and charming father was very full of it. So she learnt many things, useful and ornamental too. She was only six when she gave her little brother, Edward, a cambric shirt that she had made herself. She learnt to write a most beautiful hand. When we see her faded old yellow letters now, we wish that we could write like that. She could talk to learned men in Latin and Greek, to Frenchmen in French, to Italians in Italian. Our dear old Queen Victoria liked to stop an organ-grinder, if she met one when she was out driving, to show that she could talk to him in Italian: and Queen Elizabeth—it is one of the few points that they have in common—was very fond of showing off this accomplishment. Strange: but we have all of us these little vanities. She was but eleven years old when she wrote a letter in Italian to the last of the four stepmothers. She was taught to dance most wonderfully too—she went on dancing when she was over seventy—and she could play and sing. There were no pianos then. Her favourite instrument was called, appropriately, the virginals.

After the very disagreeable experience of having too few clothes when she was a baby, Elizabeth, as a girl of twenty, underwent the still more disagreeable experience of having too little liberty—of being shut up in prison. Her brother was dead. Her half-sister, Mary, who was queen now, was afraid that she wished to be queen. No doubt she did, but she was much too clever to say so. When next you go to the Tower of London, please ask the warder to show you Traitor's Gate. Through this gate every one who was thought to be a traitor to the queen had to pass—and to pass through that gate was very often the first chapter of a story that ended with somebody's head rolling away from somebody's body on to a scaffold. 'I am no traitor!' Elizabeth said proudly, when she was carried thither one wet Palm Sunday. One of the lords in attendance offered his cloak to keep her from the rain, but she put it back 'with a good dash,' and setting her feet on the first step of the stair, she said, 'Here landeth as true a subject, being prisoner, as ever landed at these stairs, and before Thee, O God, I speak it, having none other friend but Thee alone.' Afterwards she was in prison in the country, at Woodstock, instead of being in prison in London. Her gaoler, a gentleman named Bedingfield, was very strict; when she was going to be removed somewhere else, she took a diamond for a pen, and amused herself with scratching on a window-pane a little imaginary talk between them. Bedingfield speaks the first line:

'Much suspected by me:
Nothing proved can be,
Quoth Elizabeth, prisoner.'

When she became queen, she told Bedingfield that, if she ever wanted any one safely kept in prison, she should give that person to him. Was he pleased, do you think, or was he not? A double-edged compliment like that was very much in her line. Even her enemies—even the people who called her a serpent and a viper—confessed that she had 'a spirit full of incantation,' by which, I suppose they meant that she charmed them somehow, even while they detested her. At that time she was 'pleasing rather than beautiful,' tall and well-proportioned, her complexion somewhat olive; in her portraits she is always dazzlingly fair, but then she would not allow any shadows to be painted on her face, and as a child she is said to have smashed all the looking-glasses she could find because they did not make her pretty enough. She had beautiful eyes, full of spirit and sparkle, 'and above all a beautiful hand,' which she liked to show. Her curly hair was of a light auburn, and her nose was like the beak of an eagle. Far away, in a great old library at Durham, hangs a picture of her half-sister Mary, and I have heard it said that any one who happens to be sitting in the room while parties of visitors are being shown through, may hear very different opinions expressed about this likeness. 'Ah, poor suffering, deeply religious lady! Looks like a perfect saint,' says one man. 'O the horrid, cruel bigot! Looks like a hateful fiend!' says another. So I do not know whether you would have thought Elizabeth beautiful or not. It would have depended on your opinion of what she did, I think, for 'handsome is that handsome does.' If you had been a child you might have liked her, she was always kind to children.

When her enemies tried to puzzle her with questions, to bewilder her, to prove that she held wrong views about the Supper of the Lord, she wrote one verse which is worth all the rest of her poetry put together.

> Christ was the Word and spake it.
> He took the Bread, and brake it.
> And what the Word doth make it,
> That I believe, and take it.

Elizabeth was staying at Hatfield (where Lord Salisbury, who is of the same family as her great minister, Cecil, Lord Burghley, now lives), when the news arrived that her sister, Mary, was dead—that she was queen. Did she show how happy she was? Did she come flying up to London? Not a bit of it! She was much too clever. She sent a messenger to find out whether it was true. But before that messenger could get back again—and we may be sure that he rode as fast as his horse's legs could carry him—the lords of the council had found their way to Hatfield and greeted this young lady of twenty-three as their sovereign mistress. She fell upon her knees. 'This is the Lord's doing,' she said, 'and it is marvellous in our eyes.'

From the first she showed clearly enough that she meant to rule by the love of her people. She often appeared amongst them, she travelled hither and thither, and visited this town and that, she smiled with pleasure when they cheered, she encouraged them to come in crowds about her, she made them beautiful speeches. She led them to feel that she cared for their approval. If they disapproved strongly of anything she did, she altered her conduct. Only on one point did she hold her own. They were excessively anxious that she should marry. And she was excessively anxious that she should not.

Her brother-in-law, Philip of Spain, proposed to marry her. It would be quite easy, he said. She would only have to ask the Pope to forgive her for not having been a Roman Catholic before. She took a month to think about it—decided that it was not so easy after all—and said, No thank you.

Afterwards, at different times, there were hovering about the throne an Archduke of Austria, a Prince of Sweden, two of the sons of the King of France, one of whom she called 'her little French frog' (she used to wear a brooch made like a frog that he had given her), a Scottish Earl, a great English nobleman, Lord Leicester, who had an unenviable reputation for poisoning people he was tired of, and built the loveliest Almshouses in the world, which are still to be seen with dear old men in them at Warwick. She liked their admiration, and all the beautiful presents they gave her. She would not say Yes and she would not say No. She was just like the White Owl in the Fairy Story. 'What shall I do? I have promised to marry them all.'

'Here is a great resort of wooers and controversy among lovers,' wrote Lord Burghley. 'Would to God the Queen had one, and the rest honourably satisfied.'

The Spanish Ambassador, as was natural, expressed himself still more strongly: 'This woman is possessed with a hundred thousand devils, and yet she pretends to me that she would like to be a nun, and live in a cell, and tell her beads from morning to night.'

'I have had such a torment with the Queen's majesty as an ague hath not in five fits abated me,' says poor Lord Burghley again. And we can fancy how bad it must have been when the Queen's majesty condescended to inform him, 'I will have here but one mistress, and no master.'

I am sorry to say that when people are very vain, they often grow very jealous too. Elizabeth was extremely anxious to believe what all her lovers told her—that she was the most beautiful princess in the world; but she found it difficult, because there was another very beautiful Queen close by, Mary Stuart, Queen of Scotland, and all her courtiers said that *she* was the most beautiful princess in the world. One day she asked the ambassador from Scotland, 'Which is the most beautiful, the Queen of Scotland or myself?' That is the kind of question that never should be asked, even by Queens. The poor ambassador was very much put to it. At last he found a safe answer. 'My mistress is the most beautiful lady in Scotland,' said he, 'and your majesty is the most beautiful lady in England.' But Gloriana was not going to let him off like this. 'Which is the tallest?' she inquired. There the ambassador felt quite happy, for Mary of Scotland was the tallest. 'Then,' said Queen Elizabeth, 'she is too tall, for I myself am neither too tall nor too short. And can Queen Mary play on the virginals? Does she play well?' 'O yes,' the ambassador said, 'she plays pretty well for a Queen.' After dinner, Elizabeth arranged that he should be brought in, by chance as it were, just as she was playing herself, and playing very well indeed. She let him listen for a few minutes, and then she jumped up, very much surprised, pretended to strike him with her hand, and said she was not accustomed to play before men, she only did it when she was alone, so that she might not feel too sad. But—since he had contrived to hear them both—did Mary play better than she did, or did she play better than Mary? The ambassador was obliged to say that she played the best, but by this time he had had enough of comparisons, which might be rejected in Scotland, and he asked leave to go back. Elizabeth insisted on keeping him two days longer, however, that she might show off her dancing. She could not miss such a chance of finding out whether she or the Queen of Scotland would be looked upon as the best partner at a ball. The ambassador answered that Mary of Scotland 'danced not so high nor so disposedly as she did.' And what that means, goodness only knows. 'Oh, how I wish I could see her!' Elizabeth said; 'quietly you know, without any fuss.' 'Why not?' rejoined the ambassador. 'Why should not your majesty disguise yourself as a page, and come back to Scotland with me?' Whereupon Elizabeth heaved a sigh, and said, oh! if she only could.

The Queen of Scotland was not so particular about marrying as Queen Elizabeth. She married three times—each time more unhappily than the last—quarrelled with her great nobles— fled into England. She was bound to be Queen of England, if Elizabeth died, and many a great English nobleman, the Duke of Norfolk among the rest, aspired to be her fourth husband. But they were all afraid to mention the subject before Elizabeth; and Norfolk, at the bare idea of it, 'fell into an ague, and was fain to get him to bed without his dinner.' Remarkable how many people got the ague when they had anything to say to the Queen!

This Duke of Norfolk, finding that he dared not woo openly, made a plot to marry Queen Mary. Off went his head!

There is no doubt that, even in prison, where Elizabeth took good care to keep her, she was extremely dangerous, especially when the Pope excommunicated Queen Elizabeth, which made it lawful for any Roman Catholic to murder her. There were plots everywhere—plots among her own servants. Those who loved her—those who saw that Protestant England was growing and thriving under her wise rule—those who dreaded the most terrible confusion if she died—urged her to put Mary Stuart to death. 'I cannot put to death the bird that has flown to me for succour from the hawk,' she said. She kept the bird in a cage—in several different cages—for nineteen years. One man after another tried to get her out. One man after another failed. One head after another rolled on the scaffold.

Meanwhile, in France, the Massacre of St. Bartholomew took place, and nearly all the French Protestants were murdered. Queen Elizabeth put on mourning when she received the French Ambassador, and all the court were robed in black. It was, Lord Burghley told him, the most dreadful deed that had been done since the Crucifixion. The Protestants of England became still more alarmed about the life of their Queen, and an association was formed to protect her. At last the Queen's council urged upon her, that she *must* put Mary to death. There could be no safety, either for her or for England, while that beautiful bird lived.

'The life of Mary is the death of Elizabeth—the death of Mary is the life of Elizabeth.'

Elizabeth hesitated—shifted her ground—said she would—said she would not—hoped Mary would die of herself—wished some one would murder her without being asked to do so. Elizabeth was like a certain king in Shakespeare who 'would not play false, and yet would wrongly win.' But we cannot get rid of our perplexities in this way. Mary Stuart went on being perfectly well, and nobody tried to kill her. On the contrary, they tried to kill Elizabeth. At last her mind was made up. Even then she tried to lay all the blame on others. She could not endure to think that her people would call her what she really was—unjust and cruel. Nothing can ever make a wrong deed right. She had no business to take the life of the bird that had fled to her for succour.

Mary of Scotland had heard a sound of hammers in the hall of the Castle of Fotheringay, where she was imprisoned, and as she heard it, the picture of a scaffold rising crossed her mind—but she could not believe it. 'Day had followed day, and she heard no more.' 'The blow, when it came at last, therefore came suddenly.' Lord Shrewsbury and the Earl of Kent brought her the news.

Philip of Spain, the brother-in-law who had proposed to marry Elizabeth, made up his mind, now that Mary Queen of Scots was dead, and her son a

Protestant, to conquer England for himself. Never mind, said Queen Elizabeth's sailors, 'Twelve of her Majesty's ships are a match for all the galleys in the King of Spain's dominions.' Then was there a rush and stir throughout the realm of England. Then was there racing and chasing everywhere. Then were the beacon-fires lighted upon a hundred hills. The Armada is coming! The Armada is coming! And from the whole of England there rose a mighty shout of No!

It was Lord Howard of Effingham who commanded our fleet against the Duke of Medina Sidonia, the Commander of Spain. The winds and the waves fought upon our side—and Drake, the glorious sailor who had sailed round the world in three years in the Golden Hind, and sunk the great big ships of Spain, and brought back to the Queen £75,090 and the jewels that she wore in her crown at a state banquet after Philip had complained of his behaviour. She said the Golden Hind was to be kept for ever in memory of him, and she gave him a little golden ship that is still an heirloom in the Drake family. The ladies of Spain were so much afraid of Drake that one of them said she dared not go in a boat with the King himself upon the water, lest Drake should capture her. They said he had a magic mirror in which he could see always whatever the King of Spain did. He carried indeed the magic mirror of imagination, which enables people to see many things. In among the great big heavy lumbering vessels he sent a few old ships (no crews at all) that he had set on fire—and the great big heavy lumbering vessels blazed up, and sank.

'He blew with His breath, and they were scattered.' So ran the inscription upon the medal struck for the Armada, giving the glory to God alone. It was indeed a mighty deliverance.

Great things Queen Elizabeth did—great things she left undone. The Dutchmen, who rebelled against her brother-in-law, Philip, invited her to be their Queen. If she had accepted the invitation, it is probable that the Boer War would never have been fought. But she was very prudent. She was an excellent housekeeper. She did not think that she had money enough to fight the battles of Holland as well as those of England, and she declined the proposal. All the people of England, she said, were her husbands—perhaps she did not care to have thousands of Dutch husbands as well. She sent the Earl of Leicester to take care of them; but the only result of that was that England lost the bravest and best of all her knights, Sir Philip Sidney, the one man who dared to speak the truth to her without getting an ague. She became more and more of a tyrant. Even Sir Walter Raleigh, the gallant who first attracted her attention by spoiling a beautiful new cloak that she might not have muddy shoes—the brave discoverer who discovered potatoes, and tobacco, and a new province in America, which he called Virginia in honour of the Virgin Queen—even Sir Walter Raleigh was very much afraid.

'Fain would I climb, but that I fear to fall,' he wrote one day—as usual upon a window—as usual, I suppose, with the point of a diamond. There were so many diamonds about the world just then. And the queen took another, and underneath 'Fain would I climb, but that I fear to fall,' she wrote: 'If your heart fail you, do not climb at all.' Needless to say that Raleigh did climb—but he fell, whether his heart failed him or no. His friend Spenser sang of Elizabeth as the Fairy Queen. When Spenser died, and was buried in Westminster Abbey, it is said that all the other poets went to the funeral and dropped their pens into his grave. There lies, for all we know, the pen of Shakespeare. Shakespeare lived longer than Queen Elizabeth. He paid her a magnificent compliment in the Midsummer Night's Dream, when he said that the God of Love had no power to wound her, for, however hard he might try, 'still the imperial votaress passed on, in maiden meditation, fancy-free.'

But as the years went on he saw the imperial votaress, the Fairy Queen, grow very old and wrinkled, very capricious and cruel, and when she died he did not pretend to mourn for her.

For the last years were not the best. After the years of plenty came the years of famine. She did not like to think she was growing old—we none of us do. When the Bishop of St. David's preached before her on the text, 'Lord, teach us to number our days, that we may apply our hearts unto wisdom,' she did not thank him as was her usual custom when the sermon was over. No, no! 'You might have kept your arithmetic for yourself,' said she; 'but I see that the greatest clerks are not the wisest men.'

Lord Burghley died; and it was long before she could mention his name without tears. She seems to have cried very easily, by the way, judging from the large number of persons who enjoyed the privilege of seeing her weep. When she was really in deep distress, she did not cry, I think, she sighed. A kinsman of hers, Robert Carey, says that he heard her sigh a few days before her own death, 'forty or fifty great sighs,' just as she sighed after the death of the Queen of Scots. Burghley was dead, but still she had his son—the son whom she had made Sir Robert Cecil—to help her.

Leicester was dead, and a new favourite reigned, the Earl of Essex, but he was very disobedient, and though, after his fits of naughtiness, he said he was like Nebuchadnezzar, content to eat grass like an ox and be wet with the dew of heaven, till it should please her Majesty to restore him to his understanding, she could not make him thoroughly subservient. She did not want him to eat grass like an ox, she wanted him to do what she told him to do, and as he would not—off went his head! The people here in London loved him. He had tried to win them to come with him to the Queen, but when the moment arrived, they all got the ague. Nevertheless they could not forgive the Queen for cutting off his head. She began to lose the thing that she cared for most of all—the love of her people. Once more she made them a magnificent speech.

'It was Elizabeth's last great triumph.' The world was passing away from her. They tried to flatter and to amuse her as of old. 'When thou dost feel creeping time at thy gate,' she said to her godson, who had been writing verses for her, 'these fooleries will please thee less.' It was then that Robert Carey found her sitting on cushions on the floor sighing heavily. What was she thinking of? Not of Hatfield, not of Tilbury, not of the glorious days at Kenilworth when Leicester feasted her, not even of Essex and his rebellion and his doom. Before her eyes there stood that awful scaffold at Fotheringay—the woman, the sister Queen, the bird which had fled to her for succour and died. 'Then, upon my knowledge, she shed many tears and sighs, manifesting her innocence that she never gave consent to the death of that Queen.' In vain did Carey try to comfort her. Next day was Sunday, and she had ordered a room to be prepared for her to go to chapel. Long the courtiers waited; she did not come. At last one of the grooms of her chamber came out. She was not able to go so far as to the great room. She would have service in the private room close by. There cushions were laid for her.

Four days and nights she lay upon her cushions, neither eating nor sleeping, suffering from restlessness and thirst. She was weary of life, and yet she shrank from death. The Lord Admiral Howard, the person who had most influence, was sent for. He came and knelt beside her, kissing her hands, imploring her with tears to take some food. After a long while she let him give her a little broth; and then, encouraged by success, he ventured to urge upon her that she should go to bed.

'If you saw such things in your bed,' she said, 'as I see when I am in mine, you would not persuade me.'

At last Cecil appealed to her in the name of her people. 'To content the people,' he said, 'your Majesty must go to bed.' At this all her old spirit returned. 'The word *must* is not used to princes,' said she. 'Little man, little man, if your father had lived, you durst not have said so much, but you know I must die and that makes you presumptuous.' Cecil was bidden to go—and all the rest, except Howard. 'My lord, I am tied with a chain of iron about my neck,' she murmured. Worse and worse she grew—more and more silent, speaking only twice or thrice in the twenty-four hours—at last, for one long day and night, remaining utterly silent, her finger in her mouth, her 'rayless eyes' open. Her ladies could hardly stand the strain.

The Archbishop and her chaplains came to her. He told her that she ought to hope much in the mercy of God. Her piety—her zeal—the admirable work that she had done—and so on and so on. 'My lord,' she said, 'the crown, which I have borne so long, has given enough vanity in my time. I beseech you not to increase it in this hour, when I am so near my death.' Long and late he remained, praying by her side. At last he left her; she sank into a deep sleep from which she never awakened. 'A few hours later Robert Carey was riding hard along the North Road,' to be the first to tell the son of Mary Stuart that he was king.

It was a strange thing to stand in Westminster Abbey between the grave of Mary Stuart and the grave in which Elizabeth was laid by the side of her own half-sister, Mary. If she had never lived—had never reigned—London would not have been what it is to-day, and every one of us here in this room to-night would have been different. Every church, every chapel, would have borne a different character. The river would not have been crowded, as it is to-day, with those great ships that are the road to another England across the seas. The shops would not have been as they are now—nor the city. Up to Elizabeth's time business was carried on in the open street, or—a curious place for it—in the nave of St. Paul's Cathedral. In her time Sir Thomas Gresham built the Royal Exchange, and asked her to come and open it. Londoners, as a rule, are not fond of new inventions, and he could not feel sure whether he would be successful in letting the new shops that he had built all round. So he went, cunning man (he was the sort of man that Elizabeth could understand), to the leading shopkeepers and told them that, if they would be so kind as to come, and put out their wares in the windows, and light a few candles in honour of Her Majesty's condescension in appearing there, to make everything look prosperous and bright and pretty, he would let them have the shops rent-free for a year. Of course they came—of course they lighted the candles, of course they availed themselves of the kind permission to stay a year rent-free, of course at the end of the year they did not want to leave, they took the shops on—and you know—or perhaps you do not know—what land is worth now in the city. If Queen Elizabeth had never lived and reigned, we should not have had an excellent Poor Law. Whenever we go against it, poverty grows more, whenever we observe it, poverty grows less. If Queen Elizabeth had never lived and reigned, Shakespeare would never have written as he did, and you would not have been going to see—as I hope you do sometimes go to see—A Midsummer Night's Dream, Macbeth, Henry V., and many another wondrous play. If Queen Elizabeth had never lived and reigned, Sir Walter Scott would not have written Kenilworth, a novel that you have all read, I am sure, or one that you all mean to read some day—a finer novel than any one alive could write now. Would that we had kept the Great Eliza's love of music, and the love of it in the England of her day! In every little barber's shop there hung two instruments upon the wall, so that one customer and another might amuse himself singing and playing while the other was shaved or had his hair cut. I am afraid she and her people would not have thought much of music-halls and musical comedy; they liked better music than that, and prettier words too.

'So passes away the glory of the world!' As a dream—as a shadow—as the tinkling sound of the thin and delicate old music of Queen Elizabeth's day. 'Death lays his icy hand on kings.' They are gone, but none of the merciful forgetfulness that will shroud your name and mine is permitted to throw a veil over the ill that they have done. Terrible are their responsibilities. If they have failed and fallen, what are we that we should judge? We cannot but shudder at the cruelty of Elizabeth—we cannot but disdain her monstrous vanity. When we have done shuddering at her and despising her, let us re-member that it was she who made England what it is—and she who set the great example of love towards her native land—and she who fired the hearts of men to fight for justice.

~

The Friendly Foe
[From *The Cornhill*, March 1898]

'Not for a moment,' said the Count, with great dignity, 'did I suppose so.'

I thanked him.

He pressed my hand.

There followed one of those awkward pauses which are apt to follow on a supreme moment. He had just informed me that he did not for an instant suppose that I preferred any consideration before honour. The wind was driving the rain against my window as if it were a human thing that must be chased from the wide world without. The flames were leaping up the chimney, as if they owned some kinship with the wind and were rushing to meet him. I wanted to be alone, to enjoy the uproar in peace. How to get rid of the Count I did not know. Why the Count insisted on staying, I did not know. As he was going to shoot me, or I was going to shoot him, at eight o'clock the next morning, it seemed to me that this was waste of time; but you cannot make a remark of that kind to a guest, and he happened to be in my room.

'Let me ask you one thing!' said the Count. 'You are a generous enemy. Though not in your first youth, you are younger than I am, and you have not been out before. I would not take you at a disadvantage. Do you believe in the soul's future?'

'A most unnecessary question,' I said lightly. 'In a few hours one of us will have answered it for good and all.'

He frowned.

'You do not believe in it. I am reduced to a most unpleasant extremity. Unless you can reassure me upon this point, it is impossible for me to fight you. Unless I fight you, I am dishonoured.'

'Why should it be impossible?' I asked. But that the Count was by birth and breeding a perfect gentleman I might have suspected his courage.

'It gives me an unfair advantage,' he said, gazing steadily at me out of his deep-set eyes. 'You fight, believing death is death. I fight, believing death is birth. I know something of your chivalrous nature. If I kill you, I, in my own opinion, set free a soul. If you kill me, you, in your own opinion, commit murder. I would not have you tortured in after life by this reflection. Once more I tell you, it is impossible for me to fight unless you give me some assurance. Once more I ask you, Do you believe in eternal life?'

'I am fully sensible of your kind consideration for my feelings, but permit me to observe that I do not see what right you have to ask that question.'

'You decline to answer it?'

'I do.'

'Then our affair is settled. I also decline to fight.'

He bowed, and walked towards the door.

'Stay!' I cried. 'What are you going to do?'

He laid his hand upon a pistol.

'No,' I said. 'Why?'

'You leave me no other choice.'

It was absurd of me to object to his shooting himself when I had no objection whatever to shooting him with my own hand if I could. But it was just this one phrase *if I could* that made a difference. The alternative was too cold-blooded; I felt bound to prevent it.

'Could it not be arranged ——?' I spoke nervously, only to gain time, in the confusion of the moment.

'You are not the man I took you for,' he said.

This time he did not bow as he turned towards the door.

'You do not seem to be aware,' I remarked, 'that you are exposing me to a sense of blood-guiltiness far more onerous than that which you deprecate. If I am to be a murderer, at least allow me to feel that I did the deed myself, not that I compelled some one else to do it. Do you think that you are treating me fairly? You put a premium upon lies. You leave no other course open to me. By all that is held most sacred I swear to you that I believe in eternal life.'

And rising, I laid my hand upon my heart.

'Sir,' said the Count sternly, 'would you die with a falsehood on your lip? You do not believe it?'

'No,' I said, 'I do not. I merely wished to show you to what extremes you are driving me. But you are right. Between gentlemen this sort of thing is a mistake, even in jest. You do not leave this room till you have promised to fight me to-morrow!' and I threw myself across the door. I was the younger and the stronger man.

With perfect gravity the Count sat down in an armchair. The wind was howling more loudly than before; the flames had sunk lower.

I became conscious of the absurdity of the situation. Nothing short of flood, fire, or earthquake could put an end to it in a fitting manner. There we were bound to stay till we died of starvation, unless one or the other would compromise his dignity. As the little I knew of the Count made me feel certain that nothing would ever induce him to compromise his, I compromised mine.

'Count,' I said, 'this is a ridiculous position for both of us. My presence causes you an intolerable *gêne*, and yours, the whole night through, would scarcely be agreeable to me. Let us consider the thing dispassionately. You will not fight me because I do not hold an opinion which you, rightly or wrongly, hold to be necessary for my future happiness, if I live; *i.e.* you do not object to kill me, because you think no one can die, but you do object to poison the remainder of my mortal existence. If you do not fight me, you will shoot yourself, for you would be unable to survive your honour. That is the case on your side. Now for mine. I have an instinctive dislike of suicide, either for myself or for any one else whom I respect. It may be a mere prejudice, but so it is. If, therefore, you blow out your brains, it will seriously affect my peace of mind, inasmuch as I shall consider myself to a certain extent responsible. But fair fight is another thing altogether. It is now five o'clock. According to our agreement we meet at eight to-morrow morning. I shall need at least five hours' sleep beforehand, or I shall not take steady aim. Allowing full time to dress, breakfast, and get to the *rendezvous*, I ought not to go to bed later than two. Between five o'clock this evening and two to-morrow morning there are nine hours. Now, these nine hours I will promise you, on my word of honour as a gentleman, to spend on the investigation of a question that does not interest me in the least, and on which, but for you, I should never, in the whole course of my life, have spent nine minutes—if you, on your part, will promise to meet me at eight to-morrow. If, by that time, I can answer your question in the affirmative—and I know already that it is not by words alone that you will judge whether I speak the truth—well and good! Let us fight! Whichever way the duel ends, you will have the satisfaction of thinking that I have gained a belief which, but for you, I should not even have wished to gain. If, on the contrary, I retain my present scepticism, we will shoot ourselves instead of each other. *Voilà tout!* It is a pity: the country will lose two possible defenders instead of one, but I do not see how that can be helped. Is it a bond? Will you meet me at eight?'

The Count rose from his chair: his eyes shone.

'I have the greatest pleasure in accepting your generous proposal,' he replied, 'more especially as I am quite convinced that no one could study this question for nine hours without answering it as I myself have been taught to answer it. As for the method of study, that of course must be left to yourself. The "Phaidon" of Plato ?'

'No,' I said carelessly, moving away from the door to let him pass. 'My tastes are not philosophical. I shall sit by the fire for three hours, and think it over in my own way. (I dare not engage that my mind will not wander to other subjects. La Girouette danced adorably in the ballet last night.) Then, if you have no objection, I shall dine out and go to a ball, the invitation for which I accepted some time ago, so that my absence would be remarked: and, when the clock strikes eleven, I shall betake myself to my confessor. If serious reflection, if the sight of the vanities of this world, if the consolation of religion, all put together, cannot persuade me to believe in the immortality of the soul, it will be a hopeless affair indeed; for I am sure nothing else could.'

The Count sighed.

'It is a strange way to take,' he said; 'but let no man judge for another. I myself was led to believe by a series of events which, to any other than myself, would appear almost incredible. I pray that you may be rightly directed. In the meantime I wish you good-night. I shall not retire to rest before two o'clock.' He bowed again and went out.

When he was gone I threw myself down in the chair which he had occupied, that I might enjoy to the full the luxury of being alone. The Count's presence had become a hideous oppression to me during the last quarter of an hour. I had felt as if he would never go—as if he were a nightmare, as if he were the Old Man of the Sea, as if he were a whole crowd of people in himself, and made the room stuffy. I ran to the window and flung it open; the wind rushed in and puffed the curtains out, and rioted amongst my books and papers, bathing me, body and soul, in freedom. I heaped up faggot after faggot, and stirred them into a blaze that might have set the chimney on fire. Then, between wind and flame, down I sat, according to contract, to consider that part of myself which was more subtle than either.

I found it to the full as difficult as I had expected. The old arguments were no newer. 'We should like to go on living very much. Therefore we think we shall. But as we really do not know, we will not die till the last possible moment.' They came to little more than that, so it seemed. As I was without this strong prepossession in favour of life, I failed to recognise their cogency. Besides, to have that man going on for ever? I had a strong prepossession in favour of his extinction, even if it necessarily included my own. I loved myself less than I hated him. Not that I had any reason to hate him. He was everything that he should be, which gave a sort of zest to my abhorrence, reduced it to a fine art—made it essential, not a mere accident. Our natures were antagonistic. I could have forgiven another for murdering me more easily than I could forgive him the fact of his existence in the same universe with myself. He jarred upon my every nerve. My eyes rebelled at the sight of his face, my ears at the sound of his voice, the touch of his hand caused an electric shiver of repulsion. He annihilated all but the animal part of me; when he was in the room I knew his dog had more of a soul than I. And, by the strangest freak of fancy, it was this man who, more than any one I ever met, had the faculty of conjuring anything like it out of me, who insisted not only on my believing it was there, but that it would go on being there for ever and ever.

'No, Count,' I said, as I watched the sparks go up the chimney; 'keep your immortality to yourself! I would not share it with you for the asking,' and through my mind there flashed the old emblems of the transitoriness of life—the dream, the shadow, the morning mist, the snowflake, the flower of the grass, the bird flying out of the darkness, through the lighted hall, into the darkness again. I was reassured concerning its momentary character. 'And yet,' I said to myself, 'the Count has a very strong will. If any man had the power to insist on living, in defiance of all the rules of Nature, that man would be the Count. Perhaps it is his excessive vitality which is burdensome to ephemeral creatures like myself. It is as if he absorbed their proper part whenever he came near them.'

So thinking, I took out my pistols and cleaned them, not without a certain pleasure. I had had enough of my own society by the time the clock struck eight, and was well inclined to seek that of others.

The dinner to which I was invited was given by Princess X., who lived in an apartment on the third floor of the Hotel Z. She was going to a dance that night—the same that I meant to attend— and the party beforehand would be, she informed me, quite a small one, consisting only of myself and a few intimates. It so happened that I was rather late. Seeing the door of the lift open, I got in. The darkness had prevented me from noticing that in one corner there was already something that looked like a downy ball of white, with a very small head coming out of it. I would fain have beaten a retreat, but it was too late; the porter stepped in after me and we began to ascend.

'Oh!' said the little lady, with a gasp, putting out a small white hand to catch hold of me. I am afraid that I did not attempt to reassure her. It was all over in a minute.

The lift stopped. I made way for her to get out. She turned round to me, smiling and blushing.

'I beg your pardon,' she said, 'I never have been in one before. It is so unlike anything else—when you are not accustomed. I suppose you also are going to dine with *Marraine?*'

'I have not the pleasure of calling the Princess X. Marraine,' I replied; 'but if she has the pleasure of calling you her godchild, we are bound for one destination. Allow me to ring the bell.'

As she passed into the hall, the clearer light shone, for a moment, on her soft brown curls, and glanced, reflected, in her mirthful eyes.

We entered the drawing-room almost at the same moment. As the Princess rose to make us acquainted, she laughed again and said quickly:

'No, no, Marraine, it is too late. I was introduced by the lift, as the greatest coward this gentleman has ever known, quite three minutes ago.'

The Princess took her hand.

'Well! well!' she said, 'was there ever such a naughty debutante? It is a pity, as you took each other up so pleasantly, that you cannot take each other down also. But there I must interfere.'

'It is cruel of you, Princess. Fate was much kinder. But,'—I turned to the younger lady—'may I presume to ask your hand for the first dance?'

'You may,' she said merrily; 'but I hope you know what you are asking. It is the first dance that I have ever given any one.'

'Where is your father?' asked the Princess.

'Kept at home by a letter from the Prime Minister. He begs that you will excuse him; for nothing else would he have given up this party. He is coming later on, to take me home. I hope he will not come till very late indeed, if that is all he cares for. He did not feel sure that it was meet for me to go out to dinner alone, even to the house of my godmother, but he said that he did not want to disappoint you, and I think,' she put in candidly, though very demurely, 'he did not want to disappoint me either. I should have died of vexation if I had had to stay at home.'

The Princess laughed.

'That makes it serious. And seriously, my love, you are quite right. Unless one is dead or dying, one should keep one's dinner engagement. And, while I think of it,' she added, addressing herself to me, 'I must positively engage you to dine with me to-morrow. I expect the Prime Minister, and I cannot be left alone to entertain him. Eight o'clock, do you hear? He will have to leave early, so mind you are in time.'

'To hear is to obey. Unless I am dead or dying I will keep my dinner engagement.'

'I think I am sure of you then. You never looked better in your life.'

'Dinner is on the table,' said the Princess's butler.

The ground floor of the hotel had been engaged for the dance. The fiddles were already striking up when I, in company with the other gentlemen of the party, entered the room. My promised partner was standing beside the Princess, busily inscribing the names of various aspirants on her card. I thought she might be better employed inscribing mine, and said so. She gave me the card, and I availed myself of the vacant spaces that appeared on it.

'Quick, quick!' she cried. 'There is the music! Are you not longing to be off?'

Dancing varies inversely as the character of the lady who dances. With her it resembled nothing so much as flight. She scarcely seemed to touch the ground with her feet, she was as light as one of the feathers on her cloak. The music mounted to my brain as we went whirling round and round together. I felt as though I were a spirit chasing another spirit. I forgot everything else, and when it stopped I could not have told whether we had been dancing hours or moments. I had begun in another state of existence.

'Ah!' she said, 'your step goes well with mine.'

How I filled up the intervals when I was not dancing with her I do not know. Once, while we were standing together in the recess formed by a window, a great moth flew in and made for the lighted candelabra over our heads. There was a quick change in her.

'O save it, save it!' she cried, clasping her little hands together in wild distress.

I caught the creature in my handkerchief and let it out again. When I returned to her she was pale and trembling.

'He is quite safe,' I said. 'Do not be unhappy! After all, what would it matter if he did burn himself? In proportion, he would have lived much longer than we shall.'

'No, no,' she said. 'We live for ever.'

Her words sent a thrill of recollection through me.

'Do we?' I said in a gentler voice. 'If you tell me so, I will believe it.'

'Why yes, of course we do!' she said. 'I never heard any one say that we did not. Shall we finish this dance?'

It was the last opportunity that I had of talking to her. I think I was engaged in conversation with some one else when, later on in the evening, I heard her pleading tones close behind me.

'Only one more! O let me stay for only one more!'

In an instant she was at my side.

'I must go,' she said. 'I must have one more dance before I go. I do not know where my partner is.'

It was irresistible, though I had a humiliating sensation that she asked me only because there was no one else at hand. She broke away just when the delirium of enjoyment was at its height.

'No longer' she cried. 'Not a moment more! That was perfect. Good-night!'

She made me a tricksy sign of adieu with her fan, and tripped away; she could hardly help dancing as she moved.

I stood bewildered for a moment, then rushed to the door that I might see her as she passed to her carriage. She was leaning on her father's arm as she went down the steps. The link-man raised his torch to guide them, and a sudden glare of light showed me the features of the Count.

I drew a long breath.

'It is as well that I am going to fight that man to-morrow,' I thought. 'If not, he would inevitably have been my father-in-law. In the first place, I have not enough to marry upon; in the second, we should have made the little thing miserable between us.'

The wind detached a fragment of her swansdown cloak. I stooped and picked it up.

Practically speaking, the disposition of my time had been in no degree influenced by the Count's grotesque requirement. I had intended all along to stay at home until eight o'clock, to dine with the Princess X., to go to the dance, and to visit the dearest friend that I had in the world. He was a Dominican monk, of great learning and acuteness, resident in the monastery of S. Petrox, about half a mile off. We were old schoolfellows, and, though our ways of life were very different, he had never lost the ascendency over me which, as a boy, he had understood how to gain.

He was busy reading when I entered his cell; he laid his finger on his lips, to show me that I must not interrupt him.

After a long pause, he closed the great volume reverently and asked me what I wanted at that time of night.

'I want an immortal soul.'

'Curious!' he remarked, pushing his spectacles up on his forehead, 'I have just been studying the question of the soul.'

'Well! what is the result of your investigations?'

'My friend,' returned the Dominican, 'what would it avail were I to tell you? I know your mind upon these subjects.'

'That is more than I know myself, then—more than I should ever have wished to know but for a strange occurrence.'

I told him all the circumstances of my conversation with the Count,—not mentioning his name, of course.

'You have helped me at many a difficult pass before now,' I said. 'Help me again. Pour out the contents of that great volume upon my head!'

'You would be as wise as you were before. I know you, *amico mio*. You own no teacher save experience.'

'What is the experience that can make a man believe in that of which he has none? Tell me, that I may seek it.'

'Is there any one in the world of whom you are really fond?' said the Dominican.

For the fraction of a second I hesitated.

'Forgive the question! It is of no importance. There is one way by which you can be brought to believe, but it *may* cost you your life. Are you willing to risk it?'

'I am bound to preserve my life until to-morrow morning.'

'So far I can guarantee it, if you are careful to obey. For the rest, you are indifferent? Well and good! Understand that I, on my part, am running a great risk for your sake. If what I am about to do were to become known, I should incur excommunication. My fellow-churchmen would say that I was endangering a soul within the fold to save one that is without. So be it! You are my friend. You are, I know, an actor of some experience. Do you think that you could personate me?'

'With your instructions, I have no doubt that I could.'

He rose, and took from his cupboard a priest's robe and a little cap.

'You have just recovered from an illness; you must wear a *beretta*. You are close shaven; that is well. Under the *beretta* your hair is not too long. Be sure to recollect that you are still subject to cold—that you must on no account take it off. Before we go any further, oblige me by taking an oath—a solemn oath. First, that, whatever may happen, you will attempt no resistance; secondly, that you will never reveal the names of those amongst whom I am going to send you, nor any of the circumstances which you may be called upon to witness. Before you swear, reflect! The possession of a secret of this kind implies considerable danger. Is it worth the risk?'

'A strange question for one of your calling to ask!' I retorted; 'I am no priest, but I think it is.'

'Is there anything in the world that you hold sacred?' said the Dominican.

I drew the bit of swansdown from its resting-place, profaning the one true sentiment that was in me with a laugh. As for my friend, he never even smiled.

'That will do!' he said. 'Swear upon that!' I did so.

'You are now a penitent before me. I have heard your confession. I am about to absolve you. Take accurate note of everything that I say, and reproduce my words, as nearly as you can, when you are called in to the death-bed.'

'You spoke to me as if I were a woman,' I observed, when he had finished.

'You are quite right,' said the monk. 'Now let us reverse the parts. Do you absolve me, as if I were a woman!'

'I repeated the form of words which he had just gone through.

'*Evviva!*' he said, when I had done. 'You might have been born in a cassock.'

At the same moment I heard the hooting of an owl in the garden below. He started, and looked at the clock.

'Late!' he said. 'That is the carriage. We have not a moment to lose. Let me recommend you to keep silence from the time you leave these doors to the time when you are set down again. If you say a word more than is necessary, I will not answer for the consequences. I shall await you here on your return. Remember your oath. Then, bending forward as if he feared the very walls would hear, he added in a whisper:

'*Take no refreshment in that house.*'

He touched the back of a volume of the *Via Media* as he spoke; part of what had appeared to be the bookcase sprang open and disclosed a winding stair. Without another word, he pointed down it, taking a light to show me the way. At the last turn of the steps he left me.

I felt the cold breath of the night lifting my hair. Then I was suddenly seized and blindfolded; whether by two or more persons I could not be sure, for I was taken by surprise in the darkness. Determined to adhere to the prescribed conditions of the adventure, I made no sound and I heard a whisper:

'No need to gag him, he has his cue.'

In a moment strong arms had lifted me and were carrying me along—over the grass, as I judged, for there was no ring of footsteps. I was let down gently enough upon the seat of a carriage, and away we went like the wind. How long it took, which way we went, whether there was any one else in the carriage, I have no idea. A steady hand must have held the reins. We were going at a breakneck pace, yet we never encountered the smallest obstacle, nor did I even feel a jolt. Thus was I whirled along through the night, as little able to see as if I had been sleeping.

We stopped at last. I was helped out, and guided, as I judged by the mouldy smell, into some cellar or disused passage, at the end of which there were steps. Presumably, they led up into a house, for when we trod on level ground again, the atmosphere was dry and warm, and, to my great surprise, I heard the tones of a piano in the distance, familiar tones at the sound of which my heart beat, though it was a minute before I recollected that I had heard them last as I was leaving the ball-room. We went up many stairs, down many more and up again, the sounds growing more and more distinct as we advanced. They ceased abruptly, the bandage was removed, and I found myself standing alone in a tiny room, lit by one small red-shaded lamp. I tried the door, but it was locked; mysterious, for I had heard no turning of the key! A piano stood open, but there was no music upon it. A book lay on the sofa, as if some one had just tossed it down there. On the outer side there was no window at all; in the other wall was a recess, formed by three little windows of painted glass, through which a light from below shone dimly, by way of the Madonna and two attendant saints.

I waited a long time, but no one came. The stillness grew oppressive. I threw myself on the sofa, and tried to read, but the air was heated and magnetic—it seemed to thrust itself between me and the lines. I looked at the first page of the book to see if there were any indication of the owner, but there was none. I then tried several others, all with the same ill success. Clearly they had been read with much affection, for they were often marked with a pencil: but there was never any name in the beginning, and from one or two of them the fly-leaf had been removed.

On a sudden the light reflected from below went out; the saints became indistinguishable.

My curiosity got the better of me. I resolved, come what would, to open one of those windows; to have nothing but a pane of glass between me and the unknown was too strong a temptation. I pressed with all my strength against the woodwork of the centre one: there was a slight, a very slight, yielding; it seemed to give on darkness. I moved the lamp cautiously, so as to concentrate its beams upon the chink, and pressed again. For an instant I caught sight of the dark figure of a man, bending over a table, in front of a fireplace, far down below. Then the window gave an ominous creak. I closed it, and sat breathless. Whether the man had heard? I inclined to think that he must have. Presently there were footsteps outside.

'In half an hour,' said a man's voice.

'In half an hour,' said a woman's.

It was music echoing a discord. The key turned in the lock; the little lady of the swansdown cloak entered, and shut the door behind her. I cannot now conceive my feelings at that moment; but I had just presence of mind enough to recollect that I should be turned out if I did not sustain my part. We saluted each other in the usual way, and she knelt down before me. For the first time it darted through my mind that she was going to make a confession—and to me? A strong repugnance to hear overcame every other consideration. If I could mock that creature, I must be a fiend incarnate. Yet how, with safety to my friend—and to myself—prevent her? I took a step backward. She raised her eyes appealingly. I frowned and turned away.

'This is some jest,' I said sternly. 'I was sent for to attend a deathbed. Take me to the penitent.'

'It is I that am dying.'

'Are you mad?' I demanded. 'Many a time have I seen death; never with eyes and cheeks like these.'

'He that has not an hour to live is no nearer death than I am. I shall not see the sun rise to-morrow.'

She spoke with such conviction that I staggered back, reeling under the shock.

'You are ill,' she said solicitously, rising from her knees. 'Holy Virgin, what shall I do? Help! help!'

I summoned all the strength of mind that I possessed.

'Do not call, my daughter! It is only a passing weakness. The way hither is long. I am but lately recovered from a severe indisposition. Let me rest!'

Some excuse of this kind I think I made. Whatever it was, she accepted it, and stood watching me for a minute or two. Then, seeing that I was better, she said, with great gentleness:

'It was not good to send you out on such a wild night as this. You should have stayed at home and slept. It grieved me so to see that I have made you ill. I did not think of this when I asked my father to send for a priest. I have hardly ever been allowed one, but you are very like some one that I have seen—I cannot feel as if you were a stranger. I could believe anything that you said—I know I could. Are you glad to think how greatly it comforts me to see you?'

'I would give the remnant of my years, if that could be of any service to you,' I said, striving not to say it too fervently.

She was quiet for a moment;—then, drawing a chair close to the sofa on which I had fallen back, she resumed.

'I will not weary you with making a long confession. I think I can say what is on my mind better like this. I trust your face.'

She hesitated.

'It is a dreadful thing. At first I thought I dared not say it to any one. It was wicked of me even to think it.'

She hid her face.

'But you, you are older; you may not have very long to live either. Things look so different then. If you said it, I could believe it. I know I could.'

Once more she hesitated. The wind had risen again in all its fury, and was howling outside the window.

'Satan tempts us,' she said.

'Yes,' I said. 'Satan tempts us.'

She turned her face away, clasped her hands tightly, and went on.

'I do not know how to say it. It was like this. I was at a dance, and very happy. I think I never was so happy in my life. I never danced with any one before. There came a moth, and it was going to burn itself. He saved it; and then he said, "What matter if it had died, for we were all like moths." There is nothing more.'

'He told a lie.'

'I knew it, I knew it,' she said. 'Say that! Look at me as you say it! Say: "I believe we live again."'

'I believe that we live again,' I said solemnly, answering her gaze with perfect truthfulness. The anguish passed away; the strained hands loosened. She bent her head and closed her eyes. When she spoke again, she said in a whisper: 'It is all well. How good of you to come! He said he would believe it, if I told him. I could not tell him. He made me feel as if I did not know. If I could only—will you say this to him for me? Ah, no! I forgot. You must never tell any one.'

'You shall tell him yourself.'

A light, first of wonder, then of the happiness of those who see a vision, dawned in her eyes. I was still half in heaven with her, when the Count entered. She told him that I had been ill—that I ought not to have come out at night.

'I am greatly obliged to you for your kindness.' The Count addressed himself to me with a graceful, though condescending bow. 'The Abbot is informed of the reasons for which secrecy is imperative,' he continued. I feel sure that you will hold me excused. But we must not suffer you to go hence without a draught of wine.' His daughter went before him.

I followed, down the dark staircase into a hall—the same evidently as that into which I had peeped from the window of the boudoir. It lay in darkness now; even the fire burned low. The Count carried a lamp.

Strange figures, stranger faces, met my eyes. Goat-footed creatures were driving airy chariots over my head; Cupids and Fauns and things half man, half beast or bird, were at their wildest revelry around me. Here stood *l'homme armé*, his visor up, nothing but vacant blackness behind it. There, two colossal heads, man and woman, leered at each other. Garlands of carved fruit and flowers, amidst which squirrels, monkeys, and little owls were playing, wreathed pillar and post of the staircase by which we had come down. No two were alike.

In front of the fire stood a table; on it a tray of polished brass, holding a flask of fine Venetian work and some glasses.

He seated himself in silence. I did the same.

A French clock on its bracket struck, or rather tolled, an hour after midnight.

Lifting his dark eyes, the Count fixed them steadily upon me.

I feared his recognition too much to meet them, for he and I had looked each other in the eyes once before. It is impossible to mask the soul when she is sitting at her open windows. But he had no suspicion.

'In the course of your life,' he said, 'you have, no doubt, seen many strange things.' He waved his head in the direction of the grotesques. 'Did you ever, if I may ask the question, see a house furnished in this way before?'

'Never.'

'Could it have been so furnished by any reasonable man?'

'A poet?' I said tentatively.

The Count shrugged his shoulders.

'There are no poets in the family.'

I kept silence.

'The man shot himself. His son built the little room up above. It has no window to the front. There his wife lived until her death.'

He glanced up at a portrait on the wall, the features of which strongly resembled his own.

'No one knows what became of him.'

As he spoke, he pulled a silk tassel which hung by a long slender cord from the ceiling. A thousand lights flashed out. The heart of every carven rose became a heart of flame, stars glowed among the vine and pomegranate, eyes of fire shone from the grotesque heads. The lights, the faces, the flowers and fruit all round wreathed themselves into the first letter of the name of my enemy. Everywhere it was written. A wave of fresh, vigorous hate surged over me.

'Have you ever seen an apartment lighted in this manner before?' he asked.

'I must confess that it appears to me fantastic, though very beautiful.'

'We were not speaking of the effect, I think. It is unusual?'

'Certainly.'

'The invention is due to the father of the present owner. He fell by his own hand.'

'And the present owner?' I said.

The Count's expression changed. He looked at his daughter, who had seated herself on a low couch by the fire. She did not appear to be listening; but he lowered his voice.

'The present owner has one child—now in the flower of her youth. She does not know the dreadful fate of her ancestors. She has only been told thus much—that at the age of seventeen she will pass into another life. She feels no fear, since she is going to the mother whom, as a babe, she lost. Of the exact moment and manner of her death she has been kept in ignorance until within an hour of it. Nothing has frightened, nothing has distressed her. Pure and unspotted as she came to him, he that best loves her desires to send her back to that heaven which is more real to her than earth, to that heaven which will save her from knowing—as, but for him, she must infallibly know—that this earth is a hell. Is he right?'

'No,' I said, with a certain assurance. 'He is mad.' The Count started; but on the instant he was calm again.

'That makes the fifth generation,' he said, as if to himself. 'In the eyes of ignorant persons he may be mad perhaps. Is it not the truest sanity to prevent these horrors from culminating in a sixth? I cannot but approve his judgment.'

He turned towards the girl. She raised her face to his. I saw that it was white as marble. I thought that she was going to faint. Instinctively I seized the flask and poured out some of the wine.

'Well thought of!' said the Count. 'The Church however, comes first— even before a lady.'

He made a sign to her.

'You need refreshment more than I,' she said, offering me the glass.

I took it from her, not thinking what I did. And yet some word of hers recalled a word spoken before.

'Refreshment!'

Take no refreshment in that house.

I had but tasted. For the moment my senses still were clear. I saw the Count sprinkle drops from a phial on to his handkerchief and give it to the little lady. I saw her fall back softly on the couch.

Her father watched with rapt attention. The swansdown cloak that she had worn was hanging over the back of a chair. Suddenly he tore a bit of it away and held it to her lips. The light down never stirred.

I thought that I called out, but heard no sound. There was a weight of lead upon my eyes—the air was thick with fog. I fought with might and main to get to her. I could not stir a step. I could not even see her now.

Making one last effort to move, I missed my footing and fell—fell, as it seemed, into a yawning gulf that opened suddenly before me—fell down and down and down into the fathomless depths of that slumber wherein we spend the half of existence.

But Lethe had been meted out unevenly; to her the sleep that knew no earthly morrow—to me the sleep that ended in a few hours, leaving the rest of life a dream.

On the day after, I met the Count at eight o'clock in the morning. At eight o'clock in the evening I kept my dinner engagement.

~

Selected Passages from Letters and Diaries

Nov. 28th, 1889

How far away we are from each other. Two walls of flesh between me and the nearest person on earth! Even the eyes mysterious. I look, and see two little pictures of my outward self, when all I long for is the image of the other soul at those windows; and then, we may reduce our bodies to the same pace, sit, walk, run evenly together, but how seldom will the mind run in couples! My neighbour's mind has wings, and reaches the goal before I have so much as seen it, or mine is half-way to another goal by mistake, while my neighbour is labouring to explain where it is that he wants to go to.

June 2nd, 1890

How many a born king spends his whole life in the pursuit of asses for want of some kind prophet to tell him he is a head and shoulders taller than other people!

I have been reading Hazlitt with even keener pleasure than I meant to get out of him. It seems to me the critics of those days were flesh and blood compared to the airy-fairy creatures that carry on the trade now. They had much more solid beef and mutton books to fall back upon. The background of their minds was Shakespeare and Spenser, not Shelley and Keats, and somehow one feels the difference in the downright cut-and-thrust manliness of their style. It's not so dainty of course, but I can't help thinking it will yet manage to outlive Mat Arnold and Andrew Lang. They certainly didn't fight as one that beateth the air.

Ibsen's delicate way of unfolding character seems to me wonderful, and a man that thoroughly understands a woman was a very great man indeed. There are two or three people who can tell stories about her, and one or two who can put her into a book without killing her during the process, but how few can get her alive on to the stage not laughing only, not crying only, but doing both, and that not hundreds of years ago in blank verse, but dressed in the latest fashion, and talking prose.

March 15th, 1891

Ghosts, The Light that Failed, and a sermon fifty-six minutes long, all in the course of one week, would be too much for the patience of a female Job. I am perfectly worn out with realism and the want of it. I wish it were rather less the fashion in literature and rather more the fashion in church. Anent Ghosts, I don't know what to say. I always begin by respecting any one or anything that knocks me down, so on Friday night I was sure it must 'make for righteousness.' On Saturday morn, when I had got over the dizziness, but was still aching mentally all over from the pain of it, I didn't feel quite so sure, and by Saturday eve I felt nearly sure that it made for the very reverse. . . .

A dull, stunned sensation still clings to me. The fruit of the modern Tree of Knowledge is certainly very nasty; it may 'make one wise,' but it is not 'a thing to be desired.' E— says Ghosts is like a Greek play, because no catastrophe happens on the stage. I can't feel that. It seems to me rank where a Greek play would be strong. There's a good deal of heredity in Œdipus, and the subject is quite as revolting, but the difference of treatment prevents one from feeling it in the same way. The Greeks are wild to kill themselves because they have outraged convention, the Scandinavians are wild to kill convention, because it has outraged them. No, I don't think I 've put it fairly for the Greeks.

July 23rd, 1891

These wonderful late nights and early mornings, when there is nothing to be seen but the sky, no sound but the sea, no distinction but of sun or moon, fill all my mind for the time being, and drown the very thought of self. There is no struggle to be rid of it, no slaying of it first and rising above it. It goes. I feel so near to God, that there is no need to pray, any more than if I were one of His birds.

May 4th, 1892

When we were out this afternoon, we saw the larks descending to the ground, almost without a flutter of their wings, as if they flew upon their singing. Some people's lives are like that; they progress by harmony rather than movement.

Whether we love each other because we are like or because we are different, or—as I am far more inclined to believe—for no reason whatever, which is as much as to say for some reason so deep that the mind of man cannot fathom it—is a question to which I never find any answer that satisfies me. For I think it's very seldom that we are alike really, any two of us. The points at which we touch are almost infinitesimal compared with the vast tracts of difference. In the beginning love is often helped by the fancy that it detects a similarity which does not exist, but by the time he has found out his mistake he is far too happy to care anything about such a trifle as that.

July 13th, 1894

One gets a hunger for certain faces and to feel a certain kind of love round one. That of the ——'s is all sheltering and spoiling and yet it strengthens one, and drives one's worst self right away. I can't think how they do it. It is the very High Art of Love. There is an art of it, I 'm certain. Some people never get beyond being brilliant amateurs, and some are good serious students, always learning their lessons in it, but without any original taste. How funny an exhibition of us would be if we were all hung up as each other's 'Works'! Here a bit of character moulded by this one, there another moulded by that one, each with its own stamp on it.

April 28th, 1895

I longed for something to draw me out of myself, not to sink me down into it. If it 's lovely, it 's lovely, but if it 's not, it 's a good deal worse than nothing to me. Just during the last few minutes, these words flashed into my mind out of emptiness, 'Surely, the Lord was in this place and I knew it not.' That pleased and rested me. On the Mount of Transfiguration only can we say, 'Lord it is good for us to be here,' but of almost every bit of life we might say, 'The Lord was in this place,' and even if we do not know it at the time, it is something to know it after.

July 1896

I wonder if people who have a garden enjoy it so absurdly as Londoners enjoy one flower? The great tiger-lily that L——'s father brought wastes my time almost as well as a fire in winter.

'Pure lilies of eternal peace,' indeed! This one's a real tiger. As for the four little sunflowers in two pots on the leads—or sunleaves rather, for the flowers lie yet in the dark abyss of the future,—they have given me many a 'green thought in a *black* shade.' And I become unfriendly to the Sun himself, if I think he is scorching them, and beseech the winds of Heaven that they visit them not too roughly.

Mephisto would have had me by the wrist often enough, I have said to so many moments of life, 'Stay, thou art fair!' In solitude—à deux—even à trois. (To be happy in threes is, I believe, a great test of the capacity for being happy at all.) Only they never stayed. And you have as much chance of finding the same moment again as the same mortal. Joy is a host of happinesses, each quite unlike all the rest. A thud behind me. Only the lily falling to bits. I did so want her to stay till to-morrow, so that the St. T——s might see her. But she won't stay. She is fair.

March 21st, 1897

There's one desire I never can resist—a longing to break the great black root, a lump of coal, and free the golden flower within. What if people do call it prosaically 'poking the fire from the top'?

March 29th, 1897

To catch the sun and keep him in a book—what a hopeless business! Yet never twice the same clouds gather round him touched with the same colours; it is human to grasp at them.

> Thy sun, that Adam saw, that the last man shall see,
> Shining on thousands also shone on me.
> And one white flower of Thine born yesterday
> To wither in a sunny week away,
> Sweet to me only, to none other sweet,
> Sent up its honied fragrance at my feet.

A fragment of grey cloud showed against the gold disk like a headless cross. Then the disk was striped by little swords and daggers of light—light upon light.

For me the hero of the hour is that Duke of Parma who besieged Antwerp in the days when people wore ruffs. He dedicated the siege to the Virgin Mary and named one of his forts after her and one after his king. 'Oh, for half an hour of Alexander in the field!' the soldiers used to cry; and wherever he went they won. Alexander Farnese was his magnificent, ruff-like name. I am also more in love with Sir Philip Sidney than ever. He died of a wound in the thigh, and as he lay dying, he asked them to sing him a song called *The Broken Thigh* that he had made! So funny—so pathetic, somehow. And he was always telling the other people, who were in agonies of tears, that he didn't mind in the least—in fact he rather liked it. Have you ever read Motley? It is so fascinating. And then one turns to the *Daily Telegraph*, and there is the Kaiser giving the King thirty-two hideous silver-gilt baskets designed by himself—ugh! (I never do say *ugh!* but it 's a comfortable word to write—so much disgust in it.)

How curious that personal touch is in the great French historians. Is it for want of that that ours are such dry stuff in comparison? Michelet falls ill of overwork. '*J'ai abattu trop de rois*,' and he does another enchanting volume. Qualifications absolutely necessary for a good historian: 1. Imagination; 2. Prejudice; 3. the power of writing your own biography at the same time.

How dull is the *Life of Dean Church*! How much worse than dull the *Life of Dr. Pusey*! I think the devil writes religious biography. There's much more real religion in the *Bacchae* of Euripides, which is simply glorious—a sort of Greek Salvation Army business, all drums and cymbals and ecstasy. Macaulay says he hasn't the least idea whether Euripides meant to run up or run down fanaticism, but it's one of the finest things going. The revel of vine and ivy and bryony and wind—blown torches and roofless rocks and wild delirious joy in freedom and music and open air—is quite intoxicating. Then there's Bacchus himself, the god come down in the likeness of man, the men of Thebes refusing to understand, obstinate not to worship him, punished accordingly. There's no real tipsiness as far as I can make out. The Hallelujah Lasses get drunk on the wine of the spirit, not the wine of the grape.

From 1897 to 1907

When you spoke about sex the other night, I didn't think much about it, but to-day I did, and I know now that I didn't feel with you, and that it does seem to me to be an eternal distinction. I don't think we are separate only in body and in mind, I think we are separate in soul too, and that a woman's prayer is as different from a man's as a woman's thought or a woman's hand. I cannot think of souls that are not masculine or feminine . . . but just as the negation of sex is inconceivable to me, so is its unification; I cannot think that we shall be men as well as women, and men women as well as men. If we do not retain sex I don't see how we can retain identity. Male and female we were created; it is of the very essence of our nature.

E—— and I went to the National Gallery on Saturday. We looked at many pictures, but we thought at six—the three ideal Knights—Giorgione's, Raphael's, Velasquez's, two Madonnas, and Botticelli's 'Assumption of the Virgin.' Certainly Botticelli was one of those who saw 'Heaven opened,' though it thrills one to think how Heaven has widened and widened since the day that he finished his last golden circle of stars.

Woman with a big W bores me supremely. How γυνή would have puzzled the beautiful concrete Greeks. It is a mere abstraction born of monks and the mists of the North. A woman I know, but what on earth is Woman? She has done her best to spoil history, poetry, novels, essays, and Sir Thomas Browne and Thoreau are the only things safe from her; that's why I love them.

I read some of Medea; it stiffens one's mind to do a bit of Greek. Classic folk despise Euripides, but after all he was Milton's man. Medea is thoroughly *fin de siècle*; says she would rather go into battle three times than have a baby once, pitches into men like anything. But there's too much Whitechapel about her. How are you to be seriously interested in a woman who has murdered her mother and boiled her father-in-law before the play begins? So different from the gentle Phædra, and the wonderful Antigone and Helen.

We have got about fifty books, and if it were not for the extraordinary dulness of the Popes, I should be perfectly happy. Why is no Pope interesting except the Papa of Cæsar Borgia? Nuns are charming, monks fascinating, even an Archbishop may please, but the minute a man becomes a Pope he thinks of nothing but Bulls and Councils and slanging the Emperor of the period. I take a personal interest in the Anglo-Saxon nuns of the ninth century, because if I had happened to be born then instead of in the nineteenth, I should have had to enter a convent from the impossibility of getting books anywhere else. They were obliged by their abbesses to read two hours a day, and they wore fringes (for which the bishops had them up), and corresponded with St. Boniface, or any other saint they could find, in bad Latin, and went to Rome on pilgrimage whenever they were tired of one another, and were dreadfully afraid of meeting Saracens there. Five hundred of them once danced for joy on the grave of a novice-mistress whom they hated, till the earth sank in half a foot, and the Abbess condemned them to fast three days on account of the hardness of their hearts. My opinion is that un-married ladies had a high old time of it in those days.

Nothing has such deadly power to corrupt as unalloyed virtue.

I have spent the whole day murdering flowers. Philanthropy is like your sins, it finds you out. There was I sitting in the verandah this morning, reading of Michelet, wishing no ill to any one, when by comes nice, good Mrs. —— and inquires whether I wouldn't like to go and help her pick cowslips to be sent up to the flower-girls in the worst street of London. Having broken my back for two hours over this performance (in the course of which I made many reflections on the nature of cowslips and of nice, good women), I calculated that I must have earned about 3d. towards the hat or flannel-petticoat of Spitalfields. I should have had quite two shillings worth of pleasure out of Michelet. From a money point of view it doesn't pay. However I *dédommagéd* myself by gathering an enormous bunch of flowers afterwards for home-consumption.

Yesterday F. and I were gathering primroses. One of the dearest things about Nature to me is her secrecy. There were all those thousands of yellow stars, and yet if we had waited a year she would no more have let us see the exact moment at which every bud changed to a flower than she would have told us the very point at which Celia left off being a baby and grew into a child.

How I do love the tossing and kissing and crushing of the waves. It's like the encounter of strong-hearted friends, half play, half warfare, and half surrender; O dear! I forgot there couldn't be three halves to a thing.

The result of leaving children to the guidance of nature is so very dreadful; and the men and women who say they live according to nature are even more intolerable than the children. If I follow nature, I scream when I have a tooth out, I eat eleven strawberries when there are twelve on the table, I come down late to breakfast, there's no end to the inconvenient things that I do. Is it dreadfully Philistine to say these things? I am not—as you see—in love with nature—no doubt because I *do* live in accordance with nature myself. But I don't think the result charming.

Words could not say how deeply I agree that they are but a very superficial part of language. Where so much is played, painted, looked, touched, felt, they do seem inadequate; and it is quite true that, very often, you might as well try to paint a piece of music as to explain a picture. Still, there are certain limits, it seems to me, within which one art may lawfully help another, and such a description as Pater's, for instance, of Mona Lisa, shows literature as the hand-maid of Leonardo. The fine arts are all fine ladies, and they cannot replace each other or lay down the law for each other, but they may exchange courtesies now and again?

I believe the Elizabethan sense of love and friendship was much stronger and more sensitive, and closer to the Victorian, than anything in between.

. . . I have rapidly come to believe that construction is not nearly so important as people think. It is to a book what morality is to a person. But there are delicious books without any construction at all, and delicious people with no morality. I wrote this letter on top of a 'bus last night when all the lamps along the Brompton Road were flashing gold and mauve and crimson. Hence, you perceive, its brilliant incoherence.

How I do like *The Descent of Man!* . . . The way in which beasts, birds and fishes, all make love to each other is quite delightful. Fishes appear to be the most romantic wooers, but there don't seem to be any *constant* lovers, as far as I can make out, except pigeons, bull-finches and wild duck. Tame ducks immediately take several brides.

We read the *Life of Dickens* of an evening. There is much that attracts, and something that repels me about him; I think, for one so deep in feeling, he was curiously superficial in thought. But what a wealth of genius! How it comes tumbling, bubbling out in his private letters! He doesn't care how often he misses, because he knows he'll hit just as often, and so he has his fling at every subject in the universe. And he *lives*.

Death is become a more practical thing now it is palpably so much nearer than in the days when I thought it was going to happen to-morrow. But it seems much farther off, as practical things do.

More and more as life goes on I feel as if one of the big temptations of it were to rest content with negative ease and freedom from worry, and to forget that that's only the body of happiness and not the soul. Looking into the fluffy white heart of an oleander, the other day, a kind of rapture at its uselessness came over me, at the divine heedlessness of anything but glory and beauty at the making of it.

Self-sacrifice is the noblest thing in the world, but to sacrifice other people even for the very noblest things is as wrong as persecution.

It comes to me that what we seem to need we are not given. Joy cannot be born of necessity. There is need of patience and need of peace, but no cry of need will bring joy.

I lay for some time letting the sky wake me. From the bed you see nothing but sky. It was not 'the body of heaven' in his fulness, it was a thin wash of faint, almost transparent blue. I began to think how tremendous it would be to go out on a morning like that and stand alone with God, conscious that the earth-life would never rush in dividingly. Savonarola was in my mind— and that bit of Johannes Agricola. 'For I intend to get to God. For 'tis to God I speed so fast.' All that I felt passed into one deep human longing, I don't know how or why, except that below the surface all feeling seems to be one. There came those words, 'We never know what God is till we have given up something for him.' I have given up nothing and don't feel called to, and am as happy as can be.

Index

Angel in the House, 12, 13
Anodos, 4, 5, 6
Arnold, Edward, 7, 18–19n10
The Athenaeum, 7

Battersby, Christine, 6
Binyon, Laurence, 4
Blackwell's Victorian Women Poets: An
    Anthology, 7
Bluestockings, 4, 16
Bridges, Robert, 5; The Last Poems of
    Richard Watson Dixon, 5
Brontë, Charlotte, 4, 13, 16, 174, 192,
    194
Browne, Sir Thomas, 6, 174, 229
Browning, Robert, 3, 12

Chapman, Alison, 19n29
Coleridge, Arthur Duke, 2
Coleridge, James, 2
Coleridge, Mary Anne Jameson, 2
Coleridge, Mary E., 1–18; Becq, 5;
    "The Drawing-Room," 11; Fancy's
    Following, 4, 5, 17; Fancy's Guerdon,
    4, 5; The Fiery Dawn, 3; "The

Friendly Foe," 15; Gathered Leaves,
    15, 16, 156; The King with Two
    Faces, 3, 18–19n10; The Lady on
    the Drawingroom Floor, 2, 4, 7–12,
    18–19n10; The Last Poems of Richard
    Watson Dixon (Preface), 5; "The
    Making of Heroines," 15; "Master
    and Guest," 14; "Mrs. Gaskell," 16;
    Non Sequitur, 4, 15; "The Other
    Side of a Mirror," 6, 12–13, 20n42;
    "Recollections of Mrs. Fanny
    Kemble," 16; The Seven Sleepers of
    Ephesus, 3; The Shadow on the Wall,
    4, 18–19n10; "The Witch," 13–14;
    "Words, Words, Words!" 15
Coleridge, Samuel Taylor, 1, 2, 13, 17;
    "Christabel," 13
Coleridge, Sara, 2, 6; Phantasmion, 2
The Cornhill/Cornhill Magazine, 4, 15
Cory, William J., 3

Daniel, Charles Henry, 4
Daniel Press, 17
de la Mare, Walter, 18
Dickinson, Emily, 7

Dixon, Richard Watson, 5
Dole, Carol, 3

Eliot, George, 16, 192, 194
"eternal feminine," 2
Eton College. See Cory, William J.

feminist, 5–7, 15
Franklin, Caroline and Michael J.
    Franklin: "Victorian Gothic Poetry:
    The Corpse's [a] Text," 7

Gaskell, Elizabeth, 16, 174, 192–96;
    Mary Barton, 16, 192–93, 195
gender, 2, 6, 10, 14, 15, 16, 17
The Germ, 17
Gilbert, Sandra, 5–6
Gothic, 7, 13, 19n29
Grove Road Cemetery, 5, 19n21
Gubar, Susan, 5–6
Gustav III of Sweden, 3

Hampstead, 3
Harrogate, 5
Hazlitt, William, 17, 36, 224
Hodgkins, Violet, 5
Hunt, Holman, 5

Keats, John, 15, 16, 224
Kemble, Fanny, 16, 162–67
King's College, 3

Lind, Jenny, 2
London, 2, 7, 8
London Bach Choir, 2

MacDonald, George: Phantastes:
    A Faerie Romance for Men and
    Women, 4
The Madwoman in the Attic. See Gilbert,
    Sandra; Gubar, Susan
Manchester Guardian, 7

Matthew, Elkin: Shilling Garland, 4
McGowran, Katherine, 6–7
Merry England, 4
Millais, John Everett, 3
Mills, Cotton Mather, 16
Monthly Packet, 4
The Monthly Review, 4

Newbolt, Henry, 4, 5

Oxford, 4

The Penguin Book of Victorian Verse, 7
Percy, Thomas: Reliques, 17
"Perfect Love," 5, 19n21
Phelps, Elizabeth Stuart, 7
Pre-Raphaelite Brotherhood, 17

The Quintette, 4

The Reflector, 15
Rossetti, Christina, 7, 17
Ruskin, John, 3

Scott, Sir Walter: Minstrelsy of the
    Scottish Border, 17
"The Settee," 4–5
Shakespeare, William: King Lear, 5,
    169
Shelley, Mary, 6
Showalter, Elaine: A Literature of Their
    Own, 5
Sichel, Edith, 6, 17
Smith, Andrew and William Hughes:
    The Victorian Gothic: An Edinburgh
    Companion, 7
The Spectator, 8
Stevenson, Robert Louis, 3
Stoker, Bram: Dracula, 14

Tennyson, Lord Alfred, 3, 20n42
The Theatre, 4

Times Literary Supplement, 4
Tribune, 7
Trollope, Anthony, 3

*The Victorians: An Anthology of Poetry
and Poetics*, 7

Whistler, Theresa, 1, 4, 5, 11, 12, 17,
18; *The Collected Poems of Mary
Coleridge*, 4
woman writer, 2, 5–6, 15–16
Working Women's College, 3

Yonge, Charlotte, 4

~

About the Editor

Heather Braun is currently an assistant professor of English at the University of Akron in Ohio where she teaches nineteenth- and twentieth-century British literature, composition, literary theory, and young adult literature. Her research and teaching interests include women writers, the Gothic, the doppelgänger, and Adolescent literature. Her book *The Rise and Fall of the* Femme Fatale *in British Literature, 1790-1910* was published by Fairleigh Dickinson University Press in 2012. She has also published essays on David Mamet, Norman Mailer, Sydney Owenson, Mary E. Braddon, and Mary E. Coleridge.

www.ingramcontent.com/pod-product-compliance
Lightning Source LLC
Chambersburg PA
CBHW030639110726
47901CB00002B/504